the OTHER 3:16s

"I can't recall the last time I read a book as powerful as *The Other Three Sixteens*. It encourages the reader to dip into the harmonious waters of the greatest Book ever written and successfully tackles the task of revealing God's love and grace through the other 3:16s in the Bible, which is the central mission of The Church. I wholeheartedly recommend *The Other Three Sixteens* to both young Christian converts as well as seasoned saints. Pastors, if you are looking for sermon material, then this is a must read."

—Dr. Gary L. Phillips,
Senior Pastor, Calvary Assembly of God, El Monte, CA

"*The Other Three Sixteens* is a beautifully written study of the Word of God. It is unique and enlightening and brought out in-depth understanding of Scriptures I had never really pondered to this degree before. Malinda probes into key aspects of the Bible that remind us of God's goodness, mercy, grace, and faithfulness. This is an edifying, insightful read in solitude, or with an accountability group, and time well spent."

—Lauren Kitchens Steward,
National Radio Personality, College Professor, Motivational Speaker

"Malinda Fugate's mediations on 3:16 is a book of great sense and sapience, equally savvy and savory. I read it while looking at Donald Knuth's 3:16, where this computer scientist commissioned a different artist/calligrapher to portray in visual form each 3:16 in the Bible. The joining together of Malinda's words with Knuth's images produced a rapturous, even spellbinding experience of the transcendent that I wish were available to all readers of her charming book."

—Leonard Sweet,
Best-selling author, professor (Drew University, George Fox University, Tabor College, Evangelical Seminary), and founder/chief contributor to preachthestory.com

the OTHER 3:16s

MALINDA FUGATE

Ambassador International
GREENVILLE, SOUTH CAROLINA & BELFAST, NORTHERN IRELAND
www.ambassador-international.com

The Other Three Sixteens
©2020 by Malinda Fugate
All rights reserved

ISBN: 978-1-93550-714-7
eISBN:978-1-93550-716-1

Cover Design and Typesetting by Hannah Nichols
eBook Conversion by Anna Riebe Raats

All rights reserved. No part of this book may be used or reproduced in any manner whatsoever without written permission except in the case of brief quotations embodied in critical articles or reviews.

Unless otherwise indicated, all Scripture quotations taken from THE HOLY BIBLE, NEW INTERNATIONAL VERSION®, NIV® Copyright © 1973, 1978, 1984, 2011 by Biblica, Inc.® Used by permission. All rights reserved worldwide.

AMBASSADOR INTERNATIONAL
Emerald House
411 University Ridge, Suite B14
Greenville, SC 29601, USA
www.ambassador-international.com

AMBASSADOR BOOKS
The Mount
2 Woodstock Link
Belfast, BT6 8DD, Northern Ireland, UK
www.ambassadormedia.co.uk

The colophon is a trademark of Ambassador, a Christian publishing company.

CONTENTS

1. INTRODUCTION	9
2. GENESIS	11
3. EXODUS	15
4. LEVITICUS	21
5. NUMBERS	25
6. DEUTERONOMY	29
7. JOSHUA	33
8. JUDGES	39
9. RUTH	45
10. 1 SAMUEL	51
11. 2 SAMUEL	57
12. 1 KINGS	63
13. 2 KINGS	67
14. 1 CHRONICLES	71
15. 2 CHRONICLES	75
16. NEHEMIAH	79
17. JOB	85
18. PROVERBS	91

19. ECCLESIASTES	97
20. ISAIAH	101
21. JEREMIAH	107
22. LAMENTATIONS	113
23. EZEKIEL	119
24. DANIEL	125
25. JOEL	133
26. NAHUM	137
27. HABAKKUK	143
28. ZEPHANIAH	147
29. MALACHI	153
30. MATTHEW	159
31. MARK	165
32. LUKE	171
33. ACTS	177
34. ROMANS	183
35. 1 CORINTHIANS	187
36. 2 CORINTHIANS	191
37. GALATIANS	197
38. EPHESIANS	201
39. PHILIPPIANS	207
40. COLOSSIANS	213
41. 2 THESSALONIANS	219
42. 1 TIMOTHY	223

43. 2 TIMOTHY	229
44. HEBREWS	233
45. JAMES	237
46. 1 PETER	241
47. 2 PETER	247
48. 1 JOHN	251
49. REVELATION	257
50. JOHN, THE CONCLUSION	263
ACKNOWLEDGMENTS	269
RESOURCES CONSULTED	271
DISCUSSION QUESTIONS	273

1. INTRODUCTION

"For God so loved the world..."

Many of us could finish that sentence in our sleep. John 3:16 is a beautiful Scripture that neatly and simply sums up the message of the Gospel. It's no wonder that kids in Sunday schools across the world recite this verse constantly. It should be rooted deeply in our brains, our hearts, and our souls. But what happens when memorization leads to stale recitation? When familiarity dulls the stunning work of Christ on the cross, we begin to lose the treasure we have been given in the precious words of the Word.

John 3:16 is a central sentence, one of many anchors we find in the pages of Scripture. But every single chapter and verse has eternal value, from the eloquently poetic to the seemingly mundane historical details. The words of the Bible weave a tapestry of love, particularly the love that our Heavenly Father has for His children. A love so deep and so wide cannot be contained in one memorized phrase. It takes multiple authors of sixty-six individual books to begin to explore the mystery of God's care for us. We merely have to dive in to discover wonders, miracles, complexities, and simplicities of His unfathomably great love. Such a task is mind-boggling, an overwhelming idea that is nearly impossible to grasp. So we begin with that familiar anchor, John 3:16. "God **so** loved the world that he gave his one and only Son . . ." (author emphasis).

I propose an adventure. It will be an expedition through the living and active Scriptures we hold in our hands and yet can't truly contain. If every phrase in God's word connects us to His love, then there are gems to uncover wherever we dare to seek them. Let's take a cue from John and look at the third chapter and sixteenth verse in each book and see what we find. Now, it should be noted that "3:16" is not a magic code. The books of the Bible were written as individual documents and letters, only to have chapter and verse notations added later for our reference purposes. 3:16 will be the guide we choose for this particular quest. It could easily be any other chapter and verse, and perhaps this type of journey should be repeated with different combinations. More clues to the incredible character of God's love would certainly be revealed! But for the purposes of this study, we'll choose to follow the 3:16s and discover what is to be found there. Since not every book of the Bible has a third chapter with a sixteenth verse, we'll go ahead and skip over those when we encounter them.

We also must be sure to look around the 3:16s to keep each verse in context. It would be foolish to cherry-pick the words without connecting them to the text as a whole. To discover the true meaning behind our selected verses will mean reading through the paragraphs where they are safely nestled. We also might discover some overlapping gifts of love in multiple books. A little repetition is okay, because these are things God definitely doesn't want us to miss!

Gather your Bible and your journal and prayerfully prepare for this opportunity to glimpse snapshots of God's character, truth, and love. May the freshness of new perspective break through our familiar routine and reveal treasures we previously overlooked. Let's allow an adventurous spirit to open our hearts to what God has prepared for us—gifts He gives as we grow and mature in His rich, nurturing love.

2. GENESIS

"To the woman he said, 'I will make your pains in childbearing very severe; with painful labor you will give birth to children. Your desire will be for your husband, and he will rule over you.'"

- Genesis 3:16

Whoa. This is certainly not the beginning we expected. John 3:16 is such a lovely verse, and God's love is very good news—the best we could ever receive. But our first stop on our 3:16 journey lands at a seemingly ugly destination. Maybe this project wasn't such a great idea after all. Pack it up, call it a day, and try another approach tomorrow.

Or.

What if we endured the pain for a moment and looked for a treasure of light buried in the darkness? We've acknowledged that every piece of Scripture has divine value, so that includes the difficult sections as well. Let's not run away yet.

Genesis 3:16 is one piece in the first story we read when we open the Word. Almighty God has masterfully created an entire universe and then concentrated His efforts on planet Earth. He carefully crafted sky and sea, mountain and tree, and creatures beyond imagination. Then it was time for His most precious creation—human beings—specifically, a man named Adam and a woman named Eve. The people lived securely in the garden made just for them, caring for it as instructed, and enjoying the Lord's presence. This entire set-up was going along nicely. Then Evil entered the scene. Satanic influence and bad decisions introduced sin into the world, changing Adam and Eve's (and our) existence forever.

The devil, as a serpent, offered Eve the very fruit that God previously told His children to avoid. After brief hesitation, Eve decided that the serpent was on to something. She took the fruit and shared it with a willing Adam. Sure enough, they had new-found knowledge, but it wasn't what they probably expected. They were immediately aware of their nakedness and its resulting shame. For the first time, they tried to hide from the Lord who cared for them so greatly. They discovered that it's impossible to conceal themselves from God, and they had to face the music. No attempt at blaming one another or accusing the serpent could undo their own destructive choice. There was no avoiding the consequences of sin.

So here we are, in the darkest part of Adam and Eve's life. Wrapped in their fig leaves, they listened as their Lord explained what would happen next. First, the serpent was cursed (after all, he started it), and we still see this curse today on both the supernatural and physical level. Then, God moved to the next offender, Eve. That brings us to our first 3:16: "To the woman he said, 'I will make your pains in childbearing very severe; with painful labor you will give birth to children. Your desire will be for your husband, and he will rule over you.'" Ouch—literally. Of course, Adam was accountable for his actions as well. God told him that he must now toil and work the ground for food for the rest of his life. The effects of Adam and Eve's sin would be felt with each passing generation, reaching even through today and tomorrow.

Where's the love?

Keep reading for a couple more verses, where we spy the first glimpse of love right away. Genesis 3:21 says, "The Lord God made garments of skin for Adam and his wife and clothed them." The God of justice and order dealt with sin, but in the middle of sorting out right and wrong, He took time to replace flimsy fig leaves with warm, durable clothing. The awareness of nakedness was a natural consequence of eating the fruit from the tree in the middle of the garden. Would it have been unreasonable for the Lord Almighty to allow His wandering children to deal with their new reality on their own? Why not let them remain in their makeshift fig leaf coverings?

Because God loved Eve and Adam. The results of sin couldn't be avoided, but it didn't demolish the care the Lord has for His precious creation. Extreme disobedience called for extreme discipline, but it didn't cancel out God's love. The love of God is lasting and not able to be destroyed, not even by the sins of the very people He so loves. Adam and Eve faced a life of pain and struggle, but God remained with them through it all. We don't get the details of their new situation as Genesis moves the narrative to their children and their children's children. But we can easily imagine how God provided strength to Adam as he learned to work a land full of thistles and weeds. It's possible to envision the comfort the Lord gave Eve as she grieved the murder of one son at the hand of the other, or the joy at the sight of their newborn son, Seth. Eve and Adam left Eden, but God never once left them.

Jump back to Genesis 3:16: "To the woman he said, 'I will make your pains in childbearing very severe; with painful labor you will give birth to children. Your desire will be for your husband, and he will rule over you.'" Where is God's love in these harsh words to Eve? We must remember the subtle differences between punishment and discipline. Punishment seeks to somehow even a score, answering a negative action with another equally bleak negative action. Punishment feels like divine revenge—we hurt God, so He'll hurt us back, and now everything is balanced . . . except that's not the character of God. For one thing, human beings can never equal God in any situation. Additionally, God's character is love. Love does not delight in punishment but nurtures through discipline. Discipline allows for necessary consequences, but it makes way for growth and redemption. Relationships are damaged by punishment, but they mature through discipline. A look at a healthy parent/child relationship illustrates this reality, as a parent uses discipline to help their child grow. Meanwhile, the love between them never decreases and the parent will not stop caring for their child. Needs are still met, affection is restored, and they move forward together. The parent continues to love, and the child understands something more about life.

Hebrews 12:5-6 echoes a passage in Proverbs, saying "My son, do not make light of the Lord's discipline, and do not lose heart when he rebukes you, because the Lord disciplines the one he loves, and he chastens everyone he accepts as his son." Daughters, this goes for you, too! Both the writers of Hebrews and Proverbs point out that the Lord's discipline is proof of His love for us. If He didn't love us, He wouldn't care if we endlessly endured the natural consequences of our sins. Instead, He helps us grow so that we might avoid a cycle of suffering. Instead of a life of pain, we can live in joy and hope because of His loving discipline.

The fruit of discipline goes beyond merely avoiding future suffering. God's loving correction is ripe with forgiveness, the opportunity for repentance, and redemption. It can take us to places we'd never reach if we were simply left to our own consequences. Proverbs 29:15 reminds us that God's discipline produces wisdom while a lack of discipline leads to disgrace. Job 5:17 tells us that it brings blessings, so we shouldn't despise it. If we read further into Hebrews 12 to verse 11, we learn that the discipline of the Lord, though it might seem initially unpleasant, results in righteousness and peace.

On the surface, the curse of Genesis 3:16 appears to be nothing but pain and suffering. Yet, it is rooted in the care of a loving God who refused to cast aside His daughter, Eve, despite her disobedience. He prevents Eve from repeating this particular sin and draws her closer to Him. Meanwhile, God did not forget important parts of Adam and Eve's original calling. They would still be fruitful and multiply. They would continue to eat from the seed-bearing plants of the earth. Life would no longer be as easy as it was in the garden, but it would still happen. Our sin doesn't eliminate our calling. God still wants us to be part of His kingdom work.

Perhaps the pain of childbirth increased Eve's dependence on the Lord, or possibly the submission to Adam's leadership (as he himself was being disciplined) helped her walk closer in the Lord's ways. Until we get to heaven, we can only speculate about the rest of Eve's story based on what is written in God's Word as a whole. But we know for certain that the Lord disciplines His children because He loves them. He loved Eve. He loved Adam. And He loves you.

3. EXODUS

"Go, assemble the elders of Israel and say to them, 'The Lord, the God of your fathers—the God of Abraham, Isaac and Jacob—appeared to me and said: "I have watched over you and have seen what has been done to you in Egypt."'

- Exodus 3:16

Moses is a central character in the book of Exodus, beginning with his birth and following his journey as he led the people out of Egypt toward the Promised Land. By the time we arrive in the third chapter, Moses had left his adopted childhood home in Egypt and established a new life in Midian. He had a wife and young family to support while shepherding his father-in-law's flock of sheep. All seemed calm and quiet until he stumbled upon a strange sight on the far side of the wilderness. He found a bush, and it was ablaze with flames. However, the fire did not consume it in the usual charred and smoky fashion. This called for closer examination. As Moses peered into the fire, a voice called his name, right from the bush! Moses calmly replied, "Here I am."

The fact that this whole scene did not freak out our guy Moses is remarkable. It speaks to the calming presence of the Lord in the midst of the miraculous. But the flaming foliage was not the main event here, God was, and He had something to say. First, He established boundaries. Moses was told not to come any closer, but instead to remove his shoes in respect for the holy ground where he found himself standing. Once that's settled, the Lord continued His explanation of why He called this holy meeting. He heard the painful cries of the Israelites as they were oppressed in slavery in Egypt. He was going to deliver his people from bondage and had chosen Moses to lead them out of their captivity.

Moses had some questions, and God, of course, had the answers and more. The two were discussing details when we get to our next 3:16: "Go, assemble the elders of Israel and say to them, 'The Lord, the God of your fathers—the God of Abraham, Isaac and Jacob—appeared to me and said: I have watched over you and have seen what has been done to you in Egypt.'" Let's break this down and see where we find evidence of God's love.

The first part is straightforward; it's part of Moses' instructions. This is the beginning of an epic friendship, one that develops through the entire book of Exodus. The love between God and Moses was strengthened through adversity, plagues, miracles, and dependence. But, for now, we see God's love in the act of entrusting Moses with the weighty task of confronting Pharaoh and freeing His beloved people. It's a love that didn't simply delegate a job and walk away. Instead, God was with Moses at every step in the journey, from confronting Pharaoh to implementing the first Passover, or raising a rod to tell the Red Sea to make a path and leading an entire nation through the wilderness. Even at this very beginning, God provided direction and answered questions from a man who felt very unqualified for his job. God equips and reassures those He loves. The writer of Hebrews included this in his benediction: "Now may the God of peace . . . equip you with everything good for doing his will, and may he work in us what is pleasing to him, through Jesus Christ, to whom be glory for ever and ever. Amen" (Hebrews 13:20-21).

The second sentence holds some pretty serious weight. We frequently run across the phrase "God of Abraham, Isaac and Jacob" as we read Scripture. At face value, it's descriptive enough. In a land where multiple gods were worshiped, the Jewish people wanted to be clear when they were talking about *the* God, the same God they'd been following all their lives, the God of their fathers and ancestors. There is also another layer when we look at the relationships God had with Abraham, Isaac, and Jacob. These were relationships rooted in love.

Cruise back over to Genesis 15, and you'll find God making His initial covenant with Abraham, who was then known as Abram. After describing Himself to be Abram's shield and great reward, God promised that Abram's descendants will be too many to count. He also promised possession of the very land upon which Abram was standing. Both of these things seemed pretty unbelievable, given Abram's situation of childlessness and advanced age. But God keeps His word, and a covenant was made between the Divine and the mortal. Also, check out verses 13-16, where God gave Abram a glimpse of the very situation we find in Exodus, though hundreds of years before it happened!

True to the covenant, Abraham wouldn't remain childless. His son, Isaac, also had a relationship with God Almighty. When we jump ahead to Genesis 26:2-4, we see God renewing the covenant, this time with Isaac. In addition to the vow of offspring and land possession, the Lord told Isaac that, despite famine, he should remain where he was, and he'd be blessed. Then, Isaac's son, Jacob, also has a relationship with the Lord, though one with quite a rocky start. Despite Jacob's stubbornness and tendency to deceive, God remained faithful to the covenant He made with Jacob's father and grandfather. His words, spoken to Jacob in a heavenly vision, are recorded in Genesis 28:13-15, again echoing the promise of descendants and land. He said that all peoples on Earth will be blessed through Jacob and his offspring, then assured him that He will be with Jacob, watching over him wherever he goes. Further into his story we find Jacob in an actual wrestling match with the angel of the Lord. That's a strong commitment for a powerful God to meet Jacob in that place, going as far as to give him a new name while continuing the sacred covenant.

So what could possibly inspire the Almighty Creator of heaven and Earth to take interest in the life of a single human being? What is it that would drive a deity to make promises to His creation? Not only does He make the covenant, but He steadfastly keeps it. Deuteronomy 7:8-9 sums it up succinctly.

"But it was because the Lord loved you and kept the oath he swore to your ancestors that he brought you out with a mighty hand and redeemed you from the land of slavery, from the power of Pharaoh king of Egypt. Know therefore that the Lord your God is God; he is the faithful God, keeping his covenant of love to a thousand generations of those who love him and keep his commandments."

The answer, of course, is love. No other force would be great enough to sustain such a promise to human beings who are full of flaws and limitations. Only the perfect love of the Most High God could inspire and fulfill such a covenant to His precious children.

We're not done yet. There's one more piece of Exodus 3:16: "I have watched over you and have seen what has been done to you in Egypt." The people were suffering, and just when they thought they had reached their limit, the Egyptians increased their oppression. Yet, none of this goes unnoticed by God. Not only does He see, but He is closely watching. He was paying careful attention to the Israelites, purposely keeping His eyes on them. He was with his people; He did not abandon them.

The next question is, then, why did He allow the pain to last for so long? This is a huge inquiry that many have struggled with, and have, in fact, struggled with for all time. The account of Job is likely the oldest book in the Bible, and it centers around the question of why suffering exists. When Job called out with pleas of "why?," God answered him . . . but not necessarily with "because." Instead, He provided a glimpse of His glory and an assurance that His plans are perfect. Since then, we have learned that God's big picture and His attention to detail and timing are intentional—and ultimately in our best interest. We cling to Scriptures that promise future hope and things working for our benefit when we can't understand why things seem wrong, while trusting that God is good. The Israelites also cried out to their God. As their oppression went on, God watched with compassionate eyes. They would remain in bondage no longer; a rescue was coming.

For the Israelites, their darkness came in the form of slavery. Over the centuries, all of God's people have experienced some form of darkness. It comes in all varieties, big and small, external and internal. We face pain, bleak circumstances, injustice, catastrophes, illness, persecution, etc. These seasons are dark, and they can be long. We may feel unloved and forgotten by our Heavenly Father, but, dear child of God, He is watching. And don't for one second think that He is a passive bystander. His never-faltering presence is a light in the dark. He is in the process of making something good and beautiful out of deepest despair. God sees you. He cares about what is happening to you. He loves you. A rescue is coming.

We could stop here at our 3:16 and cling to the richness found in these short phrases. But our eyes can't help but continue down the page to find out what will happen next and how God's people will be saved. We know that they will most certainly be rescued. There was a covenant to be fulfilled. God's people would be given more than just relief from slavery; they would be given an entire blessed land of promise. They would be redeemed . . . and so will we.

4. LEVITICUS

"The priest shall burn them on the altar as a food offering, a pleasing aroma. All the fat is the Lord's."

- Leviticus 3:16

Leviticus 3:16 makes us work to understand it. It's a book of the law full of details specific to ancient Israelite life. While this was crucial during the Old Testament days, Jesus' death and resurrection eliminated the need for the law as an avenue to righteousness. Yet, because it's still included in our Bible, we know there's value in the ancient text. We must do a little research to find what God wants modern believers to glean from the old law. And if you guessed that it's love, you're on the right track.

Animal sacrifice is not a pretty subject, but it illustrates an eternal truth. Romans 6:23 articulates it by saying "the wages of sin is death." Sin separates us from God and it ultimately leads to death. The only way to redeem sin is through blood, which is why the verse in Romans is completed by "but the gift of God is eternal life in Christ Jesus our Lord." It was Christ's shed blood on the cross that forgave all sins, then, now, and forever. However, when Leviticus was written, that hadn't happened yet. So back to animal sacrifice we go.

Here's how it worked: There were different kinds of sacrifices depending on many different factors. Leviticus jumps right in with instructions on burnt offerings, followed by information on the grain offering with flour and oil. Chapter three talks about the fellowship offering, which involves animals. A fellowship offering, also called a peace offering, was given voluntarily as an expression of thanks and worship. For this sacrifice, the person could give a cow, sheep, or goat. At the doorway to the Tent of Meeting, the person giving the offering would put his hand on the animal's head. This was a symbolic gesture to express that the person was identifying themselves and their sin with that animal. This also connected the person with the animal's death. Then, it would be killed, and the blood sprinkled on the altar, because, in the ancient world, blood was a symbol of life. The specific fellowship offering discussed in our 3:16 focuses on the sacrifice of a goat. Certain parts of the animal were given to the Lord, while others were prepared as a meal for the worshiper.

Scripture frequently refers to the aroma of a sacrifice as pleasing to the Lord. While it's tempting to think the writers are just describing the smells of a holy barbecue, this expression focuses less on the physical odor and more on God's approval of a sincere offering. Leviticus 3:16 also reminds the worshiper that they were not to eat the fat because that was designated to be burned. It belonged to the Lord. The fat was sacred and the richest part of the body, which meant that the best was reserved for God.

So now that we have a basic grasp of this Old Testament ritual, how does that fit into our New Testament faith? We can learn much from our spiritual history and the lives of the believers who lived before Christ walked on earth. Many of us are naturally disturbed by the pain and suffering of the sacrificed animal, and that's only a fraction of the pain the Lamb of God endured when He died for our sins. God established His system of laws and rituals in order that His people would understand more about His nature, His justice, and His redemption. It's difficult for an earthly mind to grasp heavenly things, but the Lord is patient and intentional in helping us comprehend His ways. Romans 3:25-26 explains, "God presented Christ as a sacrifice of atonement, through the shedding of his blood—to be received by faith. He did this to demonstrate his righteousness, because in his forbearance he had left the sins committed beforehand unpunished—he did it to demonstrate his righteousness at the present time, so as to be just and the one who justifies those who have faith in Jesus."

God is the same yesterday, today, and forever. His love spans over all generations, everlasting, faithful, and unchanging. We learned in Genesis how sin entered the world and caused a great separation between the Lord and His children. Instead of declaring Adam and Eve to be failures and giving up on the human race, God made a way to reunite His people with Himself. That's the first expression of love we can see here in Leviticus 3:16, and then finally with Christ's ultimate sacrifice on the cross. A loving God powerfully provides an avenue for forgiveness and reconciliation through sacrifice. And He made it accessible! Did you notice that a worshiper had the option of offering a cow, sheep, or goat (and in some cases, grain or birds)? The choice of animal was determined by the means of the person giving the offering. Those who could afford it would choose cattle, but the average person had the option for a sheep or goat. God doesn't set high obstacles for forgiveness. In fact, He made redemption even more attainable for all by giving His Son's life for our sin. We don't need an expensive offering. We bring the humble hearts we have and give them to the Lord.

Let's also remember that there were various types of sacrifice, such as for atonement or thanksgiving. This indicates that the relationship between God and people is more complex than "sin + sacrifice = forgiveness." If that were the case, we'd merely have a divine justice system purely to determine eternal destination. Instead, the Lord develops a substantial relationship with His children. As we know, healthy relationships are not one-sided. Both parties give and take, share and receive. God gives us blessings and we receive His love. We also have the privilege to give to the Lord. And let's face it, how great is it to give someone a gift? It feels wonderful to delight someone through generosity! Now we have a gift from God in allowing us to give a gift to God, so He has blessed us through the opportunity to bless Him. Whew! Got all that?

The Psalms reveal multiple declarations of "bless the Lord, my soul!" What in the world could we possibly give to the Creator of all things, to whom all things belong? We give ourselves, our hearts. And animal sacrifice was a tangible way God gave the Israelites to express their love, gratitude, and repentance. Our modern gifts to the Lord are often financial, acts of service, and praise and worship. In fact, our entire lives can be a sacrifice to God as we devote our time and talents to Him. Dedicating ourselves to obedience to the Lord's commands and intentionally making an effort to grow in our faith is yet another way we can give to our Heavenly Father. Because God loves us so much, He fosters a deeper relationship beyond a one-sided Creator/creation dynamic. Frequent interaction between ourselves and God is much richer than one where an Almighty Judge sits to the side and supervises our attempts to live correctly. This invitation to relationship is an incredible act of love from a compassionate Heavenly Father. How He nurtures this love demonstrates even more how greatly He cares.

5. NUMBERS

"So Moses counted them, as he was commanded by the word of the Lord."

- Numbers 3:16

Were you ever chosen as a helper in elementary school? If so, do you remember the pride and excitement over being selected and then carrying out your tasks? You could say that Moses was God's special helper. Of course, his responsibilities were much greater than passing out construction paper or serving as hall monitor.

By the time we get to the book of Numbers, the Israelites had been out of Egypt for a year and were in the midst of their ambling journey to the Promised Land. Their wandering through the Sinai wilderness was not without purpose. Though the delay was a consequence of their sin, God was also using each day to ready them for the blessings of the land He had promised in the covenant. We currently find our fearless leader (he has grown a lot since that burning bush incident), Moses, being given the task to count the people.

First, he was to count all the men age twenty and older, and sort them by tribe. This was for military purposes to prepare for the conquest of the Promised Land. One tribe, however, was left out of this count—the Levites. God had another purpose for the tribe of Levi. They were assigned the great responsibility of assisting the priests in service to the tabernacle. The tabernacle was a tent where the presence of the Lord rested, a holy place of worship. While Aaron and his sons served as priests, the Levites would handle various tabernacle duties, including taking care of furnishings. They cared for the Ark of the Covenant and other articles of the sanctuary, watching over everything related to their use.

This census was the beginning of an organization process. Escaping Egypt was only the beginning. God established order through His laws and purposes for His people, and He called on Moses to lead the way. This brings us back to our 3:16. God gave Moses instructions and Moses obediently completed his task. A quick glance at the results shows us what a big task it was! There were hundreds of thousands of men to count, and scholars estimate that there were two or three million Israelites total! Yet Moses took on the challenge and served the Lord well. If we put this piece into the big picture of Moses' relationship with the Lord, we begin to find the love.

First, we see the commands themselves. These instructions were for the good of the people, as well as the glory of God and work of His kingdom. We find this pattern through Scripture, history, and in our own lives today. God doesn't arbitrarily pass out commands for no reason. He's not giving us stage directions for His amusement. God's instructions are for our benefit and for the good of His kingdom. They are blessings, which are by definition a gift of love. If the Israelites were left to chaos, what kind of disaster might have befallen them? Would they have ever reached the Promised Land? Would people look at God's miraculous Red Sea parting and say it was all for nothing? This kind of speculation is empty, because God is a God of love. He is a God who sees His work through to completion. We know the character of God is love, that all good gifts come from Him, and that He works all things together for the good of those who love Him—all these things add up to tell us that His very instructions are blessings.

Even so, the fact of the matter is that an almighty God doesn't need people—He doesn't need anything. If the Lord wanted to free the people, count the people, or do anything else directly from His own hand, it would be done. However, He allows His children to be part of the action. There are multiple reasons for this, and all of them are for our own good. Being part of the process has many advantages. We learn, grow, and mature. We take ownership, which leads to considering things more seriously and valuing our gifts. We develop a greater understanding of God's ways. Additionally, it's an honor to humbly serve our Lord.

When God gave Moses his commands, He was entrusting Moses with serious tasks. Heavy responsibility was placed upon Moses' human shoulders. Before we place this great leader on any type of pedestal, we must remember that he had flaws like everyone else. Moses became angry, made mistakes, and even disobeyed God at one point (we're looking at you, rock of Meribah). Yet, despite knowing the limitations of the people He created, God still gave Moses the job. Of course, Moses was hardly the only person to serve this way. I bet, in less than sixty seconds, you can name three other biblical examples of God entrusting people with His work. Then take another sixty seconds to think of modern day "special helpers." Entrusting people is something God does because He loves us.

In Matthew 25, Jesus tells a parable of a man who leaves bags of money with three of his servants before he goes on a trip. Each servant receives a different amount. The first two servants invest their money, but the third simply buries it in the ground for safe-keeping. When the man returns, he is delighted with his two investing servants. He exclaims that since they can be trusted with little, they will be entrusted with more! He is not pleased, however, with the third guy, who could've at least put the money on deposit with bankers and collected interest, rather than burying it in the backyard like garbage. There are many complicated principles that can be learned from this parable. But perhaps the most basic message that applies here is that God does entrust all of us with something according to our abilities. He loves us enough to put just the right amount of responsibility on our human shoulders. And, like Moses, He equips us and enables us to carry out His instructions.

When we love someone, we want them to grow. We allow them to do the things they are capable of doing and encourage them to push the boundaries a little so that they might increase their abilities. We bring them alongside our projects and include them in the rewards. We do not belittle them by doing everything for them or leaving them on the sidelines as mere spectators. Instead, we make them a part of what is important to us. Assisting causes us to feel closer to one another as the helper is entrusted with tasks that matter. This is a part of love, and we see it also in our relationship with our Lord. He is a God who can do all things, and a God who gives us loving commands that result in His blessings. This God trusts us to serve Him, and He does so because He loves.

6. DEUTERONOMY

"But to the Reubenites and the Gadites I gave the territory extending from Gilead down to the Arnon Gorge (the middle of the gorge being the border) and out to the Jabbok River, which is the border of the Ammonites."

- Deuteronomy 3:16

We're still hanging with Moses on our 3:16 journey, now in the fortieth year since the Israelites left Egypt. We get to listen in as Moses delivers a hefty speech recapping major events of the wilderness years. The initial chapters of Deuteronomy describe military victories and defeats as God's people moved through the land. As usual, things went smoothly when the Israelites were obedient to the Lord but ended in disaster when they disobeyed. As they traveled, some regions were to be left alone, as they were designated by God to different people groups (such as the descendants of Lot and Esau). Other land, however, was meant to be conquered. It can be difficult for many present-day minds to comprehend how a loving God could promote such death and destruction at the hands of His people. This is a topic that takes great time and care to explore and leads us away from our 3:16 goals. I do encourage you to prayerfully read the Old Testament texts while consulting biblical resources on the subject. Also, talk to your pastors or Bible study teachers—they love these questions! In the meantime, let's dive into our focus Scripture.

As we creep closer to the sixteenth verse in the third chapter, we begin to read about division of land, specifically to the tribes of Reuben and Gad.

If we jump back to Numbers 32, we find more details on the matter. These two tribes had a lot of livestock and felt like the land of Jazer and Gilead, just outside of the Promised Land, was a pretty good place to settle. Instead of seeing God's big picture and trusting His blessing, they liked what they saw in the moment and wanted to jump on the opportunity to claim it as theirs. So, they made a special request to Moses, the priest, and other community leaders to allow them to stay there. They agreed to continue to serve in the Israelite army and not abandon their people in the continued quest for the Promised Land. Then, when all was said and done, this land on the east side of the Jordan would be where they put down roots. Deuteronomy 3:16 marks out specific boundary lines for where the Reubenites and Gadites would remain.

Even at face value, we can see how complicated this is. For generations, God had promised a specific land to His people. It was a land of milk and honey, a place of blessing. Essentially, the tribes of Reuben and Gad were saying, "Meh, that's okay. This land right here is good enough for us." How can we relate to this? Imagine spending all day in the kitchen making a bountiful Thanksgiving feast for your family, only to have them say, "It's okay, don't worry about it. We'll just grab something from McDonald's." The Israelites were right on the doorstep of a fulfilled promise, and these two tribes were settling for something much less, essentially casting away the gift God had been preparing for them over many centuries.

Yet, God allowed it. There, my friends, is love. God did not react in anger or leave them with nothing at all. Instead, He let them live in the place they chose. The Lord did not cut off these two tribes from the rest of the people; they were still Israelites, still beloved by God. But He did allow them to experience the result of their choice and miss out on the blessings of the Promised Land. Years later, they would suffer for this choice when the Assyrians would overtake them and bring them into captivity—something that might've been avoided had they been safely on the other side of the Jordan River with the rest of their people. While they chose to put literal division between themselves and the other tribes, God did not cut them off completely.

The Reubenites and the Gadites are not rare examples of bad choices and cast-aside blessings. How many times do we make rash decisions based on our immediate perceptions instead of prayerfully seeking God's way to handle things? We see something that looks good in the moment and decide that's what we want. Without seeking wisdom from the Lord, we quickly choose the way we think is best. Yet, that doesn't separate us from the love of God. He allows us to experience the consequences of our choices, but He doesn't stop loving us or caring for us. There is room for our mistakes, our flaws, our sins; these things do not cut us off from the mercy of a loving God.

The love of God means that our foolish choices are not final. If the Lord's anger had burned against the two tribes, He could've cut them off forever from the people and focused His blessing solely on the remaining Israelites in the Promised Land. Instead of declaring the end of the story, the Reubenites and Gadites still had opportunities to follow the Lord and grow in obedience. We, too, are not ultimately defined by our mistakes. Scripture gives us endless examples of second chances. The disciple Peter denied Christ three times, but later, at a fish fry breakfast, was given three opportunities to declare his love for Jesus. Jonah refused to go to Nineveh but was given a second chance at obedience after a brief timeout in the belly of a large fish. The promises are whispered in the pages of the Old Testament, in verses such as Lamentations 3:22-23, "Because of the Lord's great love we are not consumed, for his compassions never fail. They are new every morning; great is your faithfulness." First John 1:9 reminds us that if we confess our sins, God forgives and purifies us—a clean slate. And 2 Peter 3:9, written by the disciple who truly knew about second chances, explains how the Lord is patient with us because He wants us all to come to repentance.

The actions of the Reubenites and Gadites certainly did not please the Lord, and neither do many of our choices, unfortunately. But these mistakes are not enough to separate us from the love of our Almighty God who delivers us from captivity and has blessings prepared for us. May we have the wisdom to slow down and not miss His good gifts!

7. JOSHUA

"... the water from upstream stopped flowing. It piled up in a heap a great distance away, at a town called Adam in the vicinity of Zarethan, while the water flowing down to the Sea of the Arabah (that is, the Dead Sea) was completely cut off. So the people crossed over opposite Jericho."

- Joshua 3:16

Now things are getting exciting. We open the pages of Joshua to find the Israelites facing life without Moses as their leader. God didn't leave them in aimless chaos, however. Joshua, Moses' aide, was ready to take the wheel. Not only that, but we've arrived at a big moment: the Israelites are about to enter the land of promise.

God instructed them to prepare for the journey and battles to come. Spies were sent out to get a lay of the land. They learned that the people knew of the Almighty God of Israel and were afraid of the coming conquest. It was finally time to move in . . . but there was one more obstacle. A river stood between God's people and the land He was giving them. And, of course, it was the time of year when the water was high in flood stage.

Maybe the memory of the Red Sea crossing came to mind, because there was no sign of doubt or complaint when Joshua said, "Tomorrow the Lord will do amazing things among you." When it was time, the Ark of the Covenant led the way. The ark was a holy box, about twenty-seven inches by forty-five inches and twenty-seven inches high. It was covered with gold and two gold angels sat on top of it. This was the symbol of God's presence and therefore taken extremely seriously. No one touched the Ark; it was transported by poles and only carried by the Levites, the people set apart for service in the tabernacle. In this case, the Israelites were told to keep their distance from the Ark—half a mile of distance, to be exact—as it went before them into the Promised Land.

God instructed Joshua, who led the people, step by step to the Jordan River. When the priests with the ark reached the edge of the water, they were to go stand in the river. Then, God would make a way. And that's exactly what happened.

The priests carried the ark to the river, and the moment their feet touched the water, the water from upstream stopped flowing! We've arrived at our miraculous 3:16. Once again, the God of Israel demonstrated that no obstacle is too difficult and that bodies of water are no problem. Scripture describes the phenomena by saying the waters "piled up in a heap" about 15 to 20 miles upriver. This left a dry crossing for the hundreds of thousands of Israelites to make their way to the other side. If we keep reading, we find that twelve men, one from each tribe, were chosen to come take a rock from the middle of the currently-held-up river to make a monument on the other side. This would serve as a testament to generations of the great miracle God did that day. As soon as the task was accomplished, the priests (who had been standing in the middle of the river holding a heavy Ark of the Covenant this whole time) also crossed over. At that moment, the Jordan River flowed again, all the way up to that high flood stage as it had before!

The evidence of God's love is all over this incredible event. This was a true miracle, something no human being could ever orchestrate. Even the most skilled dams take time to build or to destroy. There was no question that the Israelites' God was powerful and loved His children completely. Scholars have discovered a natural occurrence around the ancient city of Adam, where the waters "piled up in a great heap." There are limestone cliffs that occasionally fall into the water, creating a natural dam. God most certainly could have controlled the timing of such an event, making this no less a miracle. For the water to stop and go at exactly the minute of the priests approach to the water's edge points clearly to the work of the One who created the river and all that surrounded it.

Why did God go through all that trouble to rearrange the natural world? A look at Joshua 3:7 lets us listen in on the Lord's conversation with Joshua. He said that He would exalt Joshua in front of all the people, so they'd know that God was with him just as God was with Moses. While this happened, the one who was truly exalted was God Himself. Miracles always bring glory to God, and the opportunity to witness the work of His hand is a sure way to make a child of God feel loved by our Heavenly Father. Can you imagine being the recipient of such an amazing act? How humbling and encouraging!

Meanwhile, this moment in time is a snapshot of the big picture. As we read through the first few books of the Old Testament, we've watched God deliver His people from Egypt's slavery, sustain them through decades of wilderness wandering, and prepare them for this very time, the actual arrival to the Promised Land. All of this was to fulfill a covenant He had lovingly made with Abraham many generations before. Finally taking the Israelites into the Promised Land was itself an act of love.

Now, where do we find ourselves in a hard-to-believe miracle that happened thousands of years ago in a faraway land? As always, we know that our God is the same yesterday, today, and forever. He loves His children now just as fiercely as He loved those who lived in the days of Moses and Joshua. So why don't we see modern day miracles? There are books and volumes and endless discussions on this topic, and I encourage you to dig deep into them. When we seek God, He shall be found, so research on His miracles is bound to be a treasure hunt! For now, we can acknowledge the smaller-scale miracles around us every day, from displays in nature, financial blessings, perfect timing, or those things that are just too detailed to be coincidence. Perhaps we miss miracles because we aren't looking for them, or are too quick to explain them away in our modern age of cynicism and skepticism? It's been speculated that we've created for ourselves an existence that doesn't rely on God. Have we crowded Him out of our lives to leave little room for the miracles He wants to do for us? We often look for partings of the Red Sea while ignoring a multitude of daily small miracles. There are so many questions about the mysterious work of Almighty God. May we never cease to seek His love in the miraculous!

The crossing of the Jordan shows God making a way for His people. In their case, it was a literal, physical obstacle that needed to be overcome for them to continue on their path. How many times have we hit obstacles? How many challenges have seemed impossible to overcome? Many times, God holds back the waters of pressure, deadlines, adversity, or setbacks in our lives. The prophet Isaiah (in chapter 43, if you're following along) used this very imagery to explain how God did, does, and will make a way for His people. He describes God making a way through the sea and mighty waters. Isaiah speaks of God doing a new thing like making a way in the wilderness. These promises were initially for the people of that time, but, again, a constant God loves His children consistently. Psalm 34:19 says, "The righteous person may have many troubles, but the Lord delivers him from them all." The timing or result may not be what we imagined, but, dear friend, we've seen that we serve a God who is a keeper of promises. His Word has been proven true time and time again. He **will** make a way for you, no matter how high your personal river is rising.

Notice that God didn't provide a bridge for the Israelites, nor did He magically fly them over the Jordan. They had to go through it. But they didn't go alone. Remember, the Ark of the Covenant hit the riverbanks a half mile before the rest of the Israelite nation followed. God prepared a way for His people by personally going ahead of them. Then, He pushed back the flooding waters so that the path was one that all the people, including the women, children, the elderly, and even their animals could traverse. Still, the crossing had challenges. The twelve chosen men pulled rocks from the riverbed for their remembrance monument. This means that the bottom of the river was probably rocky, and the people needed to watch their step. Did any of them have doubt, as they crossed a riverbed over a hundred feet wide, that the water might come crashing back before they made it across? Because we certainly have doubts in the time that God is working in our own adversity, when we can't seem to get to the other side quickly enough. But God took them through it, and God takes us through it. He goes ahead of us and stays in that river until we are safely on the other side. He holds back the waters and helps us endure the challenges in our path. That's love.

8. JUDGES

"Now Ehud had made a double-edged sword about a cubit long, which he strapped to his right thigh under his clothing..."

Judges 3:16

The Old Testament isn't for sissies, and some of the stories in its pages are downright graphic. We've entered the age of the judges! The book begins after the death of Joshua, leaving the Israelites without a leader. They were in the process of taking over the Promised Land bit by bit and taking some liberties with God's instructions. Sometimes, a tribe would completely drive out all the inhabitants of a nation and claim the land. However, many tribes just moved in and mixed among the existing people. This went against the command the Lord had given them to not make covenants with the people of the land, but instead break down their altars (see Judges chapter 2 for more details on this). It had become so bad that the Angel of the Lord spoke to the Israelites and told them that He would no longer drive the people out for them. Instead, they would become a stumbling block to the Israelites.

Oh, what a stumbling block those people were! When the next generation of Israelites grew up, they did not serve God. Instead, they adopted the gods of the Canaanites whom they lived among. So, God didn't stop enemies from overtaking the Israelites. Things were bad, and God's people were distressed. However, despite their ignorance and waywardness, the Lord still regarded His people. Amid the Israelites' consequences, God provided judges to lead and save them. Soon, a pattern emerged. The Israelites would do their thing, ignoring God and serving Canaanite gods, until they were so oppressed by enemies that they would reach out to God for help. God would send a judge, the judge would lead them to victory, and life would improve. The Israelites would be grateful and worship their God—for a while. Then they would forget and fall back into old patterns, creating worse conditions than they were in before. That is, until they couldn't handle it anymore, called out to the Lord, received another judge . . . you get the idea. Before you criticize, don't forget that we fall into some pretty destructive patterns ourselves. Let us learn from this ancient example and break the cycle!

One such judge was a guy named Ehud. The people were doing evil again, so the Lord allowed King Eglon of Moab to take over. Israel was subject to this enemy king for eighteen years before they cried out to God, who gave them Ehud. All we know about this man is that he was from the tribe of Benjamin and that he was left-handed. Yep, those were the facts about Ehud that were important enough to preserve over centuries! But that's pretty reasonable, considering the description of King Eglon was that he was extremely obese. May our memorable qualities be more significant than merely our appearance.

Ehud was sent to King Eglon with the tribute, a required payment from the conquered people to the king. That's where we hit our 3:16—Ehud was packing heat. He had an 18-inch double-edged sword hidden, strapped to his right thigh. All went according to routine, the tribute was given, Ehud and his crew left, and they made their way toward home. Then, Ehud turned back and returned to the palace alone. He again appeared before King Eglon and claimed to have a secret message. The king was all ears and cleared the room, leaving the two of them alone and secluded. Ehud told him that he had a message from God just for Eglon, and he proceeded to hand-deliver that message, directly from his sword. This is where it gets gruesome, so here are the basics (you're welcome to dive into Judges 3 if you're curious about the details): Ehud stabbed Eglon, and the 18-inch sword wasn't even visible in such a large man. While Eglon breathed his last, Ehud sneaked out and locked the door behind him. By the time King Eglon's people realized that something happened, Ehud was long gone. The chaos of the assassination gave Israel the opportunity to turn the tables and take over the Moabites. The result was a peace that endured for eighty years.

We're looking for God's love in our 3:16. At face value, we see the Lord's hand when He answered the cry of His people and sent Ehud the judge to deliver them from Moab. The Lord loved His people and He saved the day, bringing peace. But if we dig deeper, we can find more love hidden in the brutal text.

First, there's the matter of Israel being subject to Moab at all. A God of love could certainly protect His children in a perpetual bubble of safety. But, the Almighty, in His perfect wisdom, chose to go another route. After the Israelites disobeyed, He allowed them to experience the consequences of their bad habits. We don't get the particulars, but if Scripture is using words like "evil" and "wickedness," we know this is far more serious than just forgetting to acknowledge the Lord or making a few mistakes. Like a good parent, the Lord knows that discipline and teaching His children means allowing them to experience the results of their actions. After all, they were in the Promised Land and had been granted favor by God even when they strayed from Him, so clearly a safety bubble wouldn't do much to help them follow God and experience His blessings. So, consequences it was.

Meanwhile, Judges 3 points out two other reasons God allowed Israel's enemies to overtake them. Unlike previous generations led by Joshua, the current people had zero experience in battle. They were going to need skills to follow God's plan of deliverance. With enemy opposition, they'd receive some practice fighting and then be prepared for the victorious battles to come. Additionally, the adversity from the enemies allowed God to test the Israelites in their obedience to Him. As we have seen before, a God who loves doesn't abandon us to our flaws and shortcomings. He shapes us to become who He created us to be.

And, speaking of how He created us, what about that description of Ehud? He's a Benjamite, a man from the smallest tribe. He's not coming from a background of glory like a celebrated warrior. Perhaps he had an air of humility about him? That certainly would be an advantage when he earned the trust of King Eglon while delivering his "secret message." Also, he was left-handed. Why on Earth do we need to know that? It's mentioned again in verse 21 when we see Ehud reaching with his left hand to grab the sword from his right thigh. Did this create an element of surprise since most people would reach with their right hand to their left side? Did Eglon lose the short window of opportunity to put up a fight while his brain was making sense of what was happening? Did Ehud's handedness allow him to carry out his mission? Psalm 139 says we are fearfully and wonderfully made, and Ephesians 2:10 describes us as God's handiwork made to do works prepared for us. Our loving God pays attention to details. When He created little baby Ehud in the tribe of Benjamin, He designed him to have a dominant left hand that enabled him to save an entire nation of people. What details were created in you in order to do prepared good works?

Details matter and all the little things about you that make you unique can—and will—be used by God. The possibilities are infinite. Perhaps your talents give you a platform to share the gospel. Your skill with numbers and math could bless your church finance office. Your ability to listen attentively might equip you to support a friend in need and be the hands and feet of Christ during their difficult circumstances. God created you specifically to be utilized for His kingdom. This includes the trials that He allows in our lives. Struggles like maintaining our health, managing a temper, or feeling constantly disappointed in our circumstances can be battles that equip us for victory. They make us empathetic and supportive to those who fight similar battles. Overcoming adversity strengthens us so that we conquer problems easier each time we encounter them. The skills we learn during trials enable us to face bigger challenges with bravery.

Now, let's talk about that double-edged sword, since it's the focus of the sixteenth verse. In this case, it's simply a weapon, albeit one perfectly designed to stealthily kill a chubby king. Scripture is full of references to double-edged swords, often as symbolism. We know that such a sword has the ability to work in two directions and is a powerful weapon when used by someone with experience and skill. Hebrews 4:12 uses sword imagery to describe the Word of God, saying the Word is alive, exerts power, and is sharp enough to divide soul and spirit. It can discern the intention of thoughts and heart motivation. Jumping over to Ephesians 6 will give us another reference to God's Word as a sword, packed in the middle of a discussion on spiritual warfare. Like the ancient Israelites, we, too, are in a battle. But, as Paul explains to the Ephesians, our fight isn't physically against other people. Instead, we are engaged in a war against powers of darkness. That might sound a little scary at first. Yet, like Ehud, we are equipped for battle. Our principal weapon is the "sword of the spirit," the very Word of God. Therefore, it is crucial to spend time in Scripture, learning and applying the words to our hearts and minds. It's like training with an actual sword as a weapon. If we don't know the Word, how can we use it? Knowing God's promises reassures us when life gets scary. God's wisdom and biblical examples demonstrate how to handle most situations. Like the Israelites, we do not go into battle alone. The Lord goes before us and the enemy is given into our hands. Victory is certain! We merely need to be obedient to the One who perfectly created us and provides for us. He leads us out of danger and into His blessings. He is the One who loves us.

9. RUTH

"When Ruth came to her mother-in-law, Naomi asked, 'How did it go, my daughter?' Then she told her everything Boaz had done for her..."
- Ruth 3:16

Ah, a love story. After tales of warfare and assassins, we get a rest stop on our 3:16 journey. Let's travel from Bethlehem to Moab and back again where we witness the heartbreak and healing in a faithful young woman.

The scene opens on a couple named Elimelek and Naomi during a famine. For survival's sake, they and their sons left home, landing in a neighboring country (Moab, if you're keeping track). The two sons met local women, fell in love, and married them. All seemed to be going well when tragedy struck. First, Elimelek died. Then, ten years later, both the sons passed away as well. Naomi became a widow with no sons and two also-widowed daughters-in-law.

Besides the heartbreak of losing a spouse, widowhood was extra problematic in ancient society. Women relied on men to provide for them, so without a husband or sons, Naomi was left without resources. Moreover, she was still a foreigner in Moab. Any extended family was a great distance away in Bethlehem. The situation was grim.

But Naomi was not a woman who sat back passively and allowed life to pummel her. The food situation in Bethlehem had improved and she could return home. Practically, she encouraged her daughters-in-law to return to their own families and take the opportunity to remarry. This was an emotional decision, as all three women cared deeply for each other. But with much deliberation, one daughter-in-law left and the other stayed. This is our first encounter with Ruth, a daughter-in-law who declared her loyalty to Naomi, Naomi's family, and even Naomi's God. This was a pretty big deal. Ruth was leaving behind her family, friends, home, and traditions. She gave up the assurance of remarriage. By remaining with her mother-in-law, Ruth would be relinquishing the chance at a secure life. She chose poverty with Naomi over provision without her. What inspired such loyalty? Scripture doesn't explain the "why," so we can try to imagine as we continue to watch the story unfold verse by verse.

The two women arrived in Bethlehem with very little besides their mourning hearts. For nourishment, Ruth volunteered to go to the fields to collect any scraps the harvesters left behind as they worked. If you're taking notes, this was a common practice called gleaning. It just so happened (translation: God's hand was at work) that Ruth chose a field owned by a guy named Boaz, a prominent member of Elimelek's family. Not only was Boaz successful, he was also kind. He noticed Ruth and asked about her. The answer his overseer gave him: "She is a Moabite," reminds us of yet another important detail. Not only was Ruth a widow, but she was a widow in a foreign country. The cultural differences combined with her situation were more than impractical; they were likely very isolating. Yet, like Naomi, Ruth was also not a woman who sat back passively and allowed life to pummel her. She ventured out, she was proactive, and she bravely approached that field determined to do what it took to survive.

Boaz seemed determined to help her do more than simply survive. He gave her water and something to eat. He allowed her to gather more than meager scraps, even going as far as telling his workers to leave extra on the ground for her to gather. Ruth went home to Naomi with a bounty.

Chapter three begins with Naomi thinking practically once again. She knew that Ruth needed a stable home and she thought Boaz was just the guy to provide it. Using her knowledge of their customs and Boaz's evening plans,

Naomi gave Ruth specific instructions involving sleeping arrangements and feet uncovering, which is an ancient custom that seems strange to us now. Of course, the loyal Ruth followed these precisely. Though it seems odd from our modern point of view, it was taken well by Boaz and plans are set in motion. Ruth mentioned a key detail here: Boaz is a "guardian-redeemer." Tuck that away in your mind because we'll jump back to it soon. But first, we arrive at our 3:16. Ruth returned home in the morning and reported back to her mother-in-law. "She told her everything Boaz had done for her . . ."

Let's add up all the things Boaz had done. First, he allowed her to glean from his field. He also gave her special treatment, allowing her food and water during the work day and additional amounts of grain. Ruth was also permitted to glean throughout the rest of the harvest season. Then there was the kindness shown that night. Ruth was treated with compassion and promised the care of a guardian-redeemer. He honored her by not being intimate with her but allowing her to return home early enough that it wouldn't arouse unnecessary rumors or speculation. He also filled her shawl with barley to take home to Naomi. This was a guy who went above and beyond for Ruth. Could it be true love?

There was certainly a lot of love here, and not just from Boaz. God was clearly at work in the life of Ruth. Remember, she was not an Israelite, but a Moabite. We know from our previous stories that the history with Moab was up and down as friend and foe. God made a serious covenant promise with the Israelites, but not with any other nation. So God's favor on Ruth was not because of where she was born or her heritage. Ruth chose to serve the God of Israel, the God of Naomi. She grew up with all the Moabite gods, then lived with an Israelite family for more than ten years. Ruth knew each culture well and sacrificed the comforts of a secure life in Moab in order to worship the one true God. Much like Rahab in the book of Joshua, this choice was rewarded with protection, provision, and (spoiler alert) a place in the family tree of Jesus Himself.

How great is our God? He doesn't require us to come from a certain heritage before He welcomes us in as His own. Our choice to serve and worship Him is all it takes to be one of the family. The only prerequisite to a life of the Lord's blessing is a heart that chooses Him. There's no test to pass, no burnt sacrifice to offer, no spiritual hoops to jump through. Just "declare with your mouth, 'Jesus is Lord,' and believe in your heart that God raised him from the dead, [and] you will be saved" (Romans 10:9). That's the love of our Heavenly Father.

A loving father provides for his children, and God is no exception. In fact, our Heavenly Father goes beyond what anyone on Earth could do. We see the providence of God all through the book of Ruth, beginning with the simple provision of food for Elimelek and Naomi by leading them to Moab. Naomi was inspired to return to Bethlehem when she heard that the Lord provided food for His people. Proverbs 16:9 reminds us that "In their hearts humans plan their course, but the LORD establishes their steps."

Nothing that happened to Ruth or Naomi was an accident. It was not coincidence that led Ruth to Boaz's field, nor was it happenstance that Boaz noticed her and gave her favor. Even if Naomi's idea for Ruth to visit Boaz that night was completely her idea (which, knowing how faithful Naomi was to the Lord, it's unlikely that this was out of the blue without any prayer), God allowed Boaz's response to be favorable. When we get to the end of the story, we will see more ways that God provided for His children.

Scripture tells us repeatedly that God directs us and provides for us. In His teaching, Jesus used the example of God's care for tiny sparrows to remind the disciples how valued and loved we are. After all, if the Lord gives little birds what they need, how much more will He care for His children? Examples of God's provision are spread thickly over the pages of Scripture. The very first thing God did for the very first people was give them a place to live with plenty to eat. The Israelites received manna and quail as they wandered through the wilderness. Elijah was fed by ravens (not typical wild bird behavior, so we know it was totally the Lord behind that one). Noah and his family were given instructions and shelter from the biggest storm to ever hit the Earth. Countless people were given healing for diseases and disabilities. The list is long, and it extends beyond the books of the Bible, throughout the ages to today, to the many ways God provides for everything you need . . . because He loves you.

Now, let's go back to that whole "guardian-redeemer" thing. It's also called "kinsman-redeemer," depending on which translation of the Bible you're reading. As we know, it was not great to be widowed in a time where women relied on men for daily living. So, when God set up the law, He made provisions for such situations. What was called "levirate marriage" meant that if a man died, his brother would marry his widow and pass on the family name. If there was no brother, marriage would go down a specific line of nearest relatives. This not only gave security to the widow, but a son born in the new relationship would legally be considered the son of the original man. Property would be so inherited, and the family line would continue. In many cases, such as with Ruth or Naomi, there were no brothers and no one to step in to take the place of Ruth's deceased husband. In that case, a man in the family who was a "guardian-redeemer" would help here. The title means "a family member who can buy back," such as purchasing family land that had previously been sold or buying back a member of the family from slavery. Other responsibilities might include avenging the death of a family member, helping a family member in need, or marrying a childless widow and fulfilling levirate law. Boaz was such a guardian-redeemer, and he fulfilled his role very well!

This is a great history lesson, but what does it have to do with the love of God? Oh, so much! While we don't live under levirate law today, we have a guardian- or kinsman-redeemer of our own. We are slaves to sin. There's no way around it. It's human nature to sin, and therefore the consequences are unavoidable. We are trapped. Since we can't stop sinning or fix the problems ourselves, we are left very spiritually needy. That's where Christ steps in. The Son of God is our guardian; the Son of Man who walked the Earth in the flesh is our kinsman. He stepped in to pay the price that would buy us back from the slavery of sin. That cost was the highest imaginable—His death on the cross, His life for ours. But, as Boaz loved Ruth, Jesus loves us and He redeemed us willingly, despite the sacrifice.

Ruth's story ends with a "happily ever after." Boaz married her, and they had a son. The baby continued Naomi and Elimelek's family line and extended all the way to their descendant, King David, and then to Jesus Christ, our Redeemer. God's loving provision went beyond Ruth to cover the whole world.

10. 1 SAMUEL

"... but Eli called him and said, 'Samuel, my son.' Samuel answered, 'Here I am.'"

- 1 Samuel 3:16

Samuel's story begins with his mother, Hannah. She was childless, which left her in a state of deep sorrow. Her despair was so intense that she found herself pleading with the Lord in the middle of a public place—a holy place of worship. The current of sadness flowed so strongly in Hannah that she was either not mindful or she didn't care about appearances and the usual temple social standards. Besides longing for a baby, she also endured torment from her husband's other wife and perhaps even complicated emotions about her own marriage. And so, it was there that Eli the priest found Hannah calling out to God so enthusiastically that Eli thought she was drunk.

In her prayers, Hannah made promise with the Lord. If He gave her a son, she would turn around and give that son back to Him. This baby would be dedicated to the Lord's service for his entire life. Her fervent prayers were answered, and she had a son, whom she named Samuel. True to her word, as soon as he was old enough (but still very, very young), Samuel moved into the temple and began to assist Eli.

Picture cute little boy Samuel in a kid-sized robe (that his mother brought for him each year as he, undoubtedly, quickly grew out of each one the way that little boys do), serving obediently with the adults. What kind of childhood did he have? Did he get play time, or was he constantly solemn, raised with a steadfast focus on priestly service? Did he ever laugh with other children, or was he only surrounded by serious adults? Scripture doesn't give us details about Samuel's daily life other than to say that he grew physically and in favor with God and people.

We do learn, however, that there are other sons in this story—the two sons of Eli. Though they were priests, they were bad news. The NIV calls them scoundrels, to be specific. Their priorities seemed to be their own spiritual and physical appetites and they routinely took parts of sacrifices for themselves that were designated for the Lord. In fact, they did this so often that you could tell by their excessive weight how "blessed" they were from the choice parts of the meat offerings! Additionally, they were committing sexual sin with women who served at the tent of meeting. To make matters worse, when Eli scolded them for their wicked shenanigans, they simply ignored him and continued the behavior.

Since the sons wouldn't listen to their father, God sent a prophet to make his point. A breaking point was reached and their time as priests was coming to an end. The prophet foretold the death of Eli's sons along with a promise that no one in their family line would ever serve as a priest again. Instead, the Lord would raise up a new priestly line, one that would be faithful.

Now, back to Samuel, who was growing up in this somewhat corrupt environment. Little Samuel ministered under Eli, who was aging and going blind. First Samuel 3:1 says that "the word of the Lord was rare and there were not many visions." Yet, something special happened one dark night. It began with the same bedtime routine as always: Samuel lay down near the Ark of the Covenant. In the quiet of the evening, the lamp flickered dim light on the walls when suddenly Samuel heard a voice call out his name. He responded with a very logical "Here I am," then went to Eli, thinking the priest was summoning him. Yet, Eli said he did not call, and sent young Samuel back to bed.

But when Samuel went back to bed, the voice called his name again. And again, Samuel thought it was Eli, but it wasn't Eli, and once again Eli sent Samuel back to bed . . . only for the voice to call out Samuel's name once more! Finally, Eli realized that it is the Lord who was calling Samuel, so he wisely instructed the boy to respond, "Speak, for your servant is listening." And that's just what Samuel did.

God had a message for Samuel that confirmed the words of the prophet who spoke against the scoundrel sons. The Lord verified that the previous prophecy will indeed be carried out, and judgment will come on Eli and his family for their sins. We arrive at our 3:16 the next morning, when this time Eli did call out to Samuel, who again replied, "Here I am."

Eli, of course, wanted to know what the Lord had to say. Samuel dutifully shared the bad news, and Eli, to his credit, accepted the word of the Lord.

Now that we have our context, let's find the love . . . and oh, there is a lot of love to be found. First Samuel begins with a demonstration of Psalm 34:18, "The Lord is close to the brokenhearted and saves those who are crushed in spirit." Hannah's heart was most certainly broken, and her spirit was crushed. Yet, in love, the Lord heard her cries. He had compassion on the childless woman and granted her request. Also, after Hannah faithfully dedicated Samuel to serve God, she was blessed with three more sons and two daughters! The Lord was indeed kind and loving to Hannah, and He continues to be kind and loving to His children through the ages. In His Sermon on the Mount, Jesus said, "Blessed are the poor in spirit, for theirs is the kingdom of heaven. Blessed are those who mourn, for they will be comforted" (Matthew 5:3-4). When you find yourself crushed by despair like Hannah, cry out to the compassionate God who loves you. You will find peace in Him.

The dark chapter in this story is about the sons of Eli. We see how a loving God deals with their sin by giving them fair warning before putting an end to unrighteousness. The sons were reprimanded by their father then given a serious prophecy, which was finally confirmed through Samuel's word from the Lord. Psalm 86:15 says, "But You, O Lord, are a God merciful and gracious, Slow to anger and abundant in lovingkindness and truth." He doesn't rush into punishment, but instead gives His children plenty of warning and time to repent and reverse course. However, when wickedness persists, our God of Justice acts in His perfect timing. Deuteronomy 32:4 declares, "He is the Rock, his works are perfect, and all his ways are just. A faithful God who does no wrong, upright and just is he." An almighty God who was unjust would not be a Heavenly Father who loves His children. A loving Lord does not let unrighteousness run rampant.

The most remarkable element of Samuel's story is the event in chapter three. What was it like to hear audibly the voice of God? We can use our imagination and note that it must have sounded similar to Eli whispering in the night. But once Samuel realized who was speaking, did he have chills of excitement or a supernatural peace? Regardless, he was calmly obedient and delivered the instructed response. Let's step back from the scene for a moment.

Through a wide-angle lens, we can see the holy Creator of the universe speaking to a small child. What's more, the Almighty was entrusting a substantial message with someone quite young and inexperienced. The miracle here is that such a big God would communicate with so little us. He didn't create mankind and simply deposit us on planet Earth to fend for ourselves. Instead, God is with us and takes the time to speak to us, whether miraculously audible as when He spoke to Samuel and many others in the Bible, or through His prophets or His Word. In John 10:27-28, Jesus said, "My sheep listen to my voice; I know them, and they follow me. I give them eternal life, and they shall never perish; no one will snatch them out of my hand." God spoke through the prophet Jeremiah to tell His children, "Call to me and I will answer you and tell you great and unsearchable things you do not know" (Jeremiah 33:3). Our God is not a silent deity, but a loving Lord who communicates with the people He treasures.

He is also a God full of patience. Even our best obedience falls drastically short of perfection. Our sincere efforts to serve Him don't always measure up to where we'd like to be. While our sin can be a stumbling block at times, often it is our inexperience or still-developing maturity that holds us back. Samuel was an example of innocent servanthood. He was devoted to the Lord and earnestly sought Him. However, at such a young age, he was unfamiliar with the sound of God's voice. Like Samuel, we are learning and growing. No matter where we are on our journey with the Lord, we have a long way to go. That, however, does not prevent us from being used for His holy purposes.

God was patient with Samuel when he got it wrong. When Samuel mistakenly replied to Eli, God persisted. When Samuel continually confused God's voice with that of the aging priest, God repeated the call until Samuel understood. Similarly, we see His patience with the Israelites as they wandered the desert. Deuteronomy 8:2 describes this: "Remember how the Lord your God led you all the way in the wilderness these forty years, to humble and test you in order to know what was in your heart, whether or not you would keep his commands." We can also apply 2 Peter 3:9 to our own lives when we understand that "The Lord is not slow in keeping his promise, as some understand slowness. Instead he is patient with you, not wanting anyone to perish, but everyone to come to repentance."

First Samuel 3:16 features Samuel's willingness to follow directions from God. He had quite a night, unlike anything he had ever experienced in his life! Do you think he got much sleep, or did he lie awake replaying every minute in his mind? The word of the Lord must have weighed heavily on such young shoulders. How difficult it would be to give this unpleasant news to the priest who raised and mentored him! Scripture doesn't describe a boy who hid from responsibility, but a child who answered the call of God. This required a great deal of inner strength, and we would be foolish to attribute that kind of emotional power to such a young child or even the wisest adult. The ability to serve the Lord in such a way is made possible only by the Holy Spirit. In Ezekiel 36:27, God says to Israel, "And I will put my Spirit in you and move you to follow my decrees and be careful to keep my laws." In the same way, when God gives us instructions, He enables us to follow through and complete them.

First Samuel paints a portrait of a God of love. He is a God who communicates with His creation, rules with justice and patience, compassionately cradles the brokenhearted, and works within us to accomplish His purposes and bring Him glory.

11. 2 SAMUEL

"Her husband, however, went with her, weeping behind her all the way to Bahurim. Then Abner said to him, 'Go back home!' So he went back."

- 2 Samuel 3:16

David's story is long and complicated. He began life as a shepherd boy, was anointed as a king of Israel long before he took the throne, and then he slayed a giant in order to win a battle. This is a man who had a long, complicated history with King Saul, one that involved a lot of fleeing and hiding in order to survive. The story of David's romantic relationships is also long and complicated with multiple wives and forbidden love. David was simply a complicated guy.

His first love was Saul's younger daughter, Michal. To get to 2 Samuel 3:16, we need to jump back a bit to 1 Samuel 18, where their romance began. Though, to be fair, there was also diplomacy mixed in with these two crazy kids. Saul was still king, but he knew that the Lord was with David and that David had been anointed by Samuel to take over the throne. This, of course, did not please Saul. In fact, Scripture says that Saul feared David because of this. So, Saul made a plan: he offered his oldest daughter to marry David, in exchange for David fighting a few battles against their enemy, the Philistines. The logic was that David would die in battle and all problems would be solved nicely and neatly for good ol' Saul.

David, however, refused to marry Saul's oldest daughter. He didn't have feelings for her and claimed that he wasn't worthy of being the king's son-in-law (this reasoning was possibly because his humble family could not provide the kind of dowry befitting a king's daughter). But then, plot twist! Saul's younger daughter, Michal, was in love with David, and it appeared that the feeling was mutual. Ol' Saul was back in the game with his plotting and scheming. From the king's point of view, Michal would be a distraction to David, and surely, he would be killed by the Philistines. To solve that little dowry issue, Saul asked only a simple favor, a hundred Philistine foreskins as revenge on his enemies. Then David and Michal could live happily ever after. Ah, the joys of ancient love and politics.

David was motivated by love, so he provided double what Saul asked. He and Michal were married! Meanwhile, Saul's fear of David grew. And as fear often does, it grew into an anger and hatred that led to murderous tendencies in the king. This began a pattern of Saul attempting to kill David and David escaping; a routine they would follow for years. It certainly put a damper on newlywed life. In the next chapter of 1 Samuel, Michal and her brother Jonathan protected David from their father after Saul tried to kill David with a spear. David knew he must escape in order to remain alive. His young wife helped him slip out the window, then created a "David dummy" by placing a household idol and some goat hair under a blanket. When Saul's men came to capture David, this diversion bought enough time for him to leave town safely. Love won the day!

Unfortunately, this was only a temporary victory. Saul continued to pursue David, who continued to escape with the Lord's favor. There were battles and close calls. David and Michal were separated, and time passed. Eventually, David took two more wives and King Saul gave Michal to a guy named Paltiel. We don't know much about this man, but it was likely that their marriage was a political move by Saul to seal a diplomatic alliance. This seemed to be the end of the line for David and Michal's young marriage.

After more of these escapades and then Saul's death, we finally find ourselves at 2 Samuel. David was anointed King of Judah, but Saul's son still ruled the kingdom of Israel. Predictably, there was war between the two. In this time, David and his house grew stronger, while Saul's son grew weaker. A turning point came after conflict between Saul's son and the commander of his army, named Abner. Their disagreement led to the commander's appeal to David to help him claim the kingdom. David and Abner made an agreement and David demanded one condition: that his wife, Michal, would be returned to him. This is our 3:16! Michal was taken from her second husband, Paltiel, and returned to her first husband, David. Paltiel clearly loved Michal and wept as he lost her. As a pawn in her father's political dealings, Michal was placed in a lose-lose situation—no matter which marriage prevailed, someone would get hurt.

Finding God's love in this passage takes a little bit of digging, so let's begin with the human love in this triangle. David, Michal, and Paltiel each demonstrated devotion in different ways. David went to extreme measures to marry Michal. Then, despite having other wives, he still wanted to be reunited with his first love. In all fairness, this move could have been influenced by political implications. However, as most of us know from experience, first love is a strong force. It's very possible that David longed to be with Michal again after their forced separation at the nearly homicidal hand of Saul.

Michal's love for David was greater than family loyalty. She risked becoming the object of her father's wrath in order to save David. There is no question that she was in love; it's written clearly on the pages of 1 Samuel. Tragically, Michal's affection was not lifelong. We don't know what happened during their separation or how she felt about Paltiel. We see only the end of David and Michal's romance six chapters into 2 Samuel. After David's public display of joyful dance celebrating the Ark of the Covenant, Michal despised him. After reprimanding him for what she perceived as indecency, we are told that she lived the rest of her years childless. Their young love did not pass the test of time.

What about the marriage between Paltiel and Michal? We have only two clues to spark our imaginations. The first is Paltiel's name, which means "my deliverance." Did he deliver Michal from a life of hate-fueled chaos? Did she find peace in his home, far from the manipulation and vengeance of her own family? Was there rest away from the perpetual Saul/David pursuit? Our second clue is Paltiel's intense reaction to Michal's return to David. He sobbed and followed her, turning back only when Abner, a high-ranking military official, gave orders. Clearly, he loved his wife beyond political advantage. Yet, this was the end for poor Paltiel. His love was limited in a world of diplomacy, kings, and battles over kingdoms.

David sought restoration. Paltiel passionately mourned the love he lost. And Michal's loyalty was with the object of her heart's desire. These are earthly examples of love that are merely a snapshot of the divine romance between God and His children.

The Lord is the Great Restorer. Time and again we see how God looked upon wayward Israel and brought her back to Himself. When the Israelites wandered from God in the wilderness, He brought them physically to the Promised Land as their hearts turned back to Him. Over many generations, God's people would stray, worshiping other gods and forsaking His steadfast love. And each time, keeping with the covenant established from the beginning, the Lord restored His people to Himself. He said, through the prophets Amos and Jeremiah, that He would bring the Israelites home from exile—and He did just that.

When we peruse the book of Hosea, we find both a story of the prophet and his wife as well as an illustration of Israel and their God. Hosea married a prostitute and repeatedly brought her back whenever she was unfaithful. God used this example of how, even though Israel was repeatedly unfaithful to the Lord, He always drew them back to Himself. In the last chapter of Hosea, He calls for Israel to return to the Lord their God. Then He said, "I will heal their waywardness and love them freely, for my anger has turned away from them" (Hosea 14:4).

In the New Testament, Jesus physically restored sight to the blind, hearing to the deaf, and mobility to those who could not walk. Of course, greater restoration happened in the hearts of those who heard and believed. Ultimate restoration happened on the cross, when Christ's sacrifice reunited sinful humanity with the holy God. First Peter 5:10 says, "And the God of all grace, who called you to his eternal glory in Christ, after you have suffered a little while, will himself restore you and make you strong, firm and steadfast." There is more restoration still to come, when we are reunited with Him in glory.

In our 2 Samuel story, Paltiel's great display of emotion is a teardrop in the bucket compared to the passionate love of Almighty God. Mortal words are inadequate descriptors, but God's Word gives us a glimpse at how deeply he feels. Like Paltiel, God mourns when the ones He loves are far from Him. In Genesis 6:5-6, we see how the people of Earth turned their backs on the God that created them. The Lord's "heart was deeply troubled." Generations later, the prophet Jeremiah spoke to the Israelites who had fallen so very far away from the Lord. God told Jeremiah to say, "Let my eyes overflow with tears night and day without ceasing; for the Virgin Daughter, my people, has suffered a grievous wound, a crushing blow" (Jeremiah 4:17).

As intense as His sorrow was in these passages, His love is stronger yet. First John 3:1a says, "See what great love the Father has lavished on us, that we should be called children of God!" To lavish means to bestow generously or with extravagance. Now, take that to the infinite level of God. This is an incredible love!

Need proof of how intense this is? "But God demonstrates his own love for us in this: While we were still sinners, Christ died for us" (Romans 5:8). Not only is His love passionate enough that He sacrificed His own Son, but He did it while we were in the midst of our sin. He didn't wait for us to earn it through good behavior, but instead, while we were still wallowing in the darkness, God gave us the gift of all gifts. What human being could do such a thing? There is no one like our God!

Finally, we see Michal's loyalty, so well-intentioned but so short-lived. God, however, is much more committed to the ones He loves. Moses explained this to Joshua in Deuteronomy 31 when he told him multiple times that God will never leave nor forsake him. In Isaiah 41:10, God told the people, "So do not fear, for I am with you; do not be dismayed, for I am your God. I will strengthen you and help you; I will uphold you with my righteous right hand." Later, when Jesus gave His final words to the disciples, He said, "And surely I am with you always, to the very end of the age" (Matthew 28:20). These are just a few examples of our faithful God keeping His covenant of love.

Second Samuel 3:16 is a glimpse of a messy triangle of human relationships, comprised of three people that God loved very much. As they fell extremely short of God's perfection, David, Paltiel, and Michal demonstrated how limited is the love of human beings. Praise be to our God of perfect love, a love that is restorative, passionate, and faithful.

12. 1 KINGS

"Now two prostitutes came to the king and stood before him."

- 1 Kings 3:16

After King David ruled and died, his son, Solomon, took over leadership of Israel. King Solomon was well-known for many things, particularly his wisdom. One day, after offering a thousand burnt sacrifices, the Lord visited Solomon in a vision. God said, "Ask for whatever you want," and Solomon gave this some consideration. He recognized that he was young and inexperienced yet held the great responsibility of ruling over God's people. So, he thoughtfully requested "a discerning heart in order to govern." Solomon wanted wisdom.

The Lord was pleased with this and granted Solomon his heart's desire! Additionally, Solomon was blessed with wealth, honor, and greatness among all other kings during his lifetime. Things were looking good for King Solomon!

It wasn't long before this wisdom was necessary, as we discover in our next 3:16. Two prostitutes had a terrible disagreement and sought justice from the king. The two women lived in the same house and both had infant sons. In the middle of the night, one of the babies tragically died after his mother rolled over on top of him. The mother stealthily crept over to the other woman as she slept with her own son, and then switched the two babies. Now, the sleeping woman had the dead baby while the first mother had one that was alive. Once morning came, the second mother was horrified to find that her baby had died! But upon closer examination, she realized it was not her own son. This led the two prostitutes to argue before King Solomon, each claiming that the living child was her own.

Solomon's course of action was dramatic. He called for a sword and declared that he would cut the living baby in half, giving part to each of the women. The mother of the living baby was horrified and so upset that she cried, "No! Don't kill him! Give him to the other woman!" However, the scheming mother was okay with the plan, saying that it was fair, and that neither of them should have a living son.

This was enough evidence for Solomon. He knew that the true mother would have compassion and self-sacrifice for her child. He then commanded that the baby be handed over to the first woman, who was the child's real mother. This case became well known throughout Israel, and the people saw that God granted the king wisdom to rule with justice.

Solomon's early days of reign were full of God's love. First, we see the love and favor the Lord shows the king through the offer of literally anything Solomon could ask. James wrote that "every good and perfect gift is from above, coming down from the Father of the heavenly lights, who does not change like shifting shadows" (James 1:17). Since our Heavenly Father does not change, we know that this truth remains today. The good things in our lives are gifts from above, provided by our God who loves us. Matthew 7:11 also points out that God not only gives us gifts, but they are good gifts. In this passage, Jesus taught His Sermon on the Mount. His illustration begins with a human father who gives his child fish and bread when asked. If a person, who by nature is sinful, is kind enough to give good gifts to his kids, "how much more will your Father in heaven give good gifts to those who ask him"?

Though Solomon had favor from the Lord, he wasn't unique in being loved by God. In Galatians, the apostle Paul points out that those who have faith are considered children of Abraham and blessed along with him. He reminded the reader that, when we belong to Christ, we are considered

Abraham's seed, and also heirs to God's promise. Centuries later, we who belong to Christ today also receive good gifts from our Father in heaven. Praise the Lord!

Solomon's wisdom led to a great display of justice. This was godly wisdom, and therefore his justice was also of the Lord. Scripture is full of declarations of God's justice. Isaiah 61:8 says plainly that God loves justice. Isaiah makes the connection between justice and God's love for us when he said, "Yet the Lord longs to be gracious to you; therefore he will rise up to show you compassion. For the Lord is a God of justice. Blessed are all who wait for him!" (Isaiah 30:18). The Lord is our rock, whose works are perfect, and ways are just. He does not do wrong, and He is upright and fair. In everything He does, God displays infinite, perfect justice.

This is yet another way He loves us. Psalm 140:12 explains that "the Lord secures justice for the poor and upholds the cause of the needy." God rules over the Earth with kindness and compassion while caring for His children. It would be cruel and harsh if He were *not* just. It would be more than just a matter of unfairness, but chaos and trouble from an unloving God. Thankfully, that is not our reality! As Job observed, the Lord "reveals the deep things of darkness and brings utter darkness into the light" (Job 12:22). The psalmist declared that "the Lord loves righteousness and justice; the earth is full of his unfailing love" (Psalm 33:5). His love exudes as "the Lord loves the just and will not forsake his faithful ones" (Psalm 37:28), and "when justice is done, it brings joy to the righteous" (Proverbs 21:15). In His great love, God maintains order among His people and more than meets their needs.

Finally, Solomon's story gives us an example of how God deals with us. The two women were prostitutes; their very profession was based on sin. Yet, they did not hesitate to approach the throne to seek justice. Our sin does not prevent us from the loving justice of our King. While digging into our previous 3:16, we were reminded that Christ died for us while we were sinners, which means that our perfection is not a requirement to receive God's love.

Paul describes this in Ephesians 2:4-5, saying "because of his great love for us, God, who is rich in mercy, made us alive with Christ even when we were dead in transgressions—it is by grace you have been saved." We do not have to be sinless to approach the throne of justice, but He will make us righteous by our repentance and His grace. That's what divine love does.

13. 2 KINGS

"... and he said, 'This is what the Lord says: I will fill this valley with pools of water.'"

- 2 Kings 3:16

Years passed after the wise rule of Solomon, and God's people were divided into two kingdoms: Israel and Judah. When we jump into 2 Kings, Israel was ruled by a king named Joram and Jehoshaphat reigned over Judah. Got that? So, the good news was that King Joram rid his kingdom of an idol that his father, the previous king, had established. The bad news? Straight from 2 Kings 3:2: "He did evil in the eyes of the Lord."

Ugh.

Remember Moab? At this point in history, the Moabites were subject to Israel. The king of Moab, named Mesha, raised sheep and had to pay Israel a tribute of a bunch of lambs and wool. But when Joram's father died and Joram took over the kingdom, Mesha decided he'd rather not pay such a tribute anymore. Cue the rebellion.

To deal with the uprising, King Joram reached out to King Jehoshaphat as well as the king of neighboring Edom. The three came together and made their way toward Moab. To get there, they took a route through the Desert of Edom, a strategy that offered a military advantage. Unfortunately, this strategy also meant a week-long trek through a desert, leaving them without water after seven days of marching.

The kings conferred, and Jehoshaphat suggested consulting a prophet of the Lord. It just so happened that the prophet Elisha was nearby! However, when the kings paid him a visit, his first response was, "Why do you want to involve me?" After all, King Joram was not following the one true God, but instead worshiped other gods and their idols. However, he appealed to Elisha because it was the Lord who called the three kings together. Based on his respect for King Jehoshaphat, Elisha called for a harpist and sought the Lord for a prophecy.

We find that prophecy in our 3:16. The Lord told them, through Elisha, that He would fill the dry desert valley with pools of water. There would be no storm or rain, but God Himself would provide the water so that the army and all the animals with them would be able to drink. He said that was an easy thing for the Lord to do, and He would also deliver Moab into their hands.

The next morning, water flowed into the Desert of Edom, just as the Lord said it would. As this happened, the Moabites, who had heard that the kings were on their way to fight, assembled. In the early morning sun, the water looked red, like blood. The Moabites assumed that the three kings fought each other to a bloody end, so they decided to take advantage of what they thought would be chaos. However, once they charged into the Israelite camp, the Israelites fought them until they retreated. The armies of the three kings charged into Moab and indeed took the city, as the Lord declared they would.

By now, some characteristics of God's love are becoming quite familiar to us. Again, in this story, we see God communicate with His people, provide for basic needs, and work miracles. His loving goodness never ceases to be amazing! Our God is the same yesterday, today, and forever, and we can see the patterns of His love as we turn the pages of Scripture.

What's new in this story is the situation of the divided kingdom and divided allegiances to other gods. King Joram had separated himself from the Almighty God, and almost missed out on His blessing. However, once he united with King Jehoshaphat, the story took a different turn. It reminds us of Christ's promise in Matthew 18:20, "For where two or three gather in my name, there am I with them."

This is not the first time that a person was blessed indirectly by association with one of God's people. In Genesis 30, Jacob was living with and working for his father-in-law, Laban. Jacob had been blessed by God in many ways, including with an abundance of livestock. Laban recognized this; he knew that God blessed him because of Jacob, and therefore he wanted Jacob to remain with him. Later, when we jump over to Genesis 39, we find Jacob's son, Joseph, in Egypt. After being sold into slavery by his own brothers, Joseph worked his way up to overseeing the house of an official named Potiphar. As a result, the Lord blessed the Egyptian's livelihood because of Joseph. This is one way God's promise to Abraham came to pass, as He said, "I will make you into a great nation, and I will bless you; I will make your name great, and you will be a blessing. I will bless those who bless you, and whoever curses you I will curse; and all peoples on earth will be blessed through you" (Genesis 12:2-3).

The three kings were unified, and God blessed that. We see God's love displayed through unity in the New Testament when Paul wrote to the Ephesians, "For he himself is our peace, who has made the two groups one and has destroyed the barrier, the dividing wall of hostility, by setting aside in his flesh the law with its commands and regulations. His purpose was to create in himself one new humanity out of the two, thus making peace, and in one body to reconcile both of them to God through the cross, by which he put to death their hostility" (Ephesians 2:14-16). This is referring to Christ, who is our peace. The two groups here are the Jews and the Gentiles. Though the Jews were God's chosen people, Christ opened the door to extend grace and salvation to the Gentiles as well. One thing that divided Jews and Gentiles in biblical times was the strict adherence to the Old Testament laws. However, through His work on the cross, Christ abolished the need for those laws. This passage in Ephesians points out that God united Jews and Gentiles into one family—we are all His children. Paul frequently echoes this and reminds his readers that there is neither Jew nor Gentile, for we are all one in Christ Jesus.

Like many miracles before, the act of God in 2 Kings 3:16 involved water. Specifically, God provided water to a thirsty army in the wilderness. While this hydrated them physically, we can't miss the spiritual symbolism as well. In John 4, Jesus sits by a well with a woman and explains to her that He is living water: "Indeed, the water I give them will become in them a spring of water welling up to eternal life" (John 4:14). In John 7:37-39, Jesus tells the people, "Let anyone who is thirsty come to me and drink. Whoever believes in me, as Scripture has said, rivers of living water will flow from within them." By this he meant the Holy Spirit, whom those who believed in Him were later to receive.

We can look at this from a big-picture standpoint and clearly see how our sin "dehydrates us" by separating us from God, who is life. Then Christ, the Son, the Living Water, fills us with grace and restores us to the Father again. It's no wonder that water is used symbolically in baptism not only as an acceptance of salvation, but also as a visual of being washed and cleansed by grace. We experience this flow of Living Water by the Holy Spirit that lives in us as children of God.

The blessing of Living Water can be found daily as well. Our lives often lead us to figurative desert valleys. Dire circumstances can feel like wandering a dry wilderness when trouble hits and there is no oasis in sight. During those times, when our strength is fading and solutions are out of reach, God can do great miracles. These are the days we find divine provision, hear His Word, and experience acts that can be attributed only to Him. Frequently the time when we most clearly see His hand at work is when all seems lost. This can be in the form of financial blessing, supportive friends and family, well-timed happenings that are clearly more than coincidence, and other miracles. The ways of God are creative and limitless, but always "for the good of those who love him, who have been called according to his purpose" (Romans 8:28). Just as water refreshes and is necessary for life, so is the Spirit of God. This gift is another great act of love from the Heavenly Father.

14. 1 CHRONICLES

"The successors of Jehoiakim: Jehoiachin his son, and Zedekiah."

- 1 Chronicles 3:16

At first glance, this simple verse seems empty of love. It's not even a complete sentence! But the complicated history of Judah's kings has plenty of love beneath the surface, so let's dive deeply and see what we discover.

The first king mentioned here is Jehoiakim. For more details on this guy, we refer to 2 Kings and even further into royal history. In chapter 21, we learn about the intense evil done by Jehoiakim's great grandfather, King Manasseh. We're talking idol worship, occultism, child sacrifice, and other unimaginable sins. God was more than displeased; He was livid. He promised divine disaster to Jerusalem and Judah as they followed Manasseh in his detestable behavior.

Years later, when Manasseh's grandson, King Josiah, took the crown at a young age, his faithfulness to God brought Judah back to obedience and delayed God's wrath. However, peace would not last. Egypt and Assyria joined forces against Judah and killed good King Josiah. His son inherited the throne for mere months before Egypt's pharaoh imprisoned him and imposed a levy on Judah. That's where our Jehoiakim, Josiah's other son, enters the scene.

Jehoiakim was yet another corrupt ruler who did evil in the eyes of the Lord. For a few years, Jehoiakim and the people of Judah served the king of Babylon. Apparently, they grew tired of paying tributes, because Jehoiakim eventually rebelled. Babylon was joined by a force of allies who together destroyed Judah, fulfilling the prophecy given during Manasseh's evil rule.

Once Jehoiakim died, his son, Jehoiachin, took the reign. Unfortunately, he performed just as much evil as his dad. Again, the king of Babylon took over Jerusalem, and Jehoiachin, his family, and his officials surrendered to him. The people of Jerusalem were also taken into exile. During this sad time for God's people, Jehoiachin and crew were prisoners. Of course, this meant that Jehoiachin was removed from the throne. The Babylonian king appointed Zedekiah, Jehoiakim's brother and Jehoiachin's uncle, to be the new king.

This was a family of slow learners, because Zedekiah also sinned against the Lord, and led the people to do the same. Also, like his brother, he rebelled against Babylon. The Babylonian king surrounded the city and kept them under siege for nearly two years, until famine overtook Judah. Zedekiah and his army attempted escape but were intercepted. Zedekiah was taken captive and the soldiers scattered! The punishment was severe. The last thing Zedekiah saw before the Babylonians gouged out his eyes was the murder of his sons. Then, like his nephew before him, he was taken prisoner until he eventually died.

However, there's a plot twist! Remember King Jehoiachin? After years of captivity, there was a new king in Babylon. The new king released Jehoiachin from prison and gave him a place of honor in his court. Didn't see that coming, did you?

The story is not complete without one more important element. Let's call it the Jeremiah factor. This major prophet was a voice of the Lord in a time of rampant sin. He appealed repeatedly to the kings to turn from evil and remain in the land. He warned Judah specifically that the Lord would allow the Babylonians to overcome them if they didn't get their act together and return to obedience. Jeremiah offered hope in the chaos, however. God revealed that the consequences of their sin would last only last seventy years, and then He'd bring them back home to Jerusalem.

You'd think that God's people would have appreciated the heads up, but instead they reacted with outrage. When they didn't like what he had to say, the people seized Jeremiah and sentenced him to death. God protected Jeremiah's life through imprisonments and death threats as the prophet boldly declared truth to a rebellious people. However, despite the abundant warnings and heaping helpings of truth, the kings and people of Judah refused to submit to the Lord and found themselves amid disaster.

Whew, what a story that is unearthed beneath three ancient names! Now we continue our excavation of God's love from the Scriptures. We find it in the thick of compassion, consequences, and consistency. Instead of punishing Manasseh and the people right on the spot, the Lord displayed great patience and gifted them with multiple opportunities to correct their course. Through the prophets, the people were given messages of hope: that they weren't necessarily doomed to the fate of previous evil kings. God never ceased loving His people compassionately.

But they declined the offer. As we've seen in previous stories, a fair and just God upholds the consequences of sin. If we were given unrestricted freedom to run wild, chaos would ensue. We would no longer grow and mature, but instead find ourselves hurting and causing others to hurt as well. A world without consequences—good or bad—is a world falling apart. Like a parent, God uses the consequences of our sin to guide us to obedience and blessing. Hebrews 12:11 reminds us that "no discipline seems pleasant at the time, but painful. Later on, however, it produces a harvest of righteousness and peace for those who have been trained by it."

Meanwhile, an all-powerful and sovereign universe Creator is well within His rights to run the planet as He pleases. If God wanted to operate a certain way one day and then change His mind the next without rhyme or reason, He could do so. But He doesn't. Through the Lord's consistency we see another bit of His love. "But the plans of the Lord stand firm forever, the purposes of his heart through all generations" (Psalm 33:11). The same God who handled the evils of Manasseh also honored the obedience of Josiah with peace. He sent His word to Jehoiakim, Jehoiachin, and Zedekiah in hopes that the people would seek His face again and avoid disaster. Numbers 23:19 tells us, "God is not human, that he should lie, not a human being, that he should change his mind. Does he speak and then not act? Does he promise and not fulfill?" Though He offered grace, God kept His word in how He dealt with Judah. He has kept promises consistently since the beginning of time. How could we count on a God who did not follow through? How could we trust a Heavenly Father who didn't do what He said He would? Thankfully, we serve a compassionate, consistent God who gives us the freedom to make our own choices while not allowing evil to persist chaotically without consequence.

The Almighty Lord who ultimately ruled during the days of Jehoiakim, Jehoiachin, and Zedekiah is the same Lord who rules today. The firm love, care, and discipline He gave His covenant people in the past is the same love, care, and discipline He gives us, His children, today.

15. 2 CHRONICLES

"He made wreaths of chainwork, as in the inner sanctuary, and put them on top of the pillars; and he made one hundred pomegranates, and put them on the wreaths of chainwork."

- 2 Chronicles 3:16

King David had big plans. Despite his many flaws and failings, the man after God's own heart truly wanted to please the Lord. So, David made plans to build a temple in honor of God's presence. However, his flaws and failings prevented him from carrying out the sacred project. The Lord looked upon David, who shed a lot of blood in many wars, and prohibited him from constructing such a holy place. Instead, the honor would go to David's son, Solomon, who was to be a king of peace. Solomon took over the blueprints from his father and began to build one of the grandest structures in history.

Only the finest materials and craftsmanship could be presented to the Lord Almighty. Second Chronicles begins with the now-familiar story of Solomon's request for wisdom. Not only would he need God to equip him to lead the Israelites, but also to oversee the building of the temple. The first chapter also establishes Solomon's great military and wealth. The scene is set for greatness, and, at this point in Solomon's life, the glory was going to God. He assembled a massive team of builders, then drafted a letter to the king of Tyre requesting wood and a skilled craftsman who could deftly handle the various materials of this holy place.

It's in this letter that Solomon laid out the purpose of such a magnificent building. He proclaimed that the temple would be built in the name of the Lord in order to burn incense and offerings. His words speak to a humble, heartfelt truth: "The temple I am going to build will be great, because our God is greater than all other gods. But who is able to build a temple for him, since the heavens, even the highest heavens, cannot contain him? Who then am I to build a temple for him, except as a place to burn sacrifices before him?" (2 Chronicles 2:5-6). In response, the king of Tyre praised God and agreed to send the craftsman and timber in exchange for a price Solomon promised. The building could begin.

First, the foundation was laid at Mount Moriah. This was the site where Abraham had nearly sacrificed Isaac many generations before. More recently, it was the place that held the threshing floor of Ornan. We need to cruise back to 1 Chronicles 21 to discover why this place was special to David and the people of Israel. Years before, God sent a plague over Israel in response to a great sin David had committed. After the death of thousands of men, David cried out to God to have mercy on the people and to direct wrath to David only. The Angel of the Lord appeared and instructed him to build an altar on the threshing floor of Ornan. Once David offered sacrifices there, the plague on the people was lifted. So began David's temple plans, which he prepared for Solomon. This brings us back to our story in 2 Chronicles.

The foundation was laid for a building which would be approximately ninety feet long by thirty feet wide. As the temple was constructed, the inside was overlaid with gold and decorated with carved palm trees and chainwork, and then adorned with precious stones. Carvings of angels called cherubim also graced the walls. The main room was called the Holy Place, and a smaller area was designated the Most Holy Place. This inner sanctuary would house the Ark of the Covenant and, once completed, would be entered only by the High Priest on the annual Day of Atonement. It was a special place featuring two large carved cherubim overlaid with gold. Their wings stretched across the length of the entire room. A veil made of fine linen was added, displaying hues of blue, purple, and crimson, with cherubim woven into it. The veil separated the Most Holy Place from the Holy Place. Two pillars were then constructed in front of the temple. They were decorated with the same chainwork found inside the temple but also included a hundred pomegranates. This is found in 2 Chronicles 3:16.

Why pomegranates? In Exodus, we find images of pomegranates woven into priestly garments. Pomegranates were also among the fruit the spies in Numbers 23 brought back from the Promised Land. Pomegranates were common in the region and valued for both the juice (used to make a spiced wine) as well as the rind, which could be used medicinally. The Scriptures and modern commentaries do not give specific symbolism of the fruit, but we know that it was a significant part of the intricate details that helped make Solomon's temple beautiful.

Our God is the master of details and the origin of all beauty. One way He shows His love is through His gorgeous creation. We see it above us as "the heavens declare the glory of God; the skies proclaim the work of his hands" (Psalm 19:1). The Lord's fingerprints are on mountains, trees, and beaches. His handiwork stretches from stars to ladybugs. The Earth is full of God's unfailing love. He gives us beauty in the details, and we can't help but see God's love all around us in all the things He created.

As humans, we can reflect beauty. We can't make matter from nothing, but we can pattern our work after what was made by God. The glittering details of Solomon's temple were but a whisper of the dazzling beauty of our Creator. This is the God who designed tiny wildflowers in the fields and included creative variations in thousands of animal species. He is the God who made colors in all hues and shades. Scientists continue to uncover the precise ways the universe is put together. All of these things bring glory to God first, and all of these things comprise an exquisite world created for people to inhabit. It's a world created by a God of love.

Each thoughtful detail of the carefully constructed temple honored the Lord. A powerful Creator does not require gold and statues in order to function, so these things serve another purpose, as Solomon explained humbly to the King of Tyre. This was a place to sacrifice. Could it be that the entire building was a gift—a kind of sacrifice—in its very being? Solomon paid a high price for the materials and labor. Thousands of men gave blood, sweat, and tears to erect the structure. It was all for the glory of the Lord. In Deuteronomy 16:17, God commands, "Each of you must bring a gift in proportion to the way the Lord your God has blessed you."

This instruction was in direct reference to burnt offerings for the Feast of the Tabernacle, but the principle extends beyond the Old Testament. God blesses us richly, and our response is to give back to Him. The writer of Hebrews puts this in New Testament perspective: "Through Jesus, therefore, let us continually offer to God a sacrifice of praise—the fruit of lips that openly profess his name. And do not forget to do good and to share with others, for with such sacrifices God is pleased" (Hebrews 13:15-16). These are merely a few examples of contemporary sacrifices and offerings.

Could this be part of what it means to delight in the Lord? He gives, and we give back. He models what it means to love, and we respond in kind. He is teaching us to love by His example.

For all the exquisite beauty of Solomon's temple, one fact remains. No building can contain the God who made the heavens. All the beauty and all the love of the Lord are too great to be contained by human hands or built into the structures of man. The Lord's love is so great, and His compassions never fail. His faithfulness, too, is beyond compare. The combination of God's great affection and great faithfulness is a constant supply of immense compassion. This is the greatest gift: the endless hope of infinite love.

16. NEHEMIAH

"Beyond him, Nehemiah son of Azbuk, ruler of a half-district of Beth Zur, made repairs up to a point opposite the tombs of David, as far as the artificial pool and the House of the Heroes."

- Nehemiah 3:16

God's people went through a dark time. Generations of disobedience had culminated in disaster. After grave warnings and second chances (and third chances and fourth and fifth and . . .), God allowed Israel's and Judah's enemies to overpower them. The people were taken captive and things were dismal, but only for a little while. God continued to honor the covenant He made with Abraham. After seventy years in exile, it was time for the people to go home. But it didn't all happen at once, and the Jerusalem they once knew was in ruins. The first group returned, resettled, and rebuilt the temple. Many years after that, news of the Jews in Jerusalem reached a royal cupbearer in Persia. This was Nehemiah.

Nehemiah was deeply moved by the distressing report of his people many miles away in their homeland. The walls of the city had been destroyed and now lay broken with the gate burned to the ground. After weeping in response to the news, Nehemiah fasted and prayed. He called out to God, confessing his own sins and the sins of the people, all the while reminding the Lord of the promise to gather His children once again.

Carrying the weight of despair in his heart, Nehemiah continued to serve in the palace. He couldn't hide his feelings, and the king took notice of his downcast countenance. He asked Nehemiah why he looked so horrible, which gave Nehemiah the opportunity to explain the sad situation. The king asked one more question: "What do you request?"

Nehemiah returned to prayer for the Lord's wisdom. Then, he asked the king to send him to Jerusalem to rebuild. Additionally, he needed letters of protection for safe travel as well as timber from the king's forest for building material. The king said yes to all of this and Nehemiah was on his way, now as the newly-named governor of Jerusalem.

The long journey from Persia ended at the remains of the wall. Before revealing the plans that God had laid on his heart, Nehemiah took a ride around the city under the cover of night to inspect the situation. He discovered the remains of the ruins and rallied the Jews, priests, nobles, and officials to begin the mighty task of rebuilding.

As if constructing a protective wall around an entire city wasn't daunting enough, the Jews had some enemies who weren't too thrilled about this new project. These enemies accused Nehemiah of rebelling against the king, giving him another opportunity to remind everyone that the God of heaven was in charge and would prosper them. Meanwhile, the Jews had been organized and divided into groups, each working on a different section of the wall. Nehemiah chapter three details the work crews and their specific assignments. Verse sixteen highlights another guy named Nehemiah (not the same Nehemiah who is leading the whole operation) and his section of the wall. He is one of many, all working hard for the Lord.

The work was long and difficult, and Israel's enemies did not relent. Instead, they tried various tactics to derail God's people from their mission. When fear-inducing threats were ineffective, they tried the intimidation of an army. They also attempted to outsmart and trap Nehemiah in hopes that discrediting him would bring construction to a halt. But God was with His people, strengthening them, and equipping Nehemiah to lead with wisdom. Even if it meant working with a spear in hand, ready for battle, the work would continue. Through teamwork, persistence, and the grace of the Lord, the wall was eventually built!

Chapter three verse sixteen shines a light on one of God's many obedient people. Like us, Nehemiah, son of Azbuk, was probably an average guy. The only detail we have about him was his leadership of half a district. This means he was in a place of authority, but don't let that elevate him to a place of high honor in your mind. The other wall-builders were also in positions of authority, many of them over entire districts. Nehemiah was a person with responsibilities, just as we are. There was a place for Nehemiah on the wall, a section with his name on it. He was needed for that section, as everyone else was needed for theirs. The construction of the wall required all "hands on deck" and cooperation was absolutely necessary. A wall with a gap is not very effective after all.

Teamwork is a gift from God. We know that all things that come from God are good, and the gift of help is very good! Ecclesiastes 4:9 points out that "Two are better than one, because they have a good return for their labor." What a heavy burden it is to face challenges alone! We've all struggled alone at some point, from trying to handle life's tragedies to the simple act of trying to carry in all the groceries from the car. So we teach children the value of being part of a team at an early age. From the beginning, God did not intend for us to handle life solo. When He made Adam, the Lord said it was not good for man to be alone and so Eve was created. God Himself promises never to leave us, and so we are never truly alone. But out of love, He gives us the gift of each other as well. We carry each other's burdens, and in this way, we fulfill the law of Christ (see Galatians 6:2 for more on this).

Nehemiah's story is also one of restoration. This is a recurring theme in many 3:16s, pointing to the goodness of God's love. Physically, the wall around Jerusalem was restored. Also, the people were restored to their homeland. Spiritual restoration happened as well. After the wall was completed, they read the Law aloud and the people were convicted of their sins. They also celebrated the Festival of Tabernacles once again to symbolize their return to obedience, a return to the Lord their God. We've seen God's love through restoration before and we'll continue to see it again and again. As flawed human beings, we find ourselves in a cycle of sin. Though it seems never-ending, it is no match for the Lord's infinite love. The desolate wall is a good image of those times we've hit rock bottom. We feel like the things important to us have been taken, or that in one way or another, we have been burned. It seems that our situation can't get any worse and that we are beyond repair. Until God sent Nehemiah, there were no plans to rebuild. It's possible that the Jews felt hopeless and were attempting to survive indefinitely without functional protection around their city. But God would not leave His people in despair, nor will He leave us in those dark places. God will continue to restore us to Himself as we return to Him with repentant hearts. We can call out like the prophet Jeremiah, "Heal me, Lord, and I will be healed; save me and I will be saved, for you are the one I praise" (Jeremiah 17:14). When we call, the Lord will answer.

Though God can heal hearts instantly and thoroughly as well as resolve troubled situations, He often blesses us with the opportunity to be part of the rebuilding. Just like the Jews worked tirelessly day and night to make repairs, God involves us in our own repair. Like students in a lab course, we need hands-on experience to learn and grow. The foundation for our healing is typically much stronger when we are invested in the step-by-step process rather than an overnight change. A conflict with a friend might be resolved as God gently humbles us and teaches us a more Christ-like attitude. Financial despair could be helped by winning the lottery, but a deliberate growth of our financial habits is more likely to last. God's gift of involvement is more evidence of His love for us. We are privileged to be part of His work as we experience the thorough process of divine rebuilding.

Above all, through every moment, Nehemiah prayed. He himself declared God's love in the first chapter. "Lord, the God of heaven, the great and awesome God, who keeps his covenant of love with those who love him and keep his commandments, let your ear be attentive and your eyes open to hear the prayer your servant is praying . . . " (Nehemiah 1:5-6). We've already examined the covenant love of the Lord Almighty, but something so great deserves much attention! In these few lines of prayer, we celebrate the greatness of the Lord, remember the treasure of His promise, and are comforted by the attention He gives the prayers of His people. What wondrous love! And when we step back, we find love in the simple fact that Nehemiah prayed. When he didn't know what to do, he prayed. When he needed specific instruction, he prayed. When met with challenges and opposition, Nehemiah prayed. And when the wall was done, he gathered the people . . . and they prayed.

Not once was Nehemiah disconnected from his God. We, too, experience that connection. "For the eyes of the Lord are on the righteous and his ears are attentive to their prayer . . . " (1 Peter 3:12). As the poet of Psalm 66:18-20 proclaimed, "If I had cherished sin in my heart, the Lord would not have listened; but God has surely listened and has heard my prayer. Praise be to God, who has not rejected my prayer or withheld his love from me!"

17. JOB

"Or why was I not hidden away in the ground like a stillborn child, like an infant who never saw the light of day?"

- Job 3:16

There once was a man who lived in the land of Uz. Not Oz, a place full of colorful characters and adventure, but Uz, a land so ancient that we don't know its exact location. While the book of Job sits in the middle of the Old Testament, the story takes place centuries earlier than the accounts we've been reading recently. The events are believed to have happened in the days of Abraham, Isaac, and Jacob. This tale has endured over time, resonating with suffering people throughout the ages.

Job was a righteous man, blameless and upright. He loved God and his large family, a wife, seven sons, and three daughters. Job also had a large menagerie of livestock, including sheep, camels, oxen, and donkeys. The Bible says he was the greatest of all the people in the East.

While Job was enjoying his bountiful life on Earth, a crucial conversation was developing in heaven. God and Satan were discussing Job. God pointed out to the fallen angel that Job was the shining example of righteousness. Satan replied that this was only because God had showered blessings upon the man. If Job were to lose all his wealth, surely, he would stop praising God and curse him instead! The Lord seemed to have great confidence in Job because He allowed Satan to destroy almost anything to everything that Job had. The only restriction was that the fallen angel could not touch Job himself.

And so, tragedy struck the house of the blameless and upright man. Enemies raided Job's livestock and killed his servants. Fire destroyed the remaining livestock and more servants. The most devastating blow came from a great wind that destroyed the house of his oldest son, killing all Job's children inside. Everything Job treasured was suddenly lost. In that moment of deep despair, Job tore his robe, shaved his head, and worshiped the Lord, saying, "The Lord gave and the Lord has taken away; may the name of the Lord be praised" (Job 1:21).

Once again, God and Satan discussed Job. When God pointed out that Job remained faithful despite crushing loss, Satan again had an answer. He insisted that if Job's body were to be tormented, surely, he would curse the Lord. Again, God allowed this test, restricting Satan's damage so that Job's life would be spared. Satan responded by striking Job with horrible physical ailments, including painful boils. This disease led to public shame, then Job's wife betrayed him. However, he still refused to sin against the Lord.

Three friends came to support Job in this dark time. They mourned with him and comforted him. The situation was so terrible that all they could do was sit in silence and simply remain present with Job, enduring the darkness together. Finally, after a week, Job spoke. Chapter three contains Job's lament to his listening friends.

As we can expect, his words were heavy with sorrow. While Job did not profane God, he did curse his own birth. In the poetic language characteristic of this book, Job darkly described the beginning of his existence. He wished it were never so, as the result was eventual loss and suffering in adulthood. In Job's grieving, he lamented that it would be better to never have lived than to endure his present circumstances. The sixteenth verse proclaims, "Why was I not hidden away in the ground like a stillborn child, like an infant who never saw the light of day?" Such an extreme statement can come only from a place of deep hurt.

The pace of the story then shifts to slower, deliberate dialogue. Each friend had much to say about Job's situation, mostly that it must have been something that Job did wrong. After all, they said, disaster was a consequence of sin. Job replied in protests, declaring his righteousness and appealing to face God with courtroom-style questioning.

Many of us can relate to Job because we too have big questions. We find ourselves in dark despair, staring into the face of worst-case scenarios. Our hearts have been shattered, leaving only broken pieces that can barely form the questions, let alone see the answers. It's here that we find one of the first glimpses of love in Job.

God allows us to ask questions. In Matthew 7:7, Jesus says, "Ask and it will be given to you; seek and you will find . . . " There are multiple examples of genuinely questioning God, from Abraham asking how the covenant promise would be fulfilled to Mary wondering how she, a virgin, would bear the Son of God. God welcomes questions from His children when they come from humble, reverent hearts. A King of Kings who required formality and thoughtless submission would not be a King of Love.

He also invites us to communicate with Him and be real with our emotions. David didn't merely speak to God, but said, "I cried out to him with my mouth; his praise was on my tongue" (Psalm 66:17). Scripture is full of shouts of joy, wails of anguish, and tears of sorrow. As Job spoke passionately about his dreadful circumstances, God listened. Job was not punished for his anger or struck down by holy fire because of his despair. God allowed Job to express what he was feeling about all that had happened. In the Psalms, David continued to describe God's reaction to our emotions. He said that God listens and hears our prayers. He praised God, because God did not reject his prayer or withheld love. The psalms also remind us that the state of our heart matters when we cry out to God. Being angry is one thing but being disrespectful or blasphemous to the Lord who cares for us crosses a line.

Throughout Job's ordeal, God never left him. What Job endured was *horrible*. Yet, he didn't have to withstand the pain alone. The prophet Isaiah says of the Lord, "He gives strength to the weary and increases the power of the weak" (Isaiah 40:29). Would Job have been able to survive without God sustaining him? Would any of us make it through trials without the strength of the Lord? Again, we can look to David, who also experienced devastating trials. In Psalm 119:28 he says, "My soul is weary with sorrow; strengthen me according to your word." Again, in Psalm 46:1, "God is our refuge and strength, an ever-present help in trouble." Not only is the Lord a source of strength, but He is a refuge, a place of safety. Additionally, He is an ever-present help. God was always with Job and God is always with you.

It should also be noted that God remained in control. Satan was never allowed to torment Job freely; there were limitations. God is omniscient. He knew exactly how Job would respond before everything began. He knew that Job would survive and remain faithful. While He gave the devil permission to wreak havoc, Satan still had to act within boundaries. Satan will never be in full control; he is not God's equal or counterpart, and he will never win. "The reason the Son of God appeared was to destroy the devil's work," says 1 John 3:8. The end of the story has already been written, and it includes the Lord's total victory over evil.

What did God do with all of Job's questions? What are the answers to the mysteries of suffering? One of the most difficult aspects of the book of Job is that God doesn't provide the clear-cut answers that Job seeks initially. We might also find ourselves disappointed not to receive an immediate "because" to our "why?" But God was hardly silent. After Job and friends had finished their lofty laments, the Almighty God answered Job dramatically out of a whirlwind with questions of His own. "Where were you when I laid the earth's foundation?" (Job 38:4). Wait, what? God kept going. He asked about all the intricacies of His creation, reminding Job which of them was created by the Sovereign Lord and which was created by a person with limited wisdom. He drove His point home with poetic examples of storehouses full of snow, the containment of the seas, or singing morning stars. He then recalled the wildness of nature and untamable beasts, painting a word-picture of our large, beautiful world.

This reminded Job gently but firmly of his small place in the big picture. This wasn't to minimize his pain, however. Remember that this is the God who stays close to the brokenhearted. When Christ was on Earth, He wept over Jerusalem as well as cried with His grieving friends. We are loved by a God who feels our pain. God loved Job. In fact, He loved him so much that He did not remain silent. He answered Job with wisdom, giving him just the right answer at just the right time.

Job responded humbly with his newly-received insight. Though he was not granted the privilege of knowing "why," he was reassured that his suffering was not in vain. Job said to God, "I know that you can do all things; no purpose of yours can be thwarted" (Job 42:1). There is comfort in knowing that God uses our brokenness for something greater and even beautiful. Paul explains in 2 Corinthians 12:9-10, "But he said to me, 'My grace is sufficient for you, for my power is made perfect in weakness.' Therefore I will boast all the more gladly about my weaknesses, so that Christ's power may rest on me. That is why, for Christ's sake, I delight in weaknesses, in insults, in hardships, in persecutions, in difficulties. For when I am weak, then I am strong."

When we recognize God's hand on our lives, we begin to see trials as a backdrop for God's glory. Our circumstances become the canvas where God paints His masterpiece. It may be painful for a season, and sometimes the dark seasons are dreadfully long. The big-picture reasons for suffering might be revealed, or God might only grant enough information to remind us that He remains in control and working for our good. In whatever way He decides to answer us out of our whirlwinds, we know He answers with love.

18. PROVERBS

"Long life is in her right hand; in her left hand are riches and honor."

- Proverbs 3:16

Solomon was a wise king. However, as we know, his wisdom did not come from his own thoughts or experiences. Solomon's great and world-renowned wisdom came directly from the Lord. The king had the opportunity to request anything he could wish for, and he bypassed riches, military victory, and long life. Instead, he asked God to grant him the ability to lead the people wisely. This pleased the Lord, and He gifted Solomon exactly that!

This wisdom resulted in many things, including what is now the book of Proverbs. Solomon didn't only rule wisely, but he shared his wisdom so others could also benefit. This extended beyond the scope of the Israelites. Over the centuries, Solomon's proverbs have been read across the globe. After all, the idea of a proverb is simple and cross-cultural: it's merely a small piece of truth packaged nicely in a short phrase. Some proverbs are local idioms, and some, like the sayings of Confucius, have become famous. But none have been so inspired by God Most Holy like the biblical proverbs.

Here are the things to know about the book of Proverbs. First, while it was mostly written by King Solomon, a couple of other authors contributed some chapters near the end. Also, there are some scholarly questions about who wrote the first nine chapters. While the very first words of the first chapter state "the proverbs of Solomon," this might have been an introduction for the rest of the work. However, 1 Kings 4:30-32 tells us that Solomon spoke over three thousand proverbs, so we can feel confident that, even if the beginnings of this book were penned by someone else, it's highly likely that the words came from our guy Solomon. However, it matters little, because the ultimate source of Scripture is the Lord.

In addition to being informative, Proverbs is a work of art. The text is written in a Hebrew form of poetry, adding more dimension to the words. This particular writing is characterized by repetition of themes, thoughts, and phrases. Though many of the poetic attributes are subdued or even lost in the translation, a rhythm remains. Many of the sayings exist in two lines, perhaps for easy memorization. For those who are extra academic, it's worth the time to study elements like parallelisms to deepen appreciation of Proverbs. God's Word is full of layered treasures, and the more we study, the more we unearth.

Let's dive into what this poetry is teaching us. Chapter one is a true beginning, establishing the importance of wisdom. Wisdom is more than knowledge. It is the good application of that knowledge to life's situations. Proverbs 1 links wisdom with instruction as well as doing what is "right, just, and fair." We also learn here the importance of discerning bad advice from good counsel. Evil counsel leads to extreme downfall, but wisdom from the Lord yields blessings and abundant life.

In Hebrew, as in many languages, words have either a masculine or feminine connotation. The word "wisdom" is feminine, and the writer takes this a step further by personifying wisdom as a woman. This theme persists through the book, adding more poetic value. The first chapter of Proverbs pictures wisdom as a woman calling loudly from open public spaces. She admonishes those who ignore her call and describes the grave consequences that might befall them. After all, to ignore wisdom is to willingly choose foolishness. This produces destructive results that could be avoided by heeding the call and accepting the godly instruction available to all who can hear.

Chapter two continues to strongly emphasize the value of wisdom. Beautiful language describes the various rewards of seeking knowledge of the Lord. In fact, it's again made clear that God is the only source of wisdom. Additionally, the writer points out that wisdom protects us against evil ways. This is beginning to look like a cycle. When a person chooses wisdom, they will have good rewards and a defense against evil. This allows them to continue to seek wisdom without being burdened by the consequences of folly. The increase of wisdom also increases the defense against evil, and wisdom continues to grow.

Once we reach the third chapter, we begin to see some specifics. The first few pages of Proverbs have convinced us that yes, wisdom is wonderful, and yes, we want it! But how exactly do we seek it? Verse one gives us the first step: keep the Lord's commands and do not forget His law. Proverbs 3:5-6 is well-known by many believers of all ages: "Trust in the Lord with all your heart and lean not on your own understanding; in all your ways submit to him, and he will make your paths straight."

We are instructed to trust in God with our entire heart and submit every single way to Him. Seeking wisdom is not a half-hearted commitment. It takes one hundred percent of our effort and dedication. Otherwise, we are mixing wisdom and foolishness, good and evil. These things cannot co-exist. In the same way a little bit of yeast affects a whole batch of dough, a little bit of evil corrupts good.

Next, we are told to honor the Lord with our belongings. This is followed by the value of discipline, and more emphasis on the preciousness of wisdom. This is such a big deal that it can't be said enough! We're approaching our 3:16, but to fully understand it, we need to keep it in context with verses 13-18. This is a statement of blessing. Blessed is the person who discovers wisdom. It is so much more valuable than gold, silver, or precious stones. Nothing compares to it. "Long life is in her right hand; in her left hand are riches and honor." What is in the right hand is most important—long life and health, in this case—and what is in the left hand is secondary, material wealth and character. But all of it is very good.

To finish the thought, we need to continue to verse 17, where we learn that God's wisdom is the way to peace. This can mean that the result of wisdom is receiving peace, or that making a choice that promotes peace is wise. However, given the other descriptions in this section, the emphasis seems to be on the gifts wisdom brings to us. Finally, in verse 18, wisdom is called a "tree of life." This vibrant image continues to illustrate the multi-faceted goodness of God's instruction. Trees provide shade from the hot sun. They produce oxygen that we breathe. Many trees give us fruit, and the leaves and bark often have medicinal properties. We've already seen that wisdom protects us from evil. It leads to quality of life, much like breathing in fresh air. The fruit of wisdom brings many benefits, and we also will find that we are fruitful in our works when we are choosing to seek wisdom. It's a tree of life indeed!

Among all this wisdom, there is also love. The very existence of wisdom is proof of God's care for us. Without it, we would be left to our own limited knowledge, constantly falling into mistakes and negative consequences. With it, we learn and grow. We can face new situations with confidence because God's wisdom is greater than the results of our human experiences. God declares through Isaiah, "For my thoughts are not your thoughts, neither are your ways my ways" (Isaiah 55:8). Also, "the foolishness of God is wiser than human wisdom, and the weakness of God is stronger than human strength" (1 Corinthians 1:25).

But God doesn't keep His wisdom to Himself. In a great act of love, He has made it readily available to all who seek it. How incredible that God's wisdom is given simply by asking! It is not reserved for the wealthy, the super-intelligent, or the elite. It is not exclusively granted after a harrowing quest to a mountaintop. We are simply told that "if any of you lacks wisdom, you should ask God, who gives generously to all without finding fault, and it will be given to you" (James 1:5). Then, when we receive it, we can't help but want more. We become seekers of wisdom, treasure-hunters of God's ways. "If you look for it as for silver and search for it as for hidden treasure, then you will understand the fear of the Lord and find the knowledge of God" (Proverbs 2:4-5).

Wisdom is a big deal. With it, we have beautiful gifts. It is an avenue for additional blessings, just as God gifted Solomon with long life, military victory, and great wealth in addition to the wisdom he requested! However, apart from the Lord we have evil disaster. There is a reason that wisdom is mentioned over 200 times in the Word of God. It's not optional. It's a treasure that's vital to our very existence. It is crucial. Wisdom isn't a bonus gift we can do without, but a tree of life that we need in order to survive. Wisdom is a rich expression of God's love for us, designed for blessing beyond measure.

19. ECCLESIASTES

"And I saw something else under the sun: In the place of judgment—wickedness was there, in the place of justice—wickedness was there."

- Ecclesiastes 3:16

Ecclesiastes is about questions. This book was also written by King Solomon, so to get a clear view of his perspective, let's take a quick review of his life. First Kings and 2 Chronicles detail the time of King Solomon. We've already discussed his request for wisdom and his fair rule. Additionally, King Solomon was known for his immense wealth. We're talking tens of thousands of horses and riders, tables never without a bounty of good food, and vast riches of gold, silver, precious stones, and more. He constructed the temple and his own house, and they were both dazzling buildings.

He also had seven hundred wives and three hundred concubines. Though this was another measure of success in that culture at that time, it was contrary to the law of the Lord. Therefore, it led to trouble. His wives turned his heart from God and instead to other false gods. This angered God, who allowed enemies to rise up and Solomon's own servant to rebel. The great king's story ended in sad disobedience.

Theologians believe that King Solomon wrote Ecclesiastes in the last of his days, after he repented of his sins. The book reflects on the big picture of life. Overall, King Solomon declared that life without the Lord is meaningless. He ended his musings with, "Now all has been heard; here is the conclusion of the matter: Fear God and keep his commandments, for this is the duty of all mankind" (Ecclesiastes 12:13). But that's skipping ahead. Let's slow down and return to the beginning.

Ecclesiastes starts with the revelation that everything in the world is forever the same and that there is nothing new under the sun. Just like King Solomon's previous writings, the topic again turned to the matter of wisdom. But this time, the result of knowing so much is grief. Solomon lamented that pleasure is also in vain. He despaired because both the fool and the wise man have the same ending—they both die when their time comes. So why bother being wise? What does it matter? He also felt that his work had been for nothing. Solomon did pause from his complaints to declare that the enjoyment of work comes from God, so there was some hope.

Next, he stated that there is a purpose and a season for everything, from birth and death to love and hate, as well as war and peace or mourning and dancing. This also applies to the work of the laborer. God gives gifts through work and "He has made everything beautiful in its time. He has also set eternity in the human heart; yet no one can fathom what God has done from beginning to end" (Ecclesiastes 3:11). The tone turns dark again once we reach our 3:16: "And I saw something else under the sun: In the place of judgment—wickedness was there, in the place of justice—wickedness was there."

Just like King Solomon, we observe this situation repeatedly in our fallen world. Injustice persists. Cheaters do prosper. The unrighteous achieve great success. Oppressors persecute the innocent. It's all so very unfair.

We catch a glimpse of God's love when we keep our 3:16 in the context of the chapter as a whole. Ecclesiastes 3:17 says, "God will bring into judgment both the righteous and the wicked, for there will be a time for every activity, a time to judge every deed." This is a direct answer to the cry of verse sixteen. We can't forget the poetic reminder earlier in the chapter: there is a time for every single thing on earth. That must include justice and injustice, all for the purposes of God's glory. Proverbs 16:4 point out that, "The Lord works out everything to its proper end—even the wicked for a day of disaster."

What is loving about this? We must remember that God will most certainly judge rightly. The psalms are full of reassurance of this. They declare that the Lord loves the just and He won't forsake those who are faithful. It's written in Scripture that wrongdoers will be held accountable and wickedness will be punished. God is righteous in His very nature. Yet, we see Him appear to allow sin to run rampant. How is this happening?

We must remember the truth of Ecclesiastes, that there is a time for every purpose. We know that God is detailed and every second of His timing is intentional. There is a season to tear down and a time to build up. We know that the Lord is sovereign, and He is also good. That has always been and will never change. That means that even the injustices of the world are used for His glory, in some way. Allowing wickedness to have its time is for the glory of God and the good of those He loves, despite how incredibly baffling and nearly incomprehensible it is to us.

But the time of wickedness won't last forever. Make no mistake, the wicked will be judged and God will bring justice to every person and situation. Scripture promises that. "He does not keep the wicked alive but gives the afflicted their rights," says Job 36:6. The specifics are not always as we think they should be, but we tend to think in limited earthly terms and not heavenly, eternal perspective. The unrighteous are on a time limit. Evil has an expiration date.

What good can possibly come from unrighteousness? What benefit is there to wickedness? With an all-powerful God, the possibilities are limitless. Our immediate outrage at injustice is due to concern for the victims. Wickedness does not exist in a vacuum. When unrighteousness succeeds, it is usually at the expenses of the innocent. This is, at first glance, unacceptable. Yet, we must pause and examine each situation carefully. Yes, there are many tragedies in the world that feel senseless. We will in no way make light of anyone's suffering. Extreme situations call for an overflow of compassion. But in many situations, suffering is used for the uplifting and good of the one who is hurting. We are again reminded by Peter that God, in His grace, will Himself restore us and make us strong, firm, and steadfast after we have suffered a little while. We know from James that trials produce perseverance, character, and maturity. When God allows us to walk through difficulty, we are prepared and equipped for future challenges. What is unjust initially can be turned into victory for those under the love of God.

We also discover purpose in unjust situations when we allow time for God to make things right. In that time, a new, better option can develop. When believers handle difficult situations with grace, their example can be a display of the gospel to a person who desperately needs to hear it. The story of Joseph in Genesis illustrates this perfectly. His brothers, in wickedness, sold him into slavery. Then, years later, Joseph forgave them and pointed out that they intended to harm him, but God meant it for good to accomplish the saving of many lives. In God's process, wickedness was overcome, and justice prevailed. Joseph's life was preserved, and he grew in wisdom and maturity. An entire nation was saved from famine by the hand of the Lord with Joseph as His chosen instrument. And the brothers were humbled and reconciled to both Joseph and the Lord.

This reminds us of a truth that is easy to forget. When we refer to "the wicked" or "the unrighteous," we forget the humanity of the people doing evil. All of us were created by God, and evil comes from Satan and his forces. God can redeem anyone with a heart willing to repent and follow Him. We need only to look at Saul, who once persecuted Christians to the point of death. God not only changed his heart but transformed his entire life into one that lived and breathed the gospel. In the time it appears to us that wickedness is free to roam, God can be in the very midst of changing the lives we least expect to be changed. Miracles happen even in seasons of darkness. The Light of the World is always in control. He says, "I have told you these things, so that in me you may have peace. In this world you will have trouble. But take heart! I have overcome the world" (John 16:33).

This is love. God loves us intensely and will not leave us to suffer indefinitely at the hands of the wicked. He will absolutely not allow injustice and unrighteousness to prevail. He will not permit evil to remain unrestrained. Hold tight, faithful one. Justice is on the way.

20. ISAIAH

"The Lord says, 'The women of Zion are haughty, walking along with outstretched necks, flirting with their eyes, strutting along with swaying hips, with ornaments jingling on their ankles.'"

- Isaiah 3:16

By now, we've observed that the Bible isn't arranged in exact chronological order. We traveled from David and Solomon all the way to kings taken into exile, then back to Solomon so quickly we practically got whiplash. Let's get our bearings and establish where we are in time when we meet Isaiah. This major prophet hand-delivered messages from God to His people around 750 B.C. This was after the nation of Israel divided into two kingdoms, northern (Israel) and southern (Judah). The book of Isaiah begins by listing Judah's kings of the time, so we know that we are in the days of Uzziah, Jotham, Ahaz, and Hezekiah, if we're taking historical notes.

Who was Isaiah? His name means "the Lord saves," which was very appropriate for a man whose life was dedicated to speaking the words of God. We get a bit of personal information in chapter six when we read about the beginnings of his ministry. At that time, Isaiah had a vision of the Lord on his throne, surrounded by glory. There were angels above Him, flying and calling out in worship. Everything shook and filled with smoke at the sound of their voices. Suddenly, Isaiah cried out that he was ruined because he, a person with unclean lips, saw the Lord. Then, an angel brought a live coal and touched it to Isaiah's mouth. This was symbolic for purification, taking away

Isaiah's guilt. Then the Lord's voice rang out asking, "Whom shall I send?" Isaiah boldly said, "Send me!" and his prophetic ministry began.

Besides this dramatic beginning, we know only a few other things about him. In the next couple of chapters, we learn that Isaiah was a husband and father. Scholars believe he was born into an elite family based on his ability to have close contact with kings. Other than that, biographical details are scarce. But, like many in ministry, the focus is not on the servant, but the God whom the prophet served.

We know the time and we know the prophet. Now let's examine the setting of his message. Though the prophecy is given to Judah, it also applied very much to the northern kingdom of Israel. Isaiah constantly refers to Israel when he means the whole nation of God's chosen people. Let's begin with King Uzziah. During this time, Israel was a mess, but King Uzziah was mostly a good king. He achieved military victory and successfully built towers and fortifications around Jerusalem. He had bountiful livestock, fields, and vineyards. Most importantly, he followed God. That is, of course, until power got the best of King Uzziah. Soon, pride seeped in and he became unfaithful to the Lord. He also took it upon himself to burn incense in the temple, something only priests were to do. This resulted in the punishment of leprosy until he died, and his son, Jotham, took over the kingdom. This was also when Isaiah experienced the vision that would kick-start his prophetic ministry.

King Jotham was another good king, but while he reigned, the people strayed from God's command. Like his father, he had successful building projects and military wins. His victories came from the Lord, whom Jotham followed faithfully. However, he allowed people to worship at the high places, which were sites dedicated to other gods. This clearly did not please the Lord.

Once King Jotham's son, Ahaz, took his seat on the throne, things took a sour turn. King Ahaz led the people in worshiping other gods, and he didn't stop there. He burned sacrifices to these false deities and even offered children to the fire. He adopted detestable practices from the other nations that God had removed generations before. King Ahaz went so far as to take items from the temple, giving some away, and destroying others. He then closed the temple and established mass worship of all the other gods. He led the people straight into destruction as an angry God allowed enemies to defeat Judah and take prisoners. It was a very dark time.

It is in such darkness that we find the opening chapters of the book of Isaiah. These passages document the decaying state of Israel. God's chosen people turned their backs on the very Heavenly Father to whom they owed their existence. Isaiah describes a city burned with fire with fields being stripped away. The people are compared to those of the sinful cities of Sodom and Gomorrah! Despite all their blatant sins, they still came to the temple to offer a multitude of sacrifices. This did not impress the Lord. He rejects offerings from sinful hearts that lack remorse. He instructed the people to practice justice and help the oppressed. There was still hope for redemption if only the people were obedient. But this began the words of warning: destruction would come if they continued their wayward disregard for God. The consequences were heavy but had a refining purpose. The wickedness would be removed, and justice restored to the city.

Isaiah includes a refreshing vision of a future Zion. The Lord's temple will be on the highest mountain and all people will come seek the Lord. It's a lovely image, but not for those who have turned away. Again, their pride will bring them to destruction. Isaiah describes lofty cedars, tall mountains, towering walls, and even distinguished trading ships to illustrate pride, followed by the declaration that only the Lord will be lifted up in that day. All pride of man will crumble, and life will be miserable for the previously proud.

The third chapter continues the harsh but necessary warning to unfaithful Israel. Verse sixteen is directed specifically at the wealthy women of the city. While many of the people were poor and facing oppression, these women of Zion proudly strutted about with the jangling of jewelry and flirtatious actions that drew attention to themselves. The future was not bright for these gals. The subsequent verses describe their fate: the Lord will take away all their fine things and they will be subjected to cruel captivity when they are taken prisoners on the day Israel's enemies are allowed to prevail. Not only does this describe the consequences for the women, but they also represent prideful Israel as a nation. Their beauty was superficial and easily lost, as was everything Israel attained without the Lord. Once God took away everything ungodly, Israel would have nothing left.

God's people had many issues, but the root was their pride. They stopped relying on God and instead took matters into their own hands. They decided which false gods to worship. They assumed they didn't need the laws that the Lord had given them. They knew best how to live their own lives. Unfortunately, this description doesn't apply only to the Israelites of 750 BC. How familiar is pride to us here and now? If God were to take away everything ungodly in our lives, what would be left?

Let's not confuse this pride with the satisfaction of a job well done. What we are talking about is downright arrogance. It is often unrecognizable until we see little signs creeping in. We don't really need to listen to advice because we're confident on our own. Sure, we could pray before making a decision, but really, we can handle it. We begin to credit ourselves for achievements and our material provisions; thankfulness to the Lord is a forgotten sentiment. We never see ourselves as haughty or idol worshipers like the Israelites, but our modern idols of money and ambition fill our hearts just the same. The problem of pride is not just an ancient Israelite thing. It's damaging our souls, too.

Pride takes our eyes off God and sets them firmly on ourselves. Psalm 10:4 reminds us that, "In his pride the wicked man does not seek him; in all his thoughts there is no room for God." While we are distracted by our own interests, we don't realize that we are drifting away from our Anchor. Before we know it, we are far from shore with only the lifeline of God's grace-filled love to pull us back in. This is not a good place to be. We saw how pride grew in the lives of the Israelites and caused major problems. For us, pride can lead to anger, a lack of compassion, and worry as we trust less in God and more in our own abilities. It can grow into jealousy, fear, and even hatred. Haughty pride is a sickness of the heart.

God loves us too much to allow pride to destroy us. He gets to the heart of the matter in James 4:6: "But he gives us more grace. That is why Scripture says: 'God opposes the proud but shows favor to the humble.'" He directs us to love Him first and most, then love our neighbors and our enemies. When we direct our love according to His design, there's just enough room left in our hearts to love ourselves with humility while keeping the balance healthy.

Humility is a gift from our God of love. To be humble is to see ourselves from God's perspective. It's neither a puffed-up view nor a lowly state. It's a matter-of-fact realization that we are small in the big picture while still dearly loved by the Creator. We are neither inferior nor superior to other human beings, and we are each individually precious to God's heart. This acceptance of reality, this acknowledgment of the balance of our position and value, is humility. It is a beautiful part of our design meant to shelter us from the dangers of pride. Psalm 22:4 says, "Humility is the fear of the Lord; its wages are riches and honor and life."

Christ Himself modeled humility as an example for us to follow. He wasn't flashy or charismatic. He didn't use holy power to make Himself a grand spectacle. There was no self-advertising or the hiring of a public relations firm to promote a great Teaching-And-Healing-Show. Instead, He told His disciples, "For even the Son of Man did not come to be served, but to serve, and to give his life as a ransom for many" (Mark 10:45). Jesus simply loved God and loved others. He knew He was God's Son and spoke this truth plainly when the time was right. But Christ was not prideful. There was no room for that while going about His Father's business. There is no place for self-serving pride amid pure love.

The Lord would not tolerate Israel's pride. Not only was it misplaced on idols and disobedience, but it pulled them away from their God. It disconnected a set-apart people from the Source of everything they needed. We are no different today. We require the sustaining power of our Lord. There is no life away from Him, and the barrier of pride is dangerous. Thankfully the God who calls us His chosen people won't tolerate our pride any more than He did in ancient Israel. Our loving Father creates in us humble hearts as He draws us closer to His own.

21. JEREMIAH

"'In those days, when your numbers have increased greatly in the land,' declares the Lord, 'people will no longer say, 'The Ark of the Covenant of the Lord.' It will never enter their minds or be remembered; it will not be missed, nor will another one be made.'"

- Jeremiah 3:16

Jeremiah was a priest who was called by God to be a prophet. While his calling seems slightly less dramatic than Isaiah's, it is no less precious and meaningful. Around the time King Josiah led the people of Judah, God spoke to Jeremiah. He said that even before Jeremiah was born, he was meant to be a prophet. When Jeremiah's insecurities rose to the surface, he protested based on his young age. God reassured him that he was capable because God would give him the words to speak and would be with him when he was afraid (sounds a lot like a burning bush conversation with Moses, doesn't it?).

Next the Lord touched Jeremiah's mouth and then gave Jeremiah a vision of an almond tree. This is a tree that blossoms long before the other plants in springtime. As the tree watches over the rest of the spring bloom, God was watching over Israel. The next vision was a boiling pot facing away from the north. The Lord explained to Jeremiah that catastrophe would come from the north. This would be the earthly source of God's judgment. Because this judgment was coming, it was important for Jeremiah to obediently convey God's words to the people of Israel as soon as possible.

This message seems familiar, doesn't it? Like Isaiah before him, Jeremiah would warn the people about the grave consequences of their serious sin. However, Jeremiah lived long after Isaiah. After good King Josiah came Jehoahaz, Jehoiakim, Jehoiachin, and Zedekiah. We know these names from 1 Chronicles! This is where Bible study gets fun and we can piece together details as stories overlap.

Judah had many ups and down, including some good kings who led the people in righteousness. Yet, when adversity struck, these Israelites turned to false gods and idols. Many Scriptures, including those from prophets like Hosea, compare the Israelites' unfaithfulness to prostitution and adultery. They were cheating on the God whose faithfulness to them was everlasting.

When we visited King Jehoiakim in 1 Chronicles, we learned that after ample warnings, God finally allowed Israel's enemies to overcome them. In this case, the enemy was Egypt. The pharaoh chose Jehoiakim to be king, and Judah remained subject to Egypt. To complicate matters, Babylon soon defeated Egypt and took control over Judah. Jehoiakim remained as a ruler, but now as a vassal to Babylon. This is where Jeremiah's writing enters the scene.

The message from God was given to the people through Jeremiah, just as instructed. First, the Lord recalled the good ol' days when Israel was actually faithful. But then He asked, "What happened?" What kind of reasoning could the Israelites possibly have had for wandering away and choosing other gods? Because of this, Israel was charged with idolatry and leaving the one true God (who had done so much for them) and instead choosing gods who were, in reality, nothing. Jeremiah illustrated this by pointing out that they traded in Living Water for dry, empty wells.

Israel was intended to be free but was now subject to Egypt and then Babylon as a result of their choice to worship idols. Yet, in times of great trouble, Israel would once again call out to God, only to return to idolatry when the dust settled. But enough was enough. Now, the Lord said, His people had forgotten Him. Israel had no shame.

After God continued to call out Israel for unfaithfulness, He reminded them of His persistent call to return to Him. Yet, they defiantly refused. When the northern kingdom fell, it was a testament to Judah that God meant what He said. Instead of repentance, Judah continued to sin. God declared this a worse offense and sent Jeremiah to northern Israel with this message: "'Return, faithless Israel,' declares the Lord, 'I will frown on you no longer, for I am faithful,' declares the Lord, I will not be angry forever" (Jeremiah 3:12). The Israelites were on the road to the destruction that their brothers in the North experienced, but they could avoid it by returning to the God who loved them.

God described their future. He would collect them back to Zion and give them wise leaders. Then, "in those days, when your numbers have increased greatly in the land," declares the Lord, "people will no longer say, 'The Ark of the Covenant of the Lord.' It will never enter their minds or be remembered; it will not be missed, nor will another one be made." This is our 3:16.

The lack of the Ark of the Covenant as a good thing seems counter-intuitive. However, verse 17 explains that Jerusalem will be "the Throne of the Lord" as God's presence will draw all nations to Himself. In these coming days, Judah and Israel would be reunited. The people would again call the Lord "Father" and would not stray. As God called repeatedly for His children to return to Him, He offered promises of restoration. In the thick of calling out Israel's treachery, the God of covenant extended tremendous hope.

Israel neglected God deliberately. After so many generations and a multitude of warnings, this wasn't a careless forgetfulness. Israel turned their backs on the very One who gave them everything. Their possessions, their land, and their lives were the result of divine provision. To choose another god was beyond insulting, especially one in the form of a useless idol. Allowing Israel to reap the consequences seems reasonable to us, but that wasn't God's final approach. He still cared for His children. He still loved Israel. Even though they neglected God, God refused to neglect them.

So it is with His love for us. We, too, turn our backs on our Heavenly Father. Often it begins with careless forgetfulness. But soon we are reminded of Him frequently, through the beauty of nature or a sermon in church. The occasional sign or billboard proclaims that Jesus saves. Friends speak of the Lord and books about Him sit on dusty shelves. A praise song suddenly pops into our head. God is trying to get our attention. Romans 1:20 reminds us that "since the creation of the world God's invisible qualities—his eternal power and divine nature—have been clearly seen, being understood from what has been made, so that people are without excuse." God makes Himself known to us. He will not neglect us.

Yet, we still put off church, Bible study, prayer, giving, and serving. We defiantly turn our backs on the things God commanded us to do. We think there will always be an opportunity to do it later, and tomorrow seems like a better time. When trouble arrives, we reach for God, only to look away as soon as the storm calms. We neglect God, but He will not neglect us.

Love says not to fear, because God is with us. We are not to be dismayed, because He is our God. He will strengthen, help, and keep us securely in His righteous hand. Love is in the willingness to welcome us back despite our blatant and repeated wandering. Jesus tells a story of a wandering son in a parable. The self-absorbed son convinced his dad to grant his inheritance early, while the father was still alive. This was a huge insult, but the father did it anyway. Then, the son used his new wealth to have the time of his life, partying until there was nothing left. Right about then, famine hit the country, which is a horrible time to be without a single dollar and estranged from your family. The son resorted to working as a hired farm hand, feeding pigs. The irony was that the pigs had something to eat, but the son did not! Once he reached his breaking point, the son humbly decided to return to his father, apologize, and beg for mercy. The plan was to be a hired servant in his father's house. However, when the son was still quite far from his father's house, the father saw him and ran swiftly to greet him with hugs and kisses. He called for a huge celebration to welcome home the son he once thought lost. The son was restored. Love is a father who forgives his errant child and races to embrace him once again. Love is our Father who continues to offer a future of hope despite our sin. He keeps calling us back and welcoming us home.

But does that give us a license to wander? Paul addresses this in Romans 6:1-2: "Shall we go on sinning so that grace may increase? By no means! We are those who have died to sin; how can we live in it any longer?" To take God's love and use it manipulatively would be just as heartbreaking as flagrant idolatry. Instead, God's love is for restoration, calling us for repair of our sinfulness and repentance that lasts.

The specifics of our Ark of the Covenant in this 3:16 illustrate how much our God refuses to neglect us. No longer would His presence be limited to the traditional symbol of the Ark. The Lord's presence in Zion would be among all the people, drawing all to Him. Jesus extended God's love to all people in His final instructions to His disciples, telling them to make disciples of all nations, baptize them, and teach them Christ's commands. This is immediately followed by the assurance that He'd always be with them. God's presence is not limited to Jerusalem. Because He loves us, He is with us constantly. Never for one minute are we neglected. None of our offenses eliminate the hope of being with Him. He never leaves us; it is we who wander from Him. But we can't get too far away. He calls us to return to His waiting arms the very minute we so much as avert our eye from His loving gaze.

Later in his prophecy, Jeremiah reassured the Israelites that God's judgment through captivity would not last forever. "For I know the plans I have for you," declares the Lord, "plans to prosper you and not to harm you, plans to give you hope and a future" (Jeremiah 29:11). We cling tight to this promise today. We may make the mistake of abandoning God but take heart. Our God will absolutely remain faithful, calling us back to His everlasting love.

22. LAMENTATIONS

"He has broken my teeth with gravel; he has trampled me in the dust."

- Lamentations 3:16

They didn't listen. Years of warnings from multiple prophets proved futile. The occasional good king who reignited righteousness among the people wasn't enough to make lasting change. Words from God Himself could not shake sinfulness out of the Israelite people. Because the judgment had to come, consequential disaster struck. God allowed Babylon to be victorious and the people of Judah were taken into captivity.

It's not as if the Babylonians knocked on front doors and said, "You're coming with us." No, this was the brutal deathly reality of war. Walls burned. Mothers screamed for their babies. Men shouted as they attempted in vain to defend their families and their city. The nightmare probably seemed to last an eternity and then . . . silence. The few who remained were left among the rubble of a city that was once beautiful and teeming with life. It would take everything in them to remain alive, and not everyone would survive. Jerusalem was a desolate hellscape.

Lamentations is a lament, a cry of sorrow from the depth of a soul. The writer (whom many think to be Jeremiah) expresses anguish through poetry. Judah's fall was devastating. Even knowing that it was coming could not ease the pain. Perhaps it even made it worse. This poem was not a prophecy of things to come, nor was it a glorified "I told you so." Written as an acrostic, this literary treasure is a preservation of mourning.

It begins with a description of the deserted city, personified in the poem in order that the reader might feel the universal pain of all the Israelite people. Lamentations speaks of flowing tears and betrayal by those who were once allies. Gateways were left desolate and the remaining people were consumed by grief. There was nothing left of the splendor that once adorned the temple or the bustling energy that had filled the streets. Jerusalem's ruins smoldered in shame. The remaining people scavenged for food and existed in dire suffering. The Lord had spoken and stretched out His arm of judgment. This was their new reality.

The poet makes it clear that Judah's fall was definitely the consequence of their prolonged sin. In humble acceptance, he detailed the wrath of God in response to generations of idolatry and unfaithfulness. The poet described the Lord like an enemy who had swallowed up Israel, laid waste the temple, and torn down the city wall. The people wore sackcloth, a course, scratchy material and placed ashes on their heads. This was a ritual of mourning, an expression of grief and sorrow. It could also express repentance while the mourner was humbly near to the ground. As wails of desperate sadness filled the ruined city, children were dying of hunger. There was no hope for improvement, only devastation. The sad poem continues: "The Lord has done what he planned; he has fulfilled his word, which he decreed long ago. He has overthrown you without pity, he has let the enemy gloat over you, he has exalted the horn of your foes" (Lamentations 2:17).

Chapter three shifts from the perspective of the city to the view from the eyes of the poet. This writer, too, was in mourning. He spoke of darkness, bitterness, and hardship. He felt trapped, surrounded, and weighed down as if by chains. His cries for help went unheard, only to be mocked by those around him. All of this was attributed to the Lord's judgmental wrath. Our 3:16 paints a picture of a man at rock bottom. "He has broken my teeth with gravel; he has trampled me in the dust." This could be a reference to the sackcloth and ashes display of mourning. It could also be literal abuse inflicted by those who tormented him as he grieved. Likely, it is the language of the poem attempting to make the reader understand the severity of the situation.

Where was God in all of this? Though the people felt abandoned, was that truly the case? As we sit safely in comfort centuries later, we have the benefit of big picture perspective. Our previous 3:16s have prepared us for this moment. We know that God will never truly leave His people, and though He allowed this dark season, it wasn't the end of the story for a people with a covenant promise. But did the remaining Israelites remember those words of reassurance, or did they count them as lost as their city? Was it easy for the captives from Judah to trust God as they endured the culture shock of Babylonian life, or did they give up all hope the minute they stepped foot on foreign soil? They may not have realized it in the moment, but hope was coming.

We can see that hope from the beginning, when Eve faced the results of her fruit-eating disobedience. God disciplines those He loves. As He was with Moses and Joshua, God would not truly and permanently separate Himself from His dearly loved and chosen people. As Boaz redeemed Ruth from her poverty, God would later send a Kinsman-Redeemer for all His children. Solomon reminded us that the Lord is righteous and rules with justice. While the Israelites saw only tragedy, we can see the hope.

This is not the end, but the middle of the story.

Lamentations also reminds us of Job, who also hit the ground in sackcloth and ashes, lamenting his catastrophic situation. Job's cry, however, was "why?" In this case, the poet knew exactly why Jerusalem was ruined. His mourning was one of sorrowful acceptance. But, like Job, he still cried out. And, just as in the story of Job, God was there, listening. He remained quiet for a time, but still He saw His people. God spoke in Jeremiah 33 to describe the hope for Jerusalem's future. "'Nevertheless, I will bring health and healing to it; I will heal my people and will let them enjoy abundant peace and security. I will bring Judah and Israel back from captivity and will rebuild them as they were before. I will cleanse them from all the sin they have committed against me and will forgive all their sins of rebellion against me" (Jeremiah 33:6-8).

Though we can see the hope from afar, the mourning Israelites could not. They grieved in acceptance of their judgment by taking part in the ritual of sackcloth and ashes. Rituals serve two purposes: comfort and expression of things we might otherwise have trouble articulating. There is comfort in these activities that don't require us to think clearly when the world seems to be falling apart. In these times, it takes everything in us to merely exist, let alone deal with the crushing weight of sorrow. It's soothing to know that these rituals exist because someone else walked this road before us, and others will come after us on the road of suffering. We are not alone.

Today, we have our own mourning rituals. They come in the forms of funerals and wakes, self-care through long naps and warm baths, and food. We love comfort food and we share in the grief ritual by bringing meals to those we love who are mourning. We have art, song, eulogies, and even long jogs to express our feelings through physical activity. Our modern-day sackcloth and ashes come in many forms, but our grief is no less intense. Though, as sackcloth and ashes did not heal, our mourning rituals are not the source of healing. God is. As we remember, Christ said that those who mourn are blessed and will receive comfort. Psalm 22:24 says, "He has not despised or scorned the suffering of the afflicted one; he has not hidden his face from him but has listened to his cry for help."

We can ultimately look forward to the day when God heals all. "'He will wipe every tear from their eyes. There will be no more death or mourning or crying or pain, for the old order of things has passed away" (Revelation 21:4).

Yet, as we learned in Ecclesiastes, there is a time for grief. Ecclesiastes 3:4 reminded us that there is "a time to weep and a time to laugh." Though we want to rush straight to the laughter, God is there in the grief. He is close to the brokenhearted. When Paul wrote in Romans that God works out all things for the good of those who love Him, "all things" means everything, and that includes grief. He turns our sadness into something beautiful and has a purpose for every experience and emotion. "Praise be to the God and Father of our Lord Jesus Christ, the Father of compassion and the God of all comfort, who comforts us in all our troubles, so that we can comfort those in any trouble with the comfort we ourselves receive from God" (2 Corinthians 1:3-4).

God does not invalidate our pain. Jesus wept alongside His friends, Mary and Martha, at the death of their brother. The Lord recognizes how much we hurt before He heals us. Whether our pain comes from the enemy or our own consequences, God can turn it around and fashion something beautiful in our hearts. That often comes through mourning, not despite it. The Lord can use our tears to create beauty and bring about healing. Lamentations concludes with two more chapters full of grief, and interwoven into these Scriptures of sadness are words of hope.

He says that because of the Lord's great love we are not consumed. God's compassions never fail and are faithfully new every morning. The Lord is good to those whose hope is in Him, and it's good to wait for Him. God is with us when we grieve, gently cradling our broken hearts. As He would not leave the Israelites in their brokenness, neither will He leave us. This is love.

23. EZEKIEL

"At the end of seven days the word of the Lord came to me..."
- Ezekiel 3:16

Dramatic. Mysterious. Supernatural. The beginning of Ezekiel's prophetic ministry baffles the brain and intrigues the imagination. Ezekiel was thirty years old and had been one of the Israelite captives in Babylon for five years. As he sat by a river named Kebar, God gave him a wild and fantastic glimpse of glory.

The vision began with a windstorm full of flashing lightning. Suddenly, four living creatures appeared. They appeared to be human, except they had four faces and four wings! Ezekiel tried to describe the faces, saying that they were like a person, a lion, an ox, and an eagle. They had human hands and feet like a calf, only made of bronze. The creatures were bright, glowing as if on fire and moving as quickly as the lightning of the storm.

Next, Ezekiel described wheels beside each creature, sparkling like the precious stone topaz. The wheels had more wheels within them and could go any direction with the creatures as they moved. Ezekiel described them all being connected by the same Spirit, which we know is the Holy Spirit. Above their heads was a clear crystal sky, and Ezekiel could hear a sound like rushing water as the creatures moved their wings against one another. Then, the Voice resounded.

Above the sky, Ezekiel saw a beautiful throne and a figure like a man. This figure was also glowing as if on fire, but much brighter than the creatures, the sky, or anything surrounding the throne. It was like a brilliant rainbow against a dark, cloudy sky. The glory of the Lord was so dazzling and holy that Ezekiel could only fall on his face as God spoke to him!

It was then that the Lord told Ezekiel to stand. The Holy Spirit came onto Ezekiel as he rose to his feet before the Almighty God. This is where he received his instructions from the Lord. God was sending him to the rebellious Israelites who, despite their defeat and captivity, remained stubborn. Their hearts were hard towards God. Whether or not they listened to Ezekiel's message, God called him to faithfully speak the truth and would give him the words to say. As a symbol of this arrangement, God gave Ezekiel a scroll with so many words that it filled both sides. He instructed Ezekiel to eat it! Ezekiel did so, and the scroll tasted sweet, like honey.

It was time for the prophet to go to the people. God promised to strengthen Ezekiel in preparation for the inevitable harsh rejection of the people. Then, the Spirit lifted Ezekiel as the glory of the Lord rose. Again, the rumble of the creatures' wings and the movement of the wheels echoed around him. Ezekiel found himself once more by the Kebar River where many of the Israelite exiles lived. He felt angry bitterness in his soul and remained in depression among the exiles for seven days.

We find our 3:16 at the end of that solemn week, when God spoke again to the young prophet. The Lord appointed Ezekiel as a watchman over the people. He would give His message to Ezekiel, who would in turn relay the warning to the Israelites. Feeling the hand of the Lord on him, Ezekiel followed instructions to go to a plain. This is where he again saw the glory of the Lord and fell face down in humble worship. God told him to return to his house where he would be tied up with ropes. He would not be able to speak for a period of time, but when God opened his mouth, it would be filled with prophetic words. Ezekiel's ministry had officially begun.

Whenever and wherever we encounter God, we are surrounded by love. Where God's glory resides, there, too, is love. This is because God is love in

His very being. As Ezekiel observed, it's all a bit overwhelming. So much glory is more than a human being can take without the strength of the Holy Spirit. And Ezekiel got only a small glimpse of God's glory in a vision! How incredible it will be on the day we join the Lord in glory and are completely in the midst of His presence!

God's loving fingerprints are all over Ezekiel's story as well as our own. First, they are in the vision. What a gift to have such an intense vision directly from God! Though Ezekiel is singled out here as a prophet, he is certainly not the only one to experience this. We've already read about visions given to Isaiah and Jeremiah, and other prophets received them as well. But are these holy sights limited to only a few ancient men? Perhaps not. On the day of Pentecost, after Christ died and ascended into heaven, Peter preached boldly to the people with words from the prophet Joel: "In the last days, God says, I will pour out my Spirit on all people. Your sons and daughters will prophesy, your young men will see visions, your old men will dream dreams. Even on my servants, both men and women, I will pour out my Spirit in those days, and they will prophesy" (Acts 2:17-18). God certainly has the ability to give visions to His children today. Sometimes, however, the inspiring vision God gives to us seems a little earthlier. For example, we are astounded by the intricate glory in God's creation and are moved to worship Him as the heavens declare His glory and the skies proclaim His handiwork. We also have the vision from John described in the book of Revelation about the second coming of the Lord and the end of days. God can reveal Himself through dreams and exhortations. The ways He communicates with us are unlimited, and they are always gifts of love.

The Lord also expresses His love through His perfect timing. The seven days between Ezekiel's vision and the beginning of his ministry were very intentional. A week was the traditional period of mourning, which we see in Genesis when Joseph mourned his father and in Job when his friends join him for a week of sitting in silence. Ezekiel's seven days had additional significance. We learn at the beginning of the first chapter that Ezekiel was the son of a priest and was a priest himself. The priestly career begins at age thirty—Ezekiel's age. Seven days just happens to be the time of consecration for a priest. It is in no way a coincidence that this vision coincided with the timing of Ezekiel's life. Just as God planned Jeremiah's purpose before Jeremiah's birth, so, too, did He design every moment of Ezekiel's life. That's what a God of love does for His children. His timing matters. It is often different than we desire, but, like God Himself, it is perfect. The apostle Peter wrote that to the Lord a day is like a thousand years, and a thousand years are like a day. God keeps His promises in due time. Each detail in our lives is carefully crafted by His sovereign hand. This includes every happening down to the precise second. Hardship will come and last exactly long enough. Blessings will appear just as they should. Though we often don't understand the reason, we can trust that our God has been consistently keeping time from the moment He created it.

Additionally, God gave Ezekiel another gift: the ability to withstand pressure from the rebellious Israelites. He knew that they would resist the words of the prophet. The people were predictably obstinate and cold toward the ways of the Lord, so God strengthened Ezekiel to allow him to continue to speak truth in the face of opposition. Once again, this is a gift God gives to all of us. King Solomon wrote about the way people affect us. Proverbs 13:20 says, "Walk with the wise and become wise, for a companion of fools suffers harm." But what do we do when we are surrounded by unrighteousness? David found himself in that place frequently, and wrote in Psalm 118:5-6, "When hard pressed, I cried to the Lord; he brought me into a spacious place. The Lord is with me; I will not be afraid. What can mere mortals do to me?" And in 1 Corinthians 10:13 we learn that, "No temptation has overtaken you except what is common to mankind. And God is faithful; he will not let you be tempted beyond what you can bear. But when you are tempted, he will also provide a way out so that you can endure it." Though we must resist sin and make a choice not to follow a wayward crowd, God does not leave us to a lonely battle. Like He did for Ezekiel, the Lord gives us the strength to endure.

Finally, we see that Ezekiel was designated as a watchman over the people of Israel. A watchman stood on the city wall and, as we can correctly guess, kept watch over the area. He was a lookout for any approaching danger and could sound the alarm in the event of emergency. From his vantage point, he was aware of things the people could not see from within the city. The symbolism was clear. Ezekiel was being given a supernatural perspective as God gave him the very words to speak to the people. The danger of disobedience was approaching, so Ezekiel would sound the alarm about God's judgment. Similarly, today, we have been blessed with watchmen and watchwomen in our lives. Often, we are blessed by pastors who care for people like shepherds, guiding us in God's right paths. Brothers and sisters who have walked life's path before us offer guidance and nurture. These are people who, like Ezekiel, have been called by God for such a task. Though they are human like us, we can be grateful and wisely heed their perspective—a gift from God who knows the big picture.

It's easy to be mystified by Ezekiel's strange vision. It's difficult to imagine as the prophet attempted to put into words things that aren't of this world. His descriptions might carry more symbolism than realism, but we do know for certain that they reflect God's glory. We can't let the strange and mysterious blind us to what we can see in this prophetic account. The love of God is clear and available to us now, just as it was to the people of Ezekiel's day. It is a love that transcends time and space to reach each of our hearts.

24. DANIEL

"Shadrach, Meshach and Abednego replied to him, 'King Nebuchadnezzar, we do not need to defend ourselves before you in this matter.'"

- Daniel 3:16

The exile experience varied for the people of Judah. While some slowly adjusted to their new situation far from home, others were given the royal treatment. The Babylonian king, Nebuchadnezzar, summoned young Israelite men from noble families to come serve in the palace. These boys would be trained in the language, culture, and ways of Babylonian royalty in order to work for the king. Daniel and his three friends, Shadrach, Meshach, and Abednego were among the chosen.

This didn't seem to be a bad way to spend captivity. In addition to their lessons, the young men were given fine food and wine straight from the king's table. However, there was a glitch in this plan for Daniel and friends. Jewish laws were specific about what kinds of food could be eaten and what should be avoided. Consuming the king's food violated some of those laws. When Daniel spoke up about this problem, he was unsurprisingly met with disapproval. The official in charge of the recruits explained that if the Israelite men looked worse than the others, it would be the official who was punished. So Daniel proposed a little experiment. He requested only vegetables and water for the Israelite boys over the next ten days. Then, they would evaluate the results.

When the experimental time was up, the official was left with exceedingly healthy Israelites! Not only were they now allowed to observe their laws about food, but the young men earned respect from those in charge. God blessed Daniel, Shadrach, Meshach, and Abednego, and He granted them wisdom in addition to success in their training. Daniel was also given the gift to interpret dreams and visions. Additionally, they all gained favor with King Nebuchadnezzar as they were drafted into his service. The stage was set for some very dramatic events.

The king of Babylon was a dreamer. Literally. One night, he had a disturbing dream which disrupted his sleep. He frantically called upon all his resources—advisors, magicians, astrologers, sorcerers, all the guys who specialized in understanding nightmares. When they appeared before him, Nebuchadnezzar demanded that they interpret his dream. But there was a catch. He basically said, "If you guys are so all-knowing, tell me what I dreamed." To add pressure to the situation, he decreed that if they failed to do so, they would be chopped into little pieces. He was delightful, that Nebuchadnezzar.

Of course, there was no way for the enchanted advisors to do what the king asked. How could they know another man's dream? Therefore, all the wise men were sentenced to death. Heroically, Daniel intervened! He went to the king and, with God's help, did what none of the other men could do. Not only was Daniel able to tell the king what he dreamed, but he also revealed its prophetic meaning. King Nebuchadnezzar was impressed and pleased. First, he honored Daniel and acknowledged the greatness of God. Then, Daniel, Shadrach, Meshach, and Abednego each received a promotion to a higher office.

Just when it seemed like things were going pretty well in captivity for the young men, King Nebuchadnezzar decided that he wanted a statue. This 100-foot tall gold idol was placed in a nearby field so that everyone could gather and worship. When the statue was raised, the king called for all his officials of varying ranks to come to the dedication. All the people were commanded to bow to the statue when elaborate music began playing. Anyone who refused to do so would be sentenced to death by fire in the inferno of a furnace. This was quite enough motivation for the people, so when the music began, facedown they fell! That is, except for three young Israelites: Shadrach, Meshach, and Abednego. (Daniel is not mentioned, so it's presumed that he was not present).

The king was furious. Refusal to worship this statue was openly defying the king himself. This was a guy who liked dramatic punishments, so it was rare that anyone would be so boldly disobedient. He summoned the Israelites and demanded an explanation. However, because he wasn't an unreasonable king, he gave them a second chance to bow. But if they didn't, he brashly boasted, "Then what God will be able to rescue you from my hand?"

Shadrach, Meshach, and Abednego replied in our 3:16, "King Nebuchadnezzar, we do not need to defend ourselves before you in this matter." They continued, explaining that God was able to save them from even the hottest of furnaces. But even if He chose not to deliver them, they would still refuse to worship the golden idol. Of course, this further enraged the Babylonian king and all second chances were off. He ordered the furnace to be made seven times hotter than normal. This was so extremely hot that some of the king's men died in the process of carrying out the command. Then, the three Israelites were tied up and thrown into the furnace. As the king and his men watched what was certain to be an agonizing death, they were shocked at what happened next.

Shadrach, Meshach, and Abednego were not crying out in the flames. Instead, they were walking around, unharmed, as if it were a stroll in the park! What was more, there was a fourth person in the furnace with them! This additional person looked like what Nebuchadnezzar described as "a son of the gods" (NIV). None of this made any sense to the rage-filled king, so he immediately called for the Israelites to come out of the furnace. When they complied, everyone was mystified that they were not burned. In fact, their clothing didn't even smell like smoke. This was a game-changer for King Nebuchadnezzar. He quickly changed his tune from punishing the men to praising the God they served. For good measure, he gave Shadrach, Meshach, and Abednego another promotion. This was his way of saying "sorry about that furnace incident."

Wow! What a display of God's love in this miraculous rescue! This 3:16 clearly demonstrates God's supernatural power at work in the lives of His children. God loved Shadrach, Meshach, and Abednego very much, and they loved Him. This was clear as they honored Him from day one in training for the king's service. Perhaps they recalled the words of Deuteronomy 5:33, "Walk in obedience to all that the Lord your God has commanded you, so that you may live and prosper and prolong your days." But God's love extended beyond the earthly royal favor. God protected the three men from extreme persecution. He kept them from physical harm.

This was not the first time that God rescued His children. He delivered all the Israelites from Egyptian oppression generations before. He saved David from the murderous hands of King Saul countless times. Years after the fiery furnace, God would use an obedient queen named Esther to save His people from genocide. In the New Testament, we find believers being rescued from illness, calamity, and even death. Modern accounts of supernatural protection testify to God's rescuing power. Psalm 91:14-16 gives us comforting words from God. "Because he loves me," says the Lord, "I will rescue him; I will protect him, for he acknowledges my name. He will call on me, and I will answer him; I will be with him in trouble, I will deliver him and honor him. With long life I will satisfy him and show him my salvation."

Rescue comes in many forms. Thankfully, we don't often find ourselves battling for our lives in a fiery furnace. But our fiery trials might come in the form of natural disaster, conflict at work, a child with a serious illness, trouble that threatens a marriage, or deep depression. God can rescue us from all these things. He told His children, through the prophet Isaiah, "When you pass through the waters, I will be with you; and when you pass through the rivers, they will not sweep over you. When you walk through the fire, you will not be burned; the flames will not set you ablaze" (Isaiah 43:2). God will not leave us during whatever trouble overtakes us. He reaches out to deliver us from all the things that threaten us. The rescue might not come immediately, and we might find ourselves in the fire for some time. But when all is said and done, the Lord stands with us and brings us safety, including the safety of eternal life with Him.

Shadrach, Meshach, and Abednego were protected from persecution. Similarly, God shields us from adversity. The apostle Paul modeled dependence on Christ in a life full of persecution. Because of the power of God, he says, "We are hard pressed on every side, but not crushed; perplexed, but not in despair; persecuted, but not abandoned; struck down, but not destroyed" (2 Corinthians 4:8-9). Though God allows adversity in order to help us grow, He is there with us, giving us the strength to face whatever opposes us. We will not be overcome when we have the love of God in and around us. Even though we walk through the darkest valley, we can be free from fear, because God is with us.

But, what about the times He doesn't rescue us? Sometimes, the enemies win. We don't feel victorious. Illnesses aren't healed, injustices aren't righted, and people die. Where is the rescue then? Where is the love?

We learned in Ecclesiastes that there is a time for everything; God will right the wrongs and bring justice in His time. This is a difficult truth to cling to when we can't see the results in our limited, earthly vision. In the meantime, can we stand as steadily as Shadrach, Meshach, and Abednego? When King Nebuchadnezzar brought charges against them, they did not protest the charges. They simply stood in their faith and let God fight the battle for them. They did not know that the Lord would meet them in the furnace. They had no idea what the outcome of their ordeal would be. In fact, they were prepared to die in service to their Lord and true King.

What else could account for such calm in the face of death other than divine love?

True love from God inspires this confidence as well as a trust that transcends all earthly catastrophes. A godly man named Stephen experienced this in the book of Acts. He was a man full of God's grace and power who was arrested after false testimonies from those against faith in Christ. Despite such harsh adversity, Stephen delivered a complete sermon that glorified God. This only angered his enemies more, and they hurled large stones at him, crushing his body, but not his spirit. Stephen looked to heaven and saw for himself the glory of God. He was encouraged as he looked upon Christ at the right hand of God. While he prayed, Stephen died at the hands of those who persecuted him.

We may cry out to God in outrage. We may not understand how the Lord of justice would allow the suffering of His beloved ones. These are things that we may never understand until we, too, are in glory. In His prophecy through Isaiah, God reminds us that His thoughts are not the same as our thoughts; His ways are not like our ways. But, the God of love doesn't just leave us there, longing for rescue. He reassures us that the deliverance is indeed coming in perfect time. Meanwhile, He gives us a reason to trust Him. Like Shadrach, Meshach, and Abednego, we, too, have confidence in the Lord our God. We know that He will come through for us one way or the other. How He acts and whatever He allows, it will be for our good.

"Those who know your name trust in you, for you, Lord, have never forsaken those who seek you" (Psalm 9:10). Trusting God in the scary times isn't an easy thing to do, but His love enables us to hold tightly to Him. We know He is the faithful God who keeps His covenant of love to a thousand generations of those who love Him and keep His commandments. Because He has always been faithful, we have no doubt that He will remain faithful, never letting us out of His loving grasp. When we lack the strength to cling to Him, we can cry out like the man in Mark 9:24, "I do believe; help me overcome my unbelief!" And God will do just that through the power of the Holy Spirit, giving us supernatural help that is otherwise inexplicable.

Through fire or flood, conflict or persecution, days of royal feasting or desperate famine, our loving God is there. He is a God who rescues, a God who inspires confidence. There is no other god like Him; there is no other love. Perhaps it was this knowledge that emboldened the young Israelite men to resist King Nebuchadnezzar's commands. They couldn't even entertain the thought of bowing to anyone other than the only God who loved them deeply, the God who was with them through the horror of captivity. Despite the disobedience of their people, God was still a God of deliverance. This is the same God we serve today. After experiencing His goodness, we will not dream of bowing to anyone other than the God who loves us so much that He would stand with us in the fire.

25. JOEL

"The Lord will roar from Zion and thunder from Jerusalem; the earth and the heavens will tremble. But the Lord will be a refuge for his people, a stronghold for the people of Israel."

- Joel 3:16

The Bible can feel a little unclear at times. While we are given exactly enough information to begin to learn God's ways, it sometimes feels incomplete to our inquisitive minds. So it is with Joel. We know he was a prophet. We know he spoke the words of the Lord and that he prophesied in Judah and Jerusalem. However, that's about all we know with certainty. It's not even clear precisely when this book was written! Some say that Joel lived centuries before the exile. Others believe his words were delivered around the time that Daniel was interpreting King Nebuchadnezzar's first dream. We'll keep both dates in the back of our minds while we consider Joel's message.

It began with locusts. Hundreds of locusts. Thousands of them. Swarms upon swarms. These ravenous insects devastated the land by devouring the crops, leading to ruin of the agricultural society. Fields were destroyed, grains lost, fruit trees were left bare, and the people despaired. Joel's prophecy could describe the literal aftermath of a natural disaster or a symbolic description of destruction from an enemy army. The people were mourning their great losses. But all of this was nothing compared to what was coming.

Joel declared that "The Day of the Lord" was on its way. As did most of the prophets, he warned of God's pending judgment. He described an extremely unpleasant time, advising the people to be greatly alarmed. This would be a period of darkness and terror. Images of fire and an invading army invoked feelings of panic. How much was literal and how much was symbolic would remain to be seen, but the overall message was clear: judgment was coming, and it would be terrible.

Yet, as always, God reached out to His people with hope. He invited His children to repent genuinely. "'Even now,' declares the Lord, 'return to me with all your heart, with fasting and weeping and mourning.' Rend your heart and not your garments. Return to the Lord your God, for he is gracious and compassionate, slow to anger and abounding in love, and he relents from sending calamity" (Joel 2:12-13). Then, instead of disaster, they would enjoy prosperity and safety. Rather than fear, they could rejoice. As descriptive as Joel was when communicating judgment, he also detailed the promise of restoration and blessing that were possible if the people turned their hearts back to God. Even the locust damage that had already plagued them would be reversed. Wonderful things were in store for their future.

When we reach the third chapter of Joel, God is speaking not to His chosen people, but to the nations that took the Israelites captive. While the Lord would allow for the Israelites defeat in response to their sin, those who mistreated God's people would ultimately still suffer consequences. After all, these opponents were acting in their own interests, not honoring the one true God. Through Joel, they, too, received warning of coming judgment. At the right time, the Israelites would return to Jerusalem and their enemies would be in the hands of other peoples. The captors would become captives. God told them to prepare for war, and Joel dramatically described the judgment in our 3:16: "The Lord will roar from Zion and thunder from Jerusalem; the earth and the heavens will tremble. But the Lord will be a refuge for his people, a stronghold for the people of Israel." The prophecy closes with a blessing over God's beloved people. When all is said and done, justice will be served, and the Israelites will be reconciled with their Heavenly Father.

Clearly, we see God's love in the balance of justice that eventually comes to be. We now easily recognize the loving mercy in prophecies that offer opportunities for repentance that results in blessing. The very existence of prophets, God's communication with His creation, speaks of a Creator that cares. The words of Joel solidify our previous evidence of the love of the Lord.

So what distinguishes this 3:16 from the rest? At that point in the Scripture, the prophecy is directed at the other nations, not God's people. It paints a picture of a mighty God with unfathomable power. His voice roars and the greatness of it shakes the earth. It is reminiscent of other descriptions sprinkled through biblical pages, such as Jeremiah 10:12-13: "But God made the earth by his power; he founded the world by his wisdom and stretched out the heavens by his understanding. When he thunders, the waters in the heavens roar; he makes clouds rise from the ends of the earth. He sends lightning with the rain and brings out the wind from his storehouses."

We would be mistaken to equate a loving God for a soft, weak, celestial teddy bear. The Lord is compassionate and kind, but He is also powerful and uncontainable. Just to look upon His glory is enough to overpower a human life, as we see in Old Testament stories. Our God is untamable. His very words shake the heavens and the Earth. He invokes a holy fear among all those who understand His strength and sovereignty.

Yet the Lord *is* compassionate and kind. He chooses to be so because of love. It is a love so great that He can simultaneously care for His people while remaining the Lord who makes mountains tremble. He is strong but also gentle, terrifying yet still comforting. A lesser god would be ineffective and lacking power. Could we dream of serving someone explainable? How could we worship anyone but our wild, bigger-than-our-human-brains-can-comprehend King of Kings and Lord of Lords? His overwhelming glory is magnificently beautiful.

And as the Earth shakes with the power of His voice, His hand is on His sons and daughters. God is a refuge, a shelter, a safe space. He is our strength and ever-present help in trouble. Even if the Earth gives way and the mountains fall into the heart of the sea, we don't have to fear. Waters can roar and foam and the mountains can quake with their surging, but we remain safe in Him (Psalm 46:1-3). In Exodus 33, Moses requested to see God's glory. To protect Moses from certain death, God hid him in a safe space in a rock, allowing only for a peek at God's back as He walked by. Similarly, God gives us glimpses of His glory while keeping us safe and sound. Of course, when trouble comes from outside sources, we can count on the protection of our Refuge. Before he was king, David spent many frightening days and nights escaping from King Saul's murderous pursuits. The Lord repeatedly placed David in safe places and gave him escape routes. God preserved David's life, and He extends His refuge to all whom He loves.

Even now, for us today, God provides shelter from dangers around us. At times, it is a physical safe place to flee: the home of a loved one, a homeless shelter, a hospital, a church. Refuge can be in the form of an afternoon in the forest, away from the chaos of responsibilities. Quiet time reading and reflecting on His Word becomes a safe space from the rest of the clamoring world. His truth is a refuge from injustice. It sets us free.

And so goes the love of God, over centuries and generations. His power goes hand in hand with His compassion. Praise be to the Lord who is sovereign and good, mighty and caring. His love is stronger than the dangers of our world, and He is powerful enough to be the most secure refuge, protecting His beloved children.

26. NAHUM

"You have increased the number of your merchants till they are more numerous than the stars in the sky, but like locusts they strip the land and then fly away."

- Nahum 3:16

The setting is Nineveh, the ancient capital city of Assyria. The tone is gloomy as Nahum brings a message of judgment to Israel's enemy. The prophecy is without hope. Destruction will be thorough with no promise of a happy resolution. How can we possibly find any love in the words of Nahum?

We must go back to the beginning of Nineveh's story. They weren't always void of hope and sentenced to despair. In fact, God offered great redemption to the people of Assyria. He called upon a prophet named Jonah to deliver an urgent message. The wickedness of the city had reached its limit. God wanted Jonah to warn the people that His judgment would soon be upon them. Jonah, however, decided that he'd rather not obey. From the days of our childhood, we've heard the story of the prophet's attempted escape from God's assignment. Jonah took to the sea, only to be stopped by a wild storm. The sailors who were with him believed that an offended deity was responsible for the dangerous sailing conditions. They cast lots and all signs pointed to Jonah.

Once they knew that Jonah's offense prompted God to send the wind and rain, they begged him for solution. Jonah suggested that they throw him overboard. This means that Jonah would rather drown in a violent sea than preach to the people of Nineveh! As soon as Jonah's body hit the water with a splash, the sea was calmed. But Jonah didn't die. God was not finished with His prophet and still had plans for Nineveh. The Lord sent a big fish to swallow Jonah and hold on to him for three days. This gave Jonah the opportunity to be in some serious prayer. After a three-day time-out, the fish vomited Jonah out onto the shore.

Again, God spoke to Jonah and gave instructions to prophesy. This time, Jonah obeyed. He told the people of Nineveh that God was extremely displeased with their unrighteousness and that they had forty days until the destruction of their city. Their reaction was dramatic and immediate. The Ninevites grieved and fasted. Their king exchanged his fancy robes for the sackcloth and ashes of mourning. He decreed that everyone should call on God and repent from wickedness. The Assyrians took Jonah's words very seriously as they prayed for compassion and a second chance. God heard their prayers and saw that their hearts were turning from evil, so He relented and did not destroy the city of Nineveh.

Fast forward a hundred years. The generation that cried out to God and softened their hearts had passed away. The people turned from the ways of the Lord and took wickedness to the extreme. Besides worshiping the idols of other gods, the Assyrians were known for their cruel war crimes. They were enemies of the Israelites, the very people of the God that once saved Nineveh from destruction. In fact, the Assyrians had overtaken the Israelites and taken them captive. Though God allowed this to happen as a result of Israel's disobedience, the Assyrians still acted offensively to the Lord by oppressing the Israelites and living wickedly. Such extreme sinfulness would not be tolerated for long.

This is where Nahum enters the scene. God gave him a message for Nineveh that nearly echoed Jonah's message. This time, however, it was more detailed and severe. There would be no second chances; Nineveh was toast.

"The Lord is slow to anger but great in power; the Lord will not leave the guilty unpunished" (Nahum 1:3). The prophecy began by establishing God's character and intentions. "The Lord is good, a refuge in times of trouble. He cares for those who trust in him, but with an overwhelming flood he will make an end of Nineveh; he will pursue his foes into the realm of darkness" (Nahum 1:7-8). Things weren't looking good for the forces that were passionately violent against God's people. The Assyrians were charged with plotting evil against the Lord and would now have to answer for their wicked plans. The time for Israel's discipline would soon end, resulting in restoration of the chosen nation and justice being served for wrongs committed. The crimes of the Ninevites were so extreme that their consequences would be equally extreme: total destruction. There would be no descendants to continue sinful living and idolatry. This was the end of the line.

Nahum painted a violent picture. In the warring way that Assyria conquered others, so they, too, would be conquered. Images of flashing chariots are so vivid that we can almost hear the thundering hoof beats of the horses and clattering wooden wheels racing toward Nineveh accompanied by roaring battle cries. Though the people would try to defend themselves, they would be no match for their opponents. They would be ravished and plundered. The mighty would fall to their death, leaving nothing but smoke and charred ruins.

There is no hope here, nothing but woe. This time, there would be no second chance. Perhaps this is because our omniscient God knew that their hardened hearts would show no remorse. There would be no repentance from this bloodthirsty civilization. Instead of loving God, they loved idols. Their greed led to violence as they became oppressors of many people, including the Israelites. Now, their pride would fall, and they would be brought to their knees by oppressors of their own. Nahum 3:16 describes the once-thriving city full of merchants. They came, they prospered, and then they abandoned the city to its judgment and fall. The same would be for guards and officials. They would be worthless as locusts that disappear on a sunny day. Nahum concludes his prophecy with: "Nothing can heal you; your wound is fatal. All who hear the news about you clap their hands at your fall, for who has not felt your endless cruelty?" (Nahum 3:19).

It's easy to describe a loving God when the sun is shining upon His people. Stories of redemption and provision clearly indicate that God cares for us. Yet, if we are diligent to study all of Scripture, we are confronted with God's wrath as well. With justice comes judgment, and it often feels harsh. Our limited human understanding can have difficulty comprehending the violent acts of the Lord. Old Testament battles and destructive prophecies trouble us. It doesn't seem to fit with the loving God who sent His Son to Earth to save us. What about the rest of the people? Why aren't they saved? How could a nurturing God also behave in a way that seems cruel to us? These are big questions that have no easy answers. These are the kind of inquiries that require much divine wisdom and comprehension from the Holy Spirit. Some of these answers may not come to us until we reach heaven. So, until then, we study and pray. We seek the Lord and ask for help in understanding. We can take these things a little bit at a time, piece by piece, until it all slowly comes together.

We can start with the love we see in the story of Jonah. It is a story of second chances and grace. It's also a story of hopeful generosity. The Ninevites were not Israelites. They were not part of God's chosen people; they did not serve the God of the Jews. Instead, they were Gentiles. Yet, they still mattered to God. While the Israelites were God's chosen people, we know He sent Christ for all. God said to Isaiah, "It is too small a thing for you to be my servant to restore the tribes of Jacob and bring back those of Israel I have kept. I will also make you a light for the Gentiles, that my salvation may reach to the ends of the earth" (Isaiah 49:6). Just as Ruth and Rahab were welcomed into the family of God, the Lord welcomes anyone who loves and serves Him. God's kindness is displayed in the book of Jonah as the Ninevites turn their hearts to the Lord and receive His mercy.

It wasn't God's love that failed Nineveh, but Nineveh who failed God's love. They didn't stick with their devotion. They turned back to old habits and strayed further from the Almighty Lord. It was more than just a neglect of God. Their cruel treatment of His people was a direct attack on the Lord Himself. Again, we have a front row seat to the perfect justice of our God. We've already established that love is just, even if that is difficult. We also see God's patience on display. Instead of simply wiping out the Ninevites a century before, God sent a prophet to warn them. Then, after granting them mercy, He showed great patience as they began to revert to ways of evil. As we know, unrighteousness can't exist forever. God knows exactly what the limits are and when there is no chance of repentance. He knew that Nineveh would not become a nation that honored Him. This was not a hasty decision. The Assyrians knew who God was and what it meant to follow Him. They had an entire century to pull it together, but they refused to honor the Lord and lashed out at Him instead.

God also provided justice for His oppressed people. God said, "Although I have afflicted you, Judah, I will afflict you no more. Now I will break their yoke from your neck and tear your shackles away" (Nahum 1:12-13). The fall of the Assyrians was a step closer to the freedom of the Israelites. The Lord promised that the consequences of Israel's unfaithfulness would not last forever, and He is a God who keeps His promises. This is additional evidence of His love. God does not lie or change His mind. He follows through on His words and fulfills His promises. We see that in Nahum's prophecy, which was followed by the total destruction of Nineveh at the hands of the Medes and Babylonians. God previously promised Noah (and us) that He would never again flood the Earth. We can trust Him in that. God promises never to leave or forsake us. We can trust that, too. The Bible is full of promises from a loving God, and whenever He says anything, we can count on Him. That kind of consistency is a characteristic of love.

Dark prophecies are difficult for us to accept. The suffering of His creation does not delight the Lord. He does not recreationally choose to wipe out people on a whim. He does not arrive at judgment quickly. We need help seeing His love in difficult Scriptures, but when we ask, He will provide clarity. A loving God teaches His children at just the right pace for our understanding. Will we be as patient with Him as He is with us?

27. HABAKKUK

"I heard and my heart pounded, my lips quivered at the sound; decay crept into my bones, and my legs trembled. Yet I will wait patiently for the day of calamity to come on the nation invading us."

- Habakkuk 3:16

As the remaining ruins of Nineveh smoldered, Babylon's power increased. Also known as Chaldeans, the Babylonians were notorious through the ancient land for their military conquests. While they took over nation by nation, Judah was experiencing a downslide. Good King Josiah died, and the people began to turn away from their God. This was the time of the prophet Habakkuk.

Habakkuk was a man full of questions. Like Job, he boldly spoke his mind to God, asking the burning inquiries that were on his heart. And, as in the book of Job, God had answers. This time, the Lord directly addressed the concerns brought before Him.

Habakkuk prophesied in the face of great unrighteousness. Like many others before him, he wondered when justice would be administered. This is the first question he asked the Lord, and this turned into a plea to God. How long will the prophet cry and feel unheard? How long would the violence around him go unpunished? We can relate to Habakkuk's despair in a world that seems to have unending suffering, war, and disease. How long will God allow such things to exist? Immediately, God replies. He told Habakkuk to watch, because He was going to do something big: He would allow the

Babylonians to succeed and take over. God then described the terror that would soon come from their military campaign.

From this information Habakkuk formed his second question. He asked how such a holy God could use wicked people like the Babylonians for His purposes. How can horrible violence from unrighteous people be allowed to harm someone who is righteous? God told Habakkuk to wait. The Lord's timing is perfect. Justice would come to the wicked and peril to the unrighteous. He then announced woe to the proud, to those who gain favor by evil methods, and to him who establishes a city with bloodshed and injustice. In the end, all things would be made right. God said, "For the earth will be filled with the knowledge of the glory of the Lord as the waters cover the sea" (Habakkuk 2:14). This is a way of describing total completeness. God's perfect ways will always be thorough and good.

After God's second reply, Habakkuk prayed. He responded to the Lord with intense emotion. He proclaimed the glory of the Lord and described splendor like the rising sun and bright light from his powerful hands. Habakkuk recalled mighty acts of God with allusions to the partings of the Red Sea and Jordan River, as well as the miraculous stopping of the sun during battle to help achieve victory for Joshua and the Israelites. He acknowledged God's righteous justice of the past.

All this overwhelmed Habakkuk. Our 3:16 says, "I heard and my heart pounded, my lips quivered at the sound; decay crept into my bones, and my legs trembled. Yet I will wait patiently for the day of calamity to come on the nation invading us." He concluded with the revelation that even if all seemed troubling, "yet I will rejoice in the Lord, I will be joyful in God my Savior" (Habakkuk 3:18). Habakkuk heard from God and trusted Him to act with justice. He waited on the Lord.

Love is found in relationships. Habakkuk and God had a conversation, but we witness more than a mere exchange of words. There was precious trust between the two. God trusted Habakkuk with His revelation and Habakkuk trusted God to fulfill promises and restore justice. Their conversation was full of emotion and more than a bunch of facts flying back and forth. It mattered to God how Habakkuk felt, and Habakkuk wanted to fully understand God. Theirs was hardly a superficial friendship, but an intricate relationship between prophet and Lord, servant and Master, son and Father.

In the prophecy of Habakkuk, God reinforced evidence of love we've seen in other messages: the pending justice, the care for His people, and the importance of trusting His intentional timing. Before we brush aside these things in the name of repetition, let's pause and take in the truths once more. The Lord felt that it was crucial to emphasize these messages through multiple prophets. He wanted to be sure it was heard and understood by all. This includes the people of Habakkuk's day as well as those of us reading now. It's no accident that we are looking at ancient prophecy today. Let these words strike your heart just as they impacted Habakkuk. Allow the truths of God's love to be absorbed into your soul.

How exactly did Habakkuk receive the word of the Lord? From the intensity of our 3:16, it seems to have taken over like a tidal wave. Habakkuk was in awe of this mere glimpse of God's glory. Stop again. Consider what it means to be in awe. It's an emotion that mixes reverence and wonder, inspired by something sacred. This isn't passing appreciation or simple admiration. This is knock-you-off-your-feet, take-your-breath-away, stone cold wonder. It's something too much for a human mind to process. It floods the heart with indescribable emotion and fills the eyes with tears. Words cease to adequately articulate the greatness of the Holy One and the creation is struck with . . . awe. This is what is meant when the Scriptures say "awesome," a word we casually toss around until its meaning has been forgotten.

But it's not too late. We can still reclaim the wonder. Our language may have evolved over time, but the greatness of our glorious God is unchanging. He still wants to wow us. When people witnessed the miracles of Jesus, they were constantly described as being astounded. Today, God continues to do amazing things. Psalm 65:8 says, "The whole earth is filled with awe at your wonders; where morning dawns, where evening fades, you call forth songs of joy." Are your eyes open to the incredible works of God's hand? "Come and see what God has done, his awesome deeds for mankind!" (Psalm 66:5).

The danger is when we harden our hearts and miss His blessings. Proverbs 28:14 reminds us, "Blessed is the one who always trembles before God, but whoever hardens their heart falls into trouble." The wonders are there, beloved child of God, to inspire and encourage you. His greatness will both comfort you and bring you to your knees. His love is so far beyond explanation, yet also intimately knowable in the deepest places of the heart. Let Him take your breath away as He overwhelms you with awesome love.

28. ZEPHANIAH

"On that day they will say to Jerusalem, 'Do not fear, Zion; do not let your hands hang limp.'"

- Zephaniah 3:16

From the lineage of King Hezekiah came a prophet named Zephaniah. Generations had passed since Hezekiah's rule, and Judah had been through many ups and downs as kings led them astray and then back to the Lord again. Zephaniah began to prophesy during the reign of good King Josiah. While under his leadership, Judah was returning to the ways of God once more. However, even the best of kings can't control all the people all the time. There was still enough unrighteousness lingering among the Israelites to cause great concern.

God is Lord over all the earth, and Zephaniah's message starts with a wide-angle perspective. Just as our previous prophets declared coming judgment to Israel, Zephaniah proclaimed disaster to the whole world. He jumped right in with visions of complete destruction, leaving no man, beast, bird, or fish still standing (or flying or swimming). But it all came back to Judah, God's chosen nation, His beloved people. They had especially offended God by sinning against the very One who rescued them from oppression and gifted them a rich and abundant Promised Land. Zephaniah described judgment that is now becoming familiar. While it is important to us to note whenever Scripture feels repetitious, there is something God really wants us to understand. This message was vital to the people of Judah. The words from the Lord through

Zephaniah were a matter of life and death. To ignore the repeated warnings from the prophets would result in the very disaster they predicted.

Zephaniah continued to remind anyone who would listen that judgment was not limited to Judah. In fact, his prophecy covered nations from all points of the compass: Philistia, Moab and Ammon, Cush, and Assyria. They, too, had offended the Lord of Hosts by oppressing His people, worshiping other gods, and committing other crimes. Consequences would fall upon them and destruction would obliterate any future for those who did not honor Almighty God.

Despite all the gloom and doom, Zephaniah's prophecy contained a great deal of hope. True, while Jerusalem was unrepentant, they were on a path to destruction. But the judgment had not yet fallen; there was still a chance for salvation. This was more than a message of "don't do the bad stuff and you'll avoid bad results." There were abundant blessings to be had as a natural consequence of turning their hearts back to the Lord. Chapter three describes a bright future for a remnant of Israelites who would follow God and seek his ways. "They will eat and lie down and no one will make them afraid" (Zephaniah 3:13b). Our 3:16 is similar: "On that day they will say to Jerusalem, 'Do not fear, Zion; do not let your hands hang limp.'"

The imagery of limp hands is symbolic of a posture of fear. However, in the day that God restored Israel, there would be no reason to be afraid. This is, of course, because of God's love. Despite all the sins and failings, Israel still had a hopeful future. This is easy for us to accept now, thousands of years later with clear hindsight. We're also relatively secure in our modern-day Christianity. We're not burning any incense to idols in high places at the moment (though we certainly have our own things that we hold more dearly than the Lord), but the people of Judah didn't have our perspective. They desperately needed the prophets to give them words from the Lord. They needed the hope of this message and it wasn't as easy to believe. Did they truly accept the threat of judgment as fact? Or was it because of disbelief that they continued to worship idols and disregard the Creator? Or did they think that judgment was inevitable and therefore any hope was a fairy tale?

This was an uncertain time for God's people as their loyalties were divided among multiple gods. After the forecasted judgment, it would be easy for the people to be afraid (as they very well should have been, given the circumstances). But God's love is greater than fear and it extended to His people despite the coming wrath. Similarly, God extends His fear-busting love to us today, despite any circumstances we think might prevent it from reaching us.

There are hundreds of encouragements in Scripture that tell us not to be afraid. They come indirectly as God speaks to people such as Joshua. As he prepared to lead the people into the Promised Land, God said, "Have I not commanded you? Be strong and courageous. Do not be afraid; do not be discouraged, for the Lord your God will be with you wherever you go" (Joshua 1:9). The words came to the whole nation: "But now, this is what the Lord says—he who created you, Jacob, he who formed you, Israel: Do not fear, for I have redeemed you; I have summoned you by name; you are mine" (Isaiah 43:1). Jesus spoke reassurance to His disciples when they saw Him walk on water: "Immediately he spoke to them and said, 'Take courage! It is I. Don't be afraid!'" (Mark 6:50). Paul writes to all believers, "For the Spirit God gave us does not make us timid, but gives us power, love and self-discipline" (2 Timothy 1:7) and "Be on your guard; stand firm in the faith; be courageous; be strong" (1 Corinthians 16:13).

Fear is characterized by a lack of trust and a worry about things that are happening or have yet to occur. It manifests itself physically in rapid heartbeat, sweating, shortness of breath, butterflies or a knot in the stomach, pain in the chest, and other symptoms unique to an individual. Yet, the effects of love produce very different results. When we feel loved, we are calm and secure. Our heart rate is even, our stomachs are soothed, and we can breathe freely. When we are wrapped in love, it is easier to trust the One who loves us. We know they would never bring harm upon us and would protect us to the best of their ability. So it is with the love of God. John, the disciple who truly knew the love of Jesus, wrote, "There is no fear in love. But perfect love drives out fear, because fear has to do with punishment. The one who fears is not made perfect in love" (1 John 4:18).

Imagine if it were possible to quantify fear into something we could visualize. Picture as much fear as you've ever felt or that is ever possible to feel. What does it look like? How large is it? Now, attempt to visualize the love of God. It is infinitely bigger and larger and stronger than any amount of fear we can conjure in our hearts and minds. Love greatly overpowers every ounce of fear that we might tightly grasp. We can think of many potential threats to fear, like accidents, illnesses, crime, hunger, financial ruin, or even death, but God has thought of all of that and more. He is prepared to handle each and every trial that comes our way with His infinite power, grace, and love. This is a tangible love that acts in the face of adversity. It is this love that provided manna and quail for hungry Israelites in the wilderness. This love filled Queen Esther as she fasted and prayed and later confronted an evil threatening the lives of the Jews. The powerful love of Christ healed blindness, deafness, and other physical ailments. It is a love so powerful that it can bring people back from death itself. This love even today provides financial resources and physical rescue, placing the right people in the right place at just the right time. It is the force behind stories of provision that some might be foolish enough to call coincidence. This love creates community and survives disasters. There is nothing we fear that God's love can't overcome.

The Lord did not intend to only make His people unafraid. His promises weren't simply just an absence of adversity. In Zephaniah 3:17 he says, "The Lord your God is with you, the Mighty Warrior who saves. He will take great delight in you; in his love he will no longer rebuke you, but will rejoice over you with singing." Delight, love, rejoicing . . . No rebukes but singing. These are descriptions of a nurturing Father. To nurture is to care, to help grow with attentiveness, and to provide for lovingly. Nurture is hands-on encouragement. This is a quality that we associate with parents, and in this case, care comes with heavenly intensity. God does more than just fight away the fear. The Lord cares for us and nurtures us. Christ described this care when He instructed the disciples not to worry in Matthew 6:26: "Look at the birds of the air; they do not sow or reap or store away in barns, and yet your heavenly Father feeds them. Are you not much more valuable than they?" Jesus also uses the example of the flowers of the field being clothed more beautifully than King Solomon. And, after all, they are only flowers. Won't God therefore clothe people, whom He loves all the more? It's yet another reason not to worry, because God actively provides for His children. Peter reminds us to give all anxiety to Him because He cares for us.

The Israelites had a choice. They could remain in their sin and continue to worship idols, accepting the extreme judgment that was headed their way, or they could repent of their unrighteousness and enjoy the benefits of God's blessing. Sadly, it took the fall of their cities and seventy years in exile to prepare their hearts for restoration with the Lord. We, too, have the choice between a road of fear and troubles or a path of God's comfort, confidence, and care. Our nurturing God powerfully vanquishes fear, and He is always ready to do so because of His intensely protective love.

29. MALACHI

"Then those who feared the Lord talked with each other, and the Lord listened and heard. A scroll of remembrance was written in his presence concerning those who feared the Lord and honored his name."

- Malachi 3:16

We've reached the final book of the prophets! It's been a long journey with God's holy messengers, but their words—collectively and separately—have blessed us with a rich perspective. As we examine the message of Malachi, we turn the closing pages of the Old Testament.

We know very little about the person Malachi; we have only the words he delivered from God. He holds up a figurative mirror to the hearts of the people of Israel and points out major trouble. Like petulant children, the people demanded questions of the Lord: "How have You loved us?," "Exactly how did we despise or defile You?," and other opposition to the exhortations of God's holy prophets. Of course, God, this time through Malachi, had answers.

God pointed out the difference between the nations of Edom and Israel. These people groups are descendants of twin brothers Esau and Jacob. The details of their story are found in Genesis, but for now it's important to know that Esau's people boldly rejected God and therefore Edom lacked divine blessing. The people of Israel descended from Jacob. God reminds them of the many instances of His faithfulness to them, and there's an issue. The Lord was not pleased with Israel's offerings because they brought sacrifices that were defiled and blemished in various ways. This was direct disobedience of the laws given to them at the start of their covenant with God. More than a logistical error, these subpar sacrifices reflected the attitude of their hearts. They disrespected the altar of God and the Lord Himself and couldn't be bothered to present their best or even something "good enough." In self-serving greed, they kept God's best gifts for themselves, disregarding instructions that would ultimately yield blessings.

The attention of the prophecy shifted to the priests, leaders who were intended to guide the people in the right ways of God. Instead, they went along with the half-hearted offerings and wondered why they weren't enjoying God's favor. The Lord reminded them of the covenant He made with the Levites, the tribe responsible for serving in the temple. In Malachi, we see that this was a promise of life and peace. The priests had the great responsibility of speaking truth as messengers of the Lord. However, the opposite was happening, and the people were being led astray.

But there was hope! Another messenger was coming, and He would make a way for the Lord Himself to come. Sound familiar? We're soon going to meet a man who called for the people to prepare a way, so keep these words from Malachi in mind when we soon jump ahead a few hundred years to study the New Testament. Until then, embrace the words of promise about a Messiah, a Savior who will come like a "refiner's fire." When He arrives, all things will be made right. The impure things of the world will be washed away, and the righteous will remain. God reassured them, saying, "I the Lord do not change. So you, the descendants of Jacob, are not destroyed" (Malachi 3:6). While they had this promise to cling to, the people of Israel were still called to return to the God who loved them. Remaining in sin was not an option.

After a rebuke from God about giving tithes and another complaint from the people, the tone changes at our 3:16: "Then those who feared the Lord talked with each other, and the Lord listened and heard. A scroll of remembrance was written in his presence concerning those who feared the Lord and honored his name." A group of faithful individuals existed amid a sinful nation. How remarkable to be obedient while everyone around them lived recklessly far from the Lord! And what validation poured from the heart of the God they loved, who encouraged them by noticing their obedience and promising (in verse seventeen) a lasting reward!

We experience great love when we are seen and when our efforts are noticed. For these people to continue to respect the Lord despite the society that surrounded them is nothing short of amazing. (In this verse, the word "fear" does not mean to be afraid of God, but to rightfully respect and submit to Him as we remember how great He is). There must have been occasions when they wanted to give up and take up the habits of their neighbors. It would have been easier to bring any ol' offering to the altar table and enjoy the best meat at the dinner table. Other gods might have looked inviting when the God of their fathers seemed silent. Following ancient laws took effort. They probably felt outdated. Yet these people persisted; no hardship, ridicule, inconvenience, or doubt would sway them . . . and God noticed.

He is a God who sees. A mistreated slave in the wilderness learned this in Genesis. Hagar was pregnant with Abram's child and fleeing the abuse of his wife, Sarai. It was originally Sarai's idea for her husband to have a child with her slave in an attempt to fulfill God's promise for their family. However, once the plan was in motion, Sarai had second thoughts and became bitter. Her harsh treatment was too much for Hagar, who thought the extreme conditions of the desert were better than remaining with Sarai any longer.

Hagar encountered the Angel of the Lord by a spring. He told her to return to Sarai and then encouraged her with a promise of many descendants. Her son would be a wild man and she was to name him Ishmael. Hagar's response was to give the Lord a name. She declared that He was, "The God Who Sees" and then returned to Abram and Sarai, later giving birth to baby Ishmael.

To be seen by God is a gift beyond description. There are many times we feel invisible, as if we don't matter, and think that maybe it would even be better if we weren't part of what's going on around us. Did Hagar think anyone would miss her? Or perhaps Sarai would be happier if a slave wasn't carrying her husband's baby? Running to the desert was not a happily-ever-after situation. In fact, she was likely to die without some kind of intervention. This speaks to the degree of Hagar's desperation. But that desperation became strength after she met the Lord! Simply being acknowledged and seen by the Most High was powerful enough to inspire hope in Hagar and enable her to return to an oppressive situation. If God saw a young woman running through a desert then He most certainly sees you right where you are now. He looks upon His children with loving attentiveness. Psalm 33:13-15 says, "From heaven the Lord looks down and sees all mankind; from his dwelling place he watches all who live on earth—he who forms the hearts of all, who considers everything they do."

Though His holy acknowledgement is enough to encourage our souls, God doesn't stop there. He pours out His love in blessings. These might be immediate, but even the gradual gifts are valuable and often eternal. Malachi describes the blessings that come after tithing: "'Bring the whole tithe into the storehouse, that there may be food in my house. Test me in this,' says the Lord Almighty, 'and see if I will not throw open the floodgates of heaven and pour out so much blessing that there will not be room enough to store it'" (Malachi 3:10). We experience God's favor in many areas of life, like relationships, health, or situations that have a positive outcome. However, these things are temporary in light of eternity. True love gives meaningful gifts that won't break, fade, or wear out- spiritual gifts like love, joy, peace, patience, kindness, goodness, faithfulness, gentleness, and self-control. Heaven holds many delights and rewards, the best of which is that we will be securely with God forever.

The Lord recognized His faithful children and remembered His promises. This phrase doesn't mean He ever forgot them, because God forgets nothing and knows everything. Rather, it means that He continued to honor the covenant He made with His people. He stuck by them to see them through to the other side of their disobedience. He did not overlook the minority who were obedient while the majority brought disaster on the nation. What we do as individuals matters. David writes in Psalm 62:12, "One thing God has spoken, two things I have heard: 'Power belongs to you, God, and with you, Lord, is unfailing love'; and, 'You reward everyone according to what they have done.'" God loves us each as individuals. We don't get lost in the crowd. He hears our voice and sees our face. We won't be forgotten as the world around us swirls in chaos. Love reaches down and tells us how much the Lord cares for us. He will never let us go.

30. MATTHEW

"As soon as Jesus was baptized, he went up out of the water. At that moment heaven was opened, and he saw the Spirit of God descending like a dove and alighting on him."

- Matthew 3:16

The ancient prophecies held more than judgment day warnings. The hope of Israel's future included the promise of a Savior who would deliver them. Hundreds of years after the days of the prophets, the Messiah made His earthly appearance as a helpless infant. This was hardly the way the people expected the King to arrive. Many did not believe that Jesus was the one foretold by Isaiah, Jeremiah, and Micah. Perhaps Matthew began his book with credentials of royalty in order to convince those who doubted.

When we open the pages of the New Testament, we are first greeted by a detailed genealogy. The stage is set, and Jesus Christ is the main event. Matthew made it very clear that Jesus Christ was the Messiah for whom they've been waiting, and that His lineage connected Him to David and Abraham. Jesus is the real deal. Because family lines were very important in ancient Jewish culture, Matthew demonstrated that Jesus was to be taken seriously as a descendant of King David. This qualified Him to fulfill Jeremiah's words: "'The days are coming,' declares the Lord, 'when I will raise up for David a righteous Branch, a King who will reign wisely and do what is just and right in the land'" (Jeremiah 23:5).

The King of Kings didn't slip quietly into the world on a silent night. Royal drama surrounded His birth and babyhood. We'll see the story of His mother, Mary, when we read Luke's gospel, but Matthew tells us that before Jesus was even born, He was big news. Isaiah prophesied, "Therefore the Lord himself will give you a sign: The virgin will conceive and give birth to a son, and will call him Immanuel" (Isaiah 7:14). Mary and her soon-to-be husband had not been together intimately, as they were betrothed but not yet married. Pregnancy is not a condition that can be concealed for very long, and the consequences of unwed motherhood were severe. Joseph, in an attempt to keep the law but also protect Mary, had decided to quietly leave her and break off the betrothal. However, God had other plans for this little family. An angel appeared to Joseph in a dream and confirmed that the baby she was carrying was conceived by the Holy Spirit. Joseph's instructions were to go through with the marriage to Mary and to know that she would have a son named Jesus. When Joseph awoke, he obeyed the Lord's commands.

Matthew skips ahead in the story and picks up after the Baby's birth. The story of Jesus' royalty continues with an unexpected welcoming committee. A celestial birth announcement inspired a group of Magi, or wise men, to trek a great distance to Jerusalem to see the newborn King of the Jews. Their first stop on their quest was to see the current king, Herod, to ask for directions. Herod, however, was less than pleased at the idea that anyone else would rule. He requested that the Magi give him a heads up when they found the baby so that he could also worship Him. However, he had a sinister secret agenda.

The Magi followed the same star that had alerted them to the King's birth and soon found Jesus, Mary, and Joseph in a house in Bethlehem. They worshiped Him and gave gifts appropriate for a royal baby: gold, frankincense, and myrrh. Thanks to a warning in a dream not to return to Herod, the Magi left young Jesus in safety. But that safety was temporary. Herod had no intention of allowing the perceived threat to his throne grow into manhood.

The angel of the Lord visited Joseph's dream again one night, this time with instructions to flee to Egypt. The young family left immediately, just in time to escape a cruel murder spree that took the lives of all the male children two-years-old and under in Bethlehem. Jesus and His parents stayed in Egypt until Herod died and the angel of the Lord gave the all clear for them to return home to their small village of Nazareth in the region of Galilee.

Matthew fast forwards the narrative, moving straight to Christ's adulthood. For the first time, we meet a man named John the Baptist. When we compare stories with the other gospels, we find out that John was Jesus' cousin, born only a few months before Him. John spent his days in the wilderness, clothed in camel's hair and feasting on a diet of locusts and honey. His message was loud and clear: "Repent, because the kingdom of heaven is coming. Prepare for the Lord!" John drew crowds from the whole region who eagerly listened to his proclamations. He also baptized them in the Jordan River as he continued to preach about the coming Messiah.

One day, Jesus came to the Jordan specifically to be baptized. John initially protested, saying that it should be the other way around, that Jesus should be baptizing him! But Jesus firmly explained that this was the way it needed to be to fulfill God's plan. So, John baptized his cousin, the very Messiah that he was proclaiming. It was an amazing wonder! Matthew 3:16-17 says, "As soon as Jesus was baptized, he went up out of the water. At that moment heaven was opened, and he saw the Spirit of God descending like a dove and alighting on him. And a voice from heaven said, 'This is my Son, whom I love; with him I am well pleased.'"

Before His ministry officially began, Jesus already had some remarkable events indicate that His was not an ordinary life. How many other babies from Nazareth had a star announce their birth and kings bow before them? He joined many others who were going to be baptized by John, but Christ was set apart by God Himself, announced as His Son. Can you imagine being part of the crowd that day? To see the Spirit and hear the voice of God explaining that the man who stood in the river before them was the Son of the Most High? This was the Messiah that John declared, right before their eyes!

Never had the dirty waters of the Jordan seen so much love as they did that day. Concentrated love was poured out straight from heaven onto the two men standing between its banks. Think of the tone earthly parents use when they say, "this is my child." Pride and love exude from those four simple words. They not only identify the family relationship, but they announce that the parent is glad to claim the child as their own. They approve of the person their son or daughter is now and will grow to be. They want everyone to know that this child is their offspring. We can begin to identify with parental love, but nothing compares to the love from God the Father to Christ the Son. Matthew 3:17 makes it clear that God loves Jesus and is pleased with Him.

Years later, when Jesus was speaking to His disciples, He explained, "As the Father has loved me, so have I loved you" (John 15:9). Something incredible is happening here as holy love spreads beyond the Trinity of Father, Son, and Spirit to those surrounding the Son. But the overflow of love doesn't stop with the disciples. In John 17, Jesus is praying for the disciples and then for all believers. As He talks to His Heavenly Father, He prays, " . . . then the world will know that you sent me and have loved them even as you have loved me" (John 17:23).

Stop.

Go back and read that verse again.

Let it sink in.

God loves us just as He loves Jesus. The immensity of that love is beyond description. It can't be contained on Earth but fills the universe and the heavens. If this is anything like the love of an earthly parent, that means that God is proud to call us His child and is glad that we belong to Him. Just like the love of earthly parents isn't earned by the merit of the child, it isn't our achievements or righteousness that grant us heavenly love. Paul writes in Galatians 4:6, "Because you are his sons, God sent the Spirit of his Son into our hearts, the Spirit who calls out, 'Abba, Father.'" God loves us like He loves Christ. Intensely. Passionately. Dearly. Tenderly.

With that love comes the gift of baptism. The ritual of baptism is simple, but the meaning is deep. A person is either immersed under or sprinkled by water as a symbol for being cleansed and renewed by God's grace. It's a sign of accepting the gift of salvation and being part of the church. Baptism is a sacrament, or a holy ritual of Christianity. It's an outward expression of what God is doing inside the heart. John was baptizing people in the wilderness as a sign that they were repenting of their sins. They were preparing their hearts for the coming Messiah, just as John was advising. Jesus, however, did not ever sin, and Matthew explains that His baptism was to fulfill all righteousness. This act was part of the bigger plan, one that would include death on a cross and resurrection from the dead. This was not done for Christ's own righteousness—He was blameless. It was done for ours.

Jesus' baptism is additional evidence of His love for us. He became human, like us, so that we could become righteous, like Him. God gives us the gift of baptism as part of our relationship with Him. It gives us a way to express what is happening in our hearts. It communicates to God that we are accepting His gift as well as demonstrates to others what is happening in our lives so that they might be encouraged. Colossians 2:12 paints this picture: " . . . having been buried with him in baptism, in which you were also raised with him through your faith in the working of God, who raised him from the dead." Through this imagery we can connect the relationship between Christ's death and our life, His resurrection and our eternity. Our baptism becomes a sacred reminder of the very personal gift we were given from God: the gift of forgiveness and eternal life. It is a reminder of God's grace-filled love.

31. MARK

"These are the twelve he appointed: Simon (to whom he gave the name Peter)..."

- Mark 3:16

This is where the action is. Mark jumps right into the story of Jesus and takes us breathlessly through a non-stop narrative. Hold on tight, because it's a wild ride.

The book begins with someone familiar. We again find John the Baptist fulfilling Isaiah's prophecy about a messenger preparing the way for Christ. Mark describes John as Matthew did, right down to the camel's hair, locusts, and honey. This may seem repetitious to a modern reader, but it is confirmation that these are true events being recorded by multiple sources. We can be confident that God's word is true!

After John baptized Jesus in the Jordan River, Jesus took time to prepare for His ministry. He spent forty days being tempted by Satan and ministered to by angels. After this, He began preaching about the kingdom of God in His home region of Galilee, but He didn't serve alone. Jesus befriended four fishermen and then called them to join His ministry as disciples. Simon, Andrew, James, and John left their fishing boats and followed Jesus as He continued to teach.

The Word of God is powerful, and Jesus immediately made an impact. One day, He went to the synagogue to teach and was confronted by a man with a demonic spirit. Jesus called the spirit out of the man, amazing all those present with the dramatic scene. His authority and power were clear, and word began to spread about His incredible abilities. People began following Christ as He taught, cast out demons, and healed people afflicted with various diseases. The crowds grew so large that He began traveling to neighboring towns to teach in their synagogues.

Mark highlights notable healings, such as a leper who, after being made clean, ignored instructions to keep the good news to himself. He told everyone about his miraculous healing, and soon Jesus and His disciples were unable to even enter the city. One day, Jesus preached in a house in a town called Capernaum. The crowd filled the house and spilled out the door. There were four men who wanted to bring their paralyzed friend to Jesus to be healed that night. Since they couldn't get through the crowd, they climbed to the roof, cut a hole, and lowered their friend down below! Jesus recognized their faith and told the paralyzed man that his sins were forgiven. This was quite upsetting to the Jewish scribes who were on the scene. They thought to themselves, "How is this man so blasphemous? Only God can forgive sins!" (It seems that they didn't get the memo from Jesus' baptism that He was the Son of God.) Jesus called them out on these thoughts and, to show that He has the power to forgive sins, healed the paralyzed man as well.

During all the traveling, teaching, and healing, Jesus met a tax collector (not a popular profession due to frequent cheating and greed) named Matthew. He invited Matthew to be a disciple as well, and later had dinner at Matthew's house with a group of other tax collectors and sinners. This did not sit well with the scribes or a group of Jews zealously devoted to the law called Pharisees. They didn't think it was appropriate for a righteous person to share a meal with people who were clearly sinners. Jesus again called them out and made a point that sick people need doctors, not people who are already well. In the same way, sinners desperately need the love and forgiveness of God. Later, He was criticized by the scribes and Pharisees because He and His disciples were not fasting and picked grain on the Sabbath, a holy day for resting. While Jesus was gaining popularity among the people, He was not in good favor with the Jewish leaders. Tension increased when Christ healed a man's hand in the synagogue on the Sabbath. Instead of rejoicing in the miracle, the Pharisees began to talk about ways to kill Jesus.

As His work continued, Jesus called twelve men to be close to Him. He appointed them to travel with Him and learn from Him, and He also wanted to send them out to preach, heal, and cast out demons. Jesus was expanding His ministry reach. Our 3:16 begins the list of the twelve disciples: Simon, James, John, Andrew, Philip, Bartholomew, Matthew, Thomas, another James, Thaddaeus, and another guy named Simon. Over the next couple of years, these men would have their lives changed beyond their wildest imaginations.

Can you believe that Mark packed all that into three short chapters? This was just the beginning of Jesus' revolutionary time on earth. Let's take a breath and see where we find God's love in all of this, specifically in chapter three, verse sixteen.

There were multitudes clamoring for Jesus' attention. Were they truly interested in His message of God's kingdom, or were most of them there to be healed? Were people simply dazzled by the miracles without understanding the forgiveness of sins? Nothing like this had ever been seen before in Galilee. Christ was creating a stir and angering the Jewish leaders in the process. However, in the noise and excitement, He quietly gathered His friends. Though He was fully God, Christ was also fully man. A band of brothers would not only learn from Him, but they would be a support system during the ups and downs of ministry life. These were the people who would travel with Jesus, share meals, and talk about the great mysteries of God with Him. They were also the brothers who would share jokes, witness tragedies and victories, and even try His patience from time to time. The relationship between Jesus and the disciples was like no other. They walked side by side with the Son of God and were empowered by the Lord to do great things, too.

We also have the gift of friendship with Christ. In John 15:13-15, Jesus describes this friendship to His disciples: "Greater love has no one than this:

to lay down one's life for one's friends. You are my friends if you do what I command. I no longer call you servants, because a servant does not know his master's business. Instead, I have called you friends, for everything that I learned from my Father I have made known to you." The disciples weren't the only friends of God. Moses also had a strong friendship with the Lord, talking with Him and following His instructions to lead the people of Israel. Many generations before, God had a special relationship with Abraham. The Scripture was fulfilled that says, "Abraham believed God, and it was credited to him as righteousness,' and he was called God's friend" (James 2:23). These were everyday people, just like us. They chose to put in the time and follow the words of God, then were rewarded with a deep friendship unmatched by any human relationship. We are also invited into an intimate friendship with the Lord.

To be a friend is to love. Friends know each other's favorite things and histories. They understand good moods and bad while being sensitive to what delights or upsets one another. Friends go out of their way to help and support. They talk as well as listen, often developing a shorthand communication. Little things are shared for the sole purpose of inspiring a smile. "A friend loves at all times, and a brother is born for a time of adversity" (Proverbs 17:17). Friends are there through happy occasions and sad seasons, and they don't bail out during difficulty. Advice from a caring friend is worth more than gold, and there is something sacred about simply being together. Friends enjoy a casual, comforting familiarity that doesn't exist among acquaintances. Friendship is special, and our friendship with God fits all these descriptions and more. To have such a close relationship to the Creator of the universe is remarkable! But this is what God desires for us. He loves us so deeply that He longs to be close to us. He gave everything to make that possible.

Jesus called His disciples to Him. The initial four—Peter, Andrew, James, and John—were not part of a crowd that was clamoring for a healing. In fact, they began to follow Christ before the preaching tour even began. They might have heard John the Baptist calling for repentance and preparation for the Messiah. Could they have been among the crowd that witnessed Jesus' baptism? Perhaps they were deeply moved by the Holy Spirit, or a combination of all these things. However, they were chosen, called, and invited. Similarly, God invites us to be close to Him. "He has saved us and called us to a holy life—not because of anything we have done but because of his own purpose and grace" (1 Timothy 1:9). As the Lord said to Israel through the prophet Isaiah, "Do not be afraid. I have called you by name and you are mine." We, too, are His, called by name.

Speaking of names, did you catch one final detail in Mark 3:16? When Jesus called Simon, He gave him a new name, Peter. The meanings of names are important, and they certainly matter here. Matthew 16:17-19 tells us a little more about Peter's new name. The conversation between Jesus and Simon begins with a question from Jesus: "Who do people say that I am?" followed by "Who do you say that I am?" Simon answers that Jesus is the Christ, the Son of God. In reply, Jesus tells him that he is blessed because such understanding is a revelation from God. Furthermore, Simon will now be called Peter. The name Peter comes from the word for "rock," and Jesus explains that "on this rock I will build my church, and the gates of Hades will not overcome it" (Matthew 16:18). True to this word, Peter would become an apostle and a pillar of the early church.

Our own names have meaning as well. Our parents took special care to select a name based on the literal meaning or special significance it held to them. Since God is so detail-oriented, we know that He has a reason that we bear the names that we do. As He told the prophet Jeremiah, "Before I formed you in the womb I knew you" (Jeremiah 1:5). So, too, were we known before birth and our names divinely inspired, whether or not our parents were aware of God's influence. God is in control of even the tiniest detail! In John 10, Jesus describes Himself like a shepherd caring for us, His sheep. He says,

"He calls his own sheep by name and leads them out" (John 10:3). Additionally, He gives us names like "Child," "Righteous," "New Creature," "Free," "Chosen," "Blessed," and "God's Handiwork." He also calls us "Beloved."

Jesus ministered to large crowds, but when He healed the leper, He touched him individually. The paralyzed man was lowered into a room full of people, but Jesus forgave his sins personally. Away from the crowds, Jesus connected with His disciples. In this world full of billions of people, He loves you personally and individually. He calls you by name. He gives you a new name, one that reflects that you belong to Him. You, child of God, are dearly loved.

32. LUKE

"John answered them all, 'I baptize you with water. But one who is more powerful than I will come, the straps of whose sandals I am not worthy to untie. He will baptize you with the Holy Spirit and fire.'"

- Luke 3:16

Let's revisit John the Baptist and discover an additional gift of God's love. Luke, a doctor, examined more details than Matthew and Mark, so we have a treasure trove to sift through as we search for love. He begins before John was even born, and the first person we meet is a priest named Zechariah. One particular day was special to Zechariah; it was his turn to burn incense in the temple. While he was performing his priestly duties, an angel, Gabriel, appeared. He had a message for a stunned Zechariah. The angel told him that his wife, Elizabeth, would have a baby, a son they would name John. John would be a great man who would prepare a way for the coming Messiah.

Zechariah had a few doubts, as both he and Elizabeth were elderly, and she had never been able to conceive. Because of his lack of faith, Zechariah was made mute. This made it very hard to communicate what just happened, but when he emerged from the temple, the people guessed from his signs that he saw a vision. Soon, just as the angel said, Elizabeth became pregnant and a new trajectory of their lives was set in motion.

Months later, Gabriel visited Elizabeth's cousin, Mary. His message for her was just as stunning: she would conceive and have a son as well. But Mary's baby would be called Jesus, and He would be the Son of the Most High, the

Messiah who was foretold by the prophets. Though this was an incredibly miraculous event since Mary was a virgin, she accepted the news and was willing to serve God. She did, however, pay a visit to her cousin Elizabeth and confirmed the words of the angel.

Soon, baby John was born, and Zechariah was able to speak again. He praised God and prophesied about the future for both Jesus and John. Not long after that, a census called the people to return to the town of their ancestors. For Mary, this meant traveling with her husband, Joseph, from their little village in Nazareth to the city of Bethlehem. After a long journey, they could not find lodging in the crowded city. This left only one option for the birth of the baby—a barn. There, among the straw and animals, the Savior of the world, Jesus Christ, was born.

Meanwhile, a group of shepherds were hanging out in nearby fields keeping an eye on their sheep. In a dazzling flash, an angel appeared in a blaze of glory to tell them that the Savior had been born right there in Bethlehem and was now sleeping in a feeding trough! The angel was soon joined by more glorious angels, all of whom praised God as the shepherds watched in amazement. Once the skies cleared, those shepherds wasted no time finding the newborn Jesus in the stable, lying in a manger just as the angels had described.

Luke tells us a little more about Jesus' childhood, including His presentation in the temple as a young baby and an incident where twelve-year-old Jesus was separated from Mary and Joseph on a trip to Jerusalem. It took three days, but they found Him in the temple, hanging out with the teachers. For His mother, there was never a question that Jesus was a special kid: He was the Son of God.

Luke then jumps back to John the Baptist. Years have passed since his birth and we find John as a grown man in the wilderness. By now this is a familiar scene to us. Camel's hair, locusts, honey, and preaching about the coming Messiah are John's trademarks. We know that John is fulfilling

Isaiah's prophecy about a messenger preparing the way for the Lord, but Luke supplies us with more details about John's message. First, John makes clear the need for the people to repent of their sins. It was not enough just to be descendants of Abraham. They needed to recognize how they had turned from God and receive forgiveness for their sins. The crowd was definitely listening. They asked for clarification, and John was happy to provide answers. Anyone with two shirts or extra food should share with someone who is in need. Tax collectors must only collect the required money instead of the common (but shady) practice of charging extra to keep for themselves. Soldiers are told to be happy with their pay and not extort or falsely accuse others. With all his authority and revolutionary teaching, the people began to wonder if John was the one who was the Messiah.

He set the record straight immediately, and Luke 3:16 describes the person for whom they were waiting: "John answered them all, 'I baptize you with water. But one who is more powerful than I will come, the straps of whose sandals I am not worthy to untie. He will baptize you with the Holy Spirit and fire.'"

The people had been eager to be plunged into the Jordan River. The tangible act symbolized how God washed away their sins. Their hearts were made clean and they were ready for the Messiah that was coming to save them. Water was understandable. But fire? How could one be safely dipped in fire? What did this baptism signify? The crowd did not yet understand the power of God's love and how it would soon come.

When Jesus Himself was baptized, the Holy Spirit came down like a dove as God spoke from the heavens. The people got a glimpse of the wonder of the Trinity: Father, Son, and Holy Spirit together. Another wonder would happen after Christ returned to heaven and the first church began to form. If we look ahead to Acts 2, we find the miracle at Pentecost. The believers were gathered together in Jerusalem and suddenly a sound like a mighty wind rushed from heaven. Then, they saw what looked like fire that rested on each person. Immediately, they were filled with the Holy Spirit and they all began to speak in other languages. As they proclaimed the wonders of God, they were overheard by Jews from other countries who were visiting Jerusalem. What a powerful witness!

The Holy Spirit brought more than the ability to translate the message of the kingdom of God. Before He ascended into heaven, Jesus had told the disciples, "But the Advocate, the Holy Spirit, whom the Father will send in my name, will teach you all things and will remind you of everything I have said to you" (John 14:26). The Holy Spirit would bear witness to the things of the Lord. "But when he, the Spirit of truth, comes, he will guide you into all the truth" (John 16:13). The Spirit lives in us. "In the same way, the Spirit helps us in our weakness. We do not know what we ought to pray for, but the Spirit himself intercedes for us through wordless groans" (Romans 8:26).

The gift of the Holy Spirit is a true divine present of love from our Father in heaven through the Son Jesus Christ. We've already seen some of these benefits on our 3:16 journey and they are called the fruits of the Spirit. These include joy, peace, kindness, self-control, patience, faithfulness, goodness, gentleness, and, of course, love. We aren't capable of manufacturing these qualities ourselves, no matter how hard we try. When we are filled with the Spirit of God, these parts of Him overflow from us. Like a tree produces fruit, so the Spirit produces these good things in us.

In his letter to his friend, Titus, Paul wrote, "But when the kindness and love of God our Savior appeared, he saved us, not because of righteous things we had done, but because of his mercy. He saved us through the washing of rebirth and renewal by the Holy Spirit, whom he poured out on us generously through Jesus Christ our Savior, so that, having been justified by his grace, we might become heirs having the hope of eternal life" (Titus 3:4-7). Our very salvation is by the Holy Spirit through Christ, leaving us free from the sin that held us in slavery. We will inherit His glorious riches in heaven as well as blessings here on earth.

When Isaiah described Jesus in his prophecy, he also described the Holy Spirit: "The Spirit of the Lord will rest on him—the Spirit of wisdom and of understanding, the Spirit of counsel and of might, the Spirit of the knowledge and fear of the Lord" (Isaiah 11:2). Romans 8:9 says that the Spirit is a sign that we belong to God. Paul also writes that "hope does not put us to shame, because God's love has been poured out into our hearts through the Holy Spirit, who has been given to us" (Romans 5:5). The treasures found in the Holy Spirit are endless, and some can't even be articulated by words. His very presence strengthens and comforts us, reminding us that God is near.

The imagery of fire extends to the idea of refinement, as previously mentioned in Malachi. The process of refining gold and silver involves high heat. This is necessary to remove impurities and bring out the metal's full value. Similarly, out of love, God refines us. Though we are not placed into literal flames, trials and adversity can feel like a figurative devastating inferno. God does not let these things vainly torment us. He draws a purpose out of the fire. Peter compares trials with refinement in his letter of encouragement to persecuted believers: "These have come so that the proven genuineness of your faith—of greater worth than gold, which perishes even though refined by fire—may result in praise, glory and honor when Jesus Christ is revealed" (1 Peter 1:7). Job also recognized that the Lord uses adversity to refine us, to make us stronger while displaying the glory of the kingdom of God. Paul again writes to Titus, "[Jesus Christ] gave himself for us to redeem us from all wickedness and to purify for himself a people that are his very own, eager to do what is good" (Titus 2:14). Though the refining process can be intense and painful, God remains with us from beginning to end. He grows and shapes us while we are surrounded by the fire of adversity. We emerge from the flames renewed and stronger than when we first stepped into the blaze, and then we reflect a little more of Christ. God shapes, purifies, and strengthens us for our benefit. To leave us a weak, impure mess would not be kind. It would not be nurturing. Thankfully, God loves us with the intensity of a refiner's fire.

33. ACTS

"By faith in the name of Jesus, this man whom you see and know was made strong. It is Jesus' name and the faith that comes through him that has completely healed him, as you can all see."

- Acts 3:16

There is healing in Jesus' name.

The statement resounds through worship songs and sermons, echoed in Bible studies and spoken encouragement. We cling to its hope yet often fear a disappointing outcome. How can we understand a supernatural miracle? Why don't healings follow an expected pattern or formula? The book of Acts is full of wonders, so perhaps we can find answers among these pages also written by our friend, Luke.

Acts follows the four gospels and begins with Jesus' return to heaven. The ascension was a wonder itself. One minute, He and the disciples were all standing around talking. The next, Jesus was rising up into the clouds until He was out of sight, leaving two angels in white to snap the disciples out of their gaze and remind them that Christ will come again.

Before He left, Jesus gave the disciples plenty of instructions. His command in the final chapter of Matthew is now called the Great Commission because He told them to go to all the nations and make more disciples. Jesus also gave them a heads-up about the coming of the Holy Spirit, as we previously learned. The Spirit arrived as a sign that could not be missed. After many heard the believers speaking in various tongues, some were amazed, some were confused, and others chalked it up to drunkenness. Peter stood up and set the record straight. They were not drunk, and, for that matter, it was only nine in the morning! He reminded the people of Joel's prophecy: the Spirit would be poured out in the last days. He pointed out that Jesus' miracles and signs were proof of His divine nature, and then he reviewed His death and resurrection. Peter proclaimed that the speaking of languages and evidence of the Holy Spirit was from God and that Jesus was Lord. These were bold statements that reached the hearts of the crowd: three thousand people became believers in Christ that day.

Sometime later, Peter and John were headed to the temple to pray when they encountered a man who couldn't walk. This man sat at the temple gate daily to beg for money. As Peter and John passed by, the man asked them for a donation. Peter replied that he didn't have money, but he had a better idea: "In the name of Jesus Christ, get up and walk."

And walk the man did! He also leaped! He praised God right there in the temple! Everyone recognized him as the crippled man who had been begging every day for years and years. The reaction was big; everyone was astonished. Now that God had everyone's attention, Peter stood up in the aftermath of the miracle and began preaching. He gave all credit and glory to God for the healing while yet again declaring the death and resurrection of Christ. Peter explained that it was through Christ that the beggar's healing had happened. "By faith in the name of Jesus, this man whom you see and know was made strong. It is Jesus' name and the faith that comes through him that has completely healed him, as you can all see" (Acts 3:16). The remainder of Peter's sermon called for the people to repent of sin and follow Christ.

Many of the people saw only the healing miracle, but Peter wanted them to know that it was not the main event. Jesus is what matters. The abilities to walk, see, or hear are secondary to the wellness of the soul. A person with a physical ailment can have a spiritual heart that is healed by Christ while another person with the highest level of physical fitness could miss the redemption of Christ if their heart is cold and their ears don't listen. When we focus only on physical healing, we are in danger of neglecting the health of our spirit. As we consider this gift of God's love, let us keep a perspective that gives God glory while remembering that a heart forgiven and redeemed by Christ is the ultimate healing.

Physical restoration was—and is—a great gift of God's love. While on earth, Jesus healed crowds of people. He restored sight to eyes, hearing to ears, and gave the ability to walk to some who had never before taken a step. Issues of blood, demonic spirits, and even death were erased by His miracles. Then, God used the disciples (and seventy-two other followers in Luke 10) to preach and heal. Such miracles were frequent in the early church, and stories of supernatural healing continue through the centuries even today. In these supernatural events, we see God's love in tangible ways.

When we are physically suffering, it's difficult to concentrate on anything else. A basic headache can ravish an entire work day and a tiny cold virus can knock us off our feet for days. Major illnesses and chronic pain consume our entire lives. Perhaps one reason that God sometimes utilizes physical healing is to eliminate something that hinders us from giving our full attention to Him. We also know that healings display God's abilities and compassion, not just for the healed, but for all who witness the event as well as friends and family who experience the effects of a changed life. In addition to the gift of the healing itself, it is an honor to be the canvas on which God paints His work. Those who are healed are a walking display of the wonders of the Lord. Since every person is unique and every situation is different, it's impossible to list all the reasons why God chooses to heal someone physically. But we can begin to understand that it is a small part of the big-picture purpose for His glory and good for those He loves. The Lord often uses our pain to draw us closer to Him and show us how to depend on Him for everything we need. In the times He relieves our suffering, we learn to trust Him for provision and solutions to problems. We are free to love, serve, and worship Him while allowing Him to handle our burdens.

God's healing is not limited to physical ailments. We can also be healed of mental and spiritual issues. Conflicts can be soothed, fears calmed, and emotional brokenness repaired. God's care for us is attentive, kind, and thorough. Psalm 103:2-4 says, "Praise the Lord, my soul, and forget not all his benefits—who forgives all your sins and heals all your diseases, who redeems your life from the pit and crowns you with love and compassion." We can depend on Him. The psalmist also declared, "Lord my God, I called to you for help, and you healed me" (Psalm 30:2).

We can joyfully celebrate God's healing and easily proclaim His love when we are made well. But what about the times when healing doesn't happen? Why isn't everyone automatically made whole and suffering eliminated? These are questions that have been asked for generations over many centuries. We find some guidance in books like Job, Ecclesiastes, and Psalms when we see God's timing and know that His plan goes beyond what our earthly eyes can see. God is doing a good work, but sometimes it's different than what we imagine as the best scenario. He can use our pain to craft something beautiful. In John 9, Jesus meets a man who had been blind since birth. Many questioned why he had been born that way. They even suggested that it was a consequence of his parents' sin, but Jesus explained that his condition was part of God's work. It had always been God's plan to use this man to demonstrate His glory.

Your pain has a purpose. You are not forgotten, even when the hurt seems to go on for too long. Through His perfect timing, God "who began a good work in you will carry it on to completion until the day of Christ Jesus" (Philippians 1:6). In the meantime, He will never leave you to handle the burdens on your own. Psalm 9:9 says, "The Lord is a refuge for the oppressed, a stronghold in times of trouble." He is your safe place as you weather the storm when the healing doesn't seem to come. We may not understand his timing until glory, but when the pain and sickness seem to last, He keeps His loving arms around us as He makes us whole. The process of healing might take a lifetime, but He has not forgotten or neglected a single one of His children.

Acts 3:16 includes the role of our faith in the healing process. Peter said that it was through faith in Christ that the beggar was healed. He emphasized this by saying that the healing happened through Jesus' name and the faith that comes through Him. This indicates that there is a relationship between faith and healing. During Jesus' earthly ministry, there were times when He didn't heal due to a lack of faith (see Mark 6). In Mark chapter 5, He tells a sick woman that her faith has made her well after she reached out and touched his robe. This does not mean that we manufacture our own healing by the power of our own beliefs. A lack of healing does not indicate a lack of faith. We do see through these and similar examples that faith is an avenue for healing, but where does such faith come from? From the loving Lord Himself! In Mark 9, a father brought his son to Jesus in hopes that the son would be healed from demon possession. When the man expressed some doubt, he exclaimed to Jesus that he did believe, but begged the Lord to help him with his unbelief! The passionate cry was heard, and Jesus healed the son. We, too, can call out during our human doubt.

James 5:14-15 encourages us: "Is anyone among you sick? Let them call the elders of the church to pray over them and anoint them with oil in the name of the Lord. And the prayer offered in faith will make the sick person well; the Lord will raise them up. If they have sinned, they will be forgiven." This connection between faith and healing is another way that God involves us in the process of His work. It is for His glory and our benefit, and another way He loves us.

When all is said and done, we will be healed. Revelation 21 describes our future in a new heaven and new earth. We will be with God in beautiful glory. He will wipe every tear from our eyes, and eliminate death, mourning, crying, and pain. He will make everything new and whole. Though we may be in a season of darkness now, there is a happy ending coming our way. The God of love is the God who heals, yesterday, today, and forever.

34. ROMANS

"... ruin and misery mark their ways ... "

- Romans 3:16

The threats to Christ-followers became so severe they were murderous. Saul was not merely angry at the people preaching about Jesus; he was filled with rage. He was ready to do whatever necessary to silence what he considered blasphemy to the Lord. The persecution at his hand was excessive and feared by all who followed Christ. Then Saul was confronted by Jesus Himself.

A bright light was the least dramatic thing about Saul's walk down the road to Damascus. That light was blinding, but it was the voice from the sky that cut straight through to his heart and completely transformed all hate into love. It affected him physically; he couldn't eat or drink for days. Perhaps he felt an incredible weight had been lifted from his burdened soul when he was filled with the Holy Spirit. But did intense remorse settle in when he realized the great harm he caused God's people? How long before he felt the reassurance of forgiveness strongly enough to walk securely on the path the Lord set before him?

Saul changed his name to Paul to signify his remarkable transformation. Then, he obediently preached the gospel of Christ throughout the land. He hopped on a boat and sailed to places like Cyprus, Antioch, Philippi, and Lystra. Every time his foot stepped onto new soil, he proclaimed the saving truth of Jesus Christ. New churches began, and Paul equipped the people to live in Christ. When his missionary journey took him away to new locations, he wrote letters to encourage the new believers and strengthen their relationship with God as well as one another.

But he couldn't be everywhere at once. Paul also wrote to people he hoped to visit one day. The letter to the believers in Rome was such a message. His priority was to declare that Jesus was the Son of God who had been resurrected from the dead. He said that it was through Jesus that God's people received grace. The very words he once punished were now the truths he held most dearly! After expressing a desire to visit Rome in the near future, Paul jumped into some pretty deep theology. He talked about the extreme sin of the people and the way God allowed them to experience the consequences. Paul painted quite a bleak picture.

Next, he discussed the Lord's judgment. He said that God's kindness is meant to lead a person to repentance, and a day is coming when each person will be judged. Those who seek God's glory will receive life, but those who reject truth will experience God's anger. However, the Lord is still faithful to His promises, even when His people are unfaithful.

The truth is that a righteous person does not exist. The people had been debating about Jewish laws and the faith of the Gentiles. As they argued, they didn't realize that it didn't matter to which group a person belonged, they were still a sinner. Paul describes humanity in Romans 3:10-18 with words like worthless, deceitful, and full of bitterness. "Ruin and misery mark their ways" (Romans 3:16). They do not have peace, nor do they fear God.

Where is the love in such a dismal evaluation of mankind? It is in Christ. Based on our qualifications alone, we are not worthy of God's love. It would make perfect sense for a holy Deity to concern Himself only with what is already righteous and pure. Anything less would be rejected. But that's not the reality of love. Romans 3:23-24 explains, "for all have sinned and fall short of the glory of God, and all are justified freely by his grace through the redemption that came by Christ Jesus." The story doesn't end at our depravity.

God loves us despite our sinfulness. He also loves us in the thick of that unrighteousness. As we examined in a previous 3:16, Christ demonstrated His love for us by dying for us while we were still sinners. This means that while we were lying, God loved us. When we were in the middle of adultery, God loved us. When we misused other people to get a promotion at work, God loved us. Despite our abuse of drugs and alcohol, God didn't love us any less. There's not a single sin that can scare God away. We won't frighten or disgust our loving Heavenly Father.

However, we must be righteous to be in the presence of holiness, so Christ made us righteous. Romans 3:25-26 explains that Jesus was the sacrifice that paid the price and atoned for the sins of each and every human being. God was patient and left previous sins unpunished so that Christ would take the punishment in our place. This allowed His beloved children to be redeemed and set free. It prepared us to be with our holy Heavenly Father.

Love did not wait for us to get our act together. Love was not disgusted at us, and Love did not abandon the unworthy. Instead, Love reached down and got His hands dirty when He rescued us from the miry pit. Love endured the horrors of sin just to be with us.

So often in human life, we require others to earn our favor and affections. Good behavior yields positive results, while negative actions call for extensive boundaries that eventually sever relationships. Sometimes this is a reaction to hurt, while other times, it's necessary for our own health and well-being. We expect so much of life to be merit-based, and our way of dealing with sinfulness is often limited by our human abilities. We can't safely navigate the worst of people because we are not God. We are not strong enough or capable of withstanding the darkness of sin on our own. That takes the mighty power of a holy Lord. Because of His great love, He chooses to fight the battle against evil in order to reach us and pull us into the safety of His presence.

Humanity rejects what isn't "good enough," but the Lord embraces His wayward children. This Perfect Love is not afraid of imperfections. In fact,

He confronts those imperfections and transforms us. This was done when Jesus Christ died on the cross. "For by one sacrifice he has made perfect forever those who are being made holy" (Hebrews 10:14). Did you hear that? We are being made holy. We are not lost in sin; we are not banished from God's presence because of our flaws and mistakes. We are being perfected by the very God who loves us passionately enough to do this detailed work in the heart of each individual. We are not forced to better ourselves before being acknowledged by God. We do not earn our way into eternal life. Instead, Love comes to clean us up and restore us to our intended place, forever with our Lord.

What God did in Paul's heart was not unique. This is how He operates in each of us. Paul's example is evidence that there is no sin too great for the transformative power of God. Love is a tremendous force that changes even the hardest of hearts.

35. 1 CORINTHIANS

"Don't you know that you yourselves are God's temple and that God's Spirit dwells in your midst?"

- 1 Corinthians 3:16

The diverse Greek city of Corinth was well-known, mostly due to excessive immorality. They worshiped many gods, and Aphrodite, the goddess of love, was among their favorites. At first, this sounds like the last place an apostle would want to hang out. However, it's a place that desperately needed the good news of Christ, so Paul sailed to Corinth. When he arrived, he met a Jewish couple named Aquila and Priscilla, who were tentmakers. It just so happened that Paul was also a tentmaker, so they began working together. During this time, he went to the synagogue to talk to both Jews and Gentiles about Christ. Acts 18:4 says he reasoned with them, which was a reflection on how their culture valued logic and rhetoric. This was the best way to communicate the gospel message to the people of Corinth!

Unfortunately, the Corinthian Jews did not want to hear that Jesus was the Messiah. They opposed this so forcefully that Paul declared that he would then only preach to the Gentiles. From there, many of the people believed and were baptized, and the church at Corinth was born. God encouraged Paul in a vision, letting him know that he was safe there and to keep speaking. After all, God Himself was with Paul. For a year and half, Paul remained and taught the word of God to the Corinthians. When it was time, he sailed for

Syria and then Ephesus. However, the Corinthian church was not forgotten. Sometime later, he wrote his first letter to them.

Based on the contents of 1 Corinthians, it was clear that this church had some major issues. Paul addressed matters such as sexual immorality, lawsuits among believers, and marriage. He began the letter gently, reminding them of the spiritual gifts with which God had blessed them. He encouraged them to be united and not allow themselves to be divided by loyalties to their various teachers. Some were claiming to be followers of Paul, others of Peter, and still others were loyal to the teachings of a man named Apollos. Paul urged them to remember that it is Christ that they are following. Paul, Peter, and Apollos were coworkers in the work of the spreading the gospel, but they were not the source of grace! Paul illustrated this point by saying that he planted the seeds of God's word; Apollos watered them as he taught and encouraged them, but it was God who made them grow. All glory and devotion should be directed toward God, not a human teacher.

Additionally, Paul spoke of the wisdom of the Lord and the great contrast of the message of the cross against the ways of the world. Compared to God, the greatest wisdom of the world was nothing but foolishness. Imagine how this hit home with a people who valued logic and searched for wisdom through intellectual discussion! Paul wrote that though the crucifixion and resurrection of Christ defy all reason, they are powerful and the ultimate expression of wisdom. Therefore, glory is due to God and God alone. In fact, Paul pointed out that he didn't come to the Corinthians with excellent polished speaking skills or a fountain of wisdom he earned himself. He purely preached the good news of Jesus Christ, which is wonderful enough on its own.

He continued to focus on wisdom, something he knew that this church valued. He described the wisdom of God as mysterious and hidden. Yet, God is gracious in revealing His wisdom through the Holy Spirit so that we can know the things He has given us freely. Because man cannot teach the things that only the Spirit knows, we require the help of the Spirit to understand the things of God. This is truly a gift of love.

Then, Paul reminded the church that they were still growing in their faith. He used the illustration of feeding them milk because, due to their spiritual immaturity, they weren't ready for solid food. He wanted them to understand again that he and the other teachers were working together to serve the church; the teachers are the workers and the church is like a field or a building being constructed. Jesus Christ is the foundation that teachers build upon. This analogy leads to our 3:16: "Don't you know that you yourselves are God's temple and that God's Spirit dwells in your midst?"

Repeat that: God's Spirit dwells in our midst. He is in the church, and He is with us individually. God loves us so much that He wants to be close to us, and so He dwells within us. This is a long-term arrangement; He lives, stays, and abides in us. He doesn't come and go, nor does He visit occasionally. God is in it for the long run, all the time. He's not only ahead of us, behind us, and next to us, but within us. He makes our hearts His residence. It's no mistake that Paul described the church as a temple. The temple in Jerusalem was built as a place for the Lord. The innermost rooms were so thick with His presence that only the consecrated few could even enter. After the redemptive sacrifice of Christ on the cross, God's presence was found in His church. He said that where two or three gather in His name, He would be with them. First Corinthians 3:16 echoes this confirmation of the Holy Spirit in the midst of the people.

When we are away from the body of Christ, when we are not gathered with two or more, does that exclude us from God's presence? Absolutely not. When we accept our place as His children, God's spirit dwells in us individually as well. Paul wrote to a pastor named Timothy about treasuring the message and gift of salvation from God. In doing so, he also mentioned that the Holy Spirit is in us: "Guard the good deposit that was entrusted to you—guard it with the help of the Holy Spirit who lives in us" (1 Timothy 1:14). In his letter to the Romans, Paul also wrote, "And if the Spirit of him who raised Jesus from the dead is living in you, he who raised Christ from the dead will also give life to your mortal bodies because of his Spirit who lives in you" (Romans 8:11). This confirms not only that the Holy Spirit dwells in us, but He is powerful and full of life. Power and life are in us because the Holy Spirit is in us! This gift keeps on giving as we realize the Spirit's unlimited benefits.

A culture that worshiped the goddess of love certainly valued love. Paul wanted them to realize that they had encountered real, pure love in Christ alone. In order to clarify truth, Paul dedicated a portion of his letter to the subject of love. He wanted the Corinthians to recognize the genuine love of God, lest it be confused with the false version they were worshiping. He said that love was patient, kind, and free of pride, envy, and boasting. It cares about and honors others over self. Love does not become angry quickly and it definitely doesn't keep a scorecard of wrongs committed. Love does not enjoy evil, but instead celebrates what is true. It always trusts, protects, perseveres, and hopes. First Corinthians 13 is full of details about love! God's love is real, and these are the characteristics that help us recognize it. Anything else is merely another emotion posing in disguise or is a cheap knock-off affection full of charm and flattery. Such imitations typically have ulterior motives lurking beneath the surface. Not so with actual love. Love can be taken at face value and is motivated simply by Christ Himself. "We love because he first loved us" (1 John 4:19).

The new believers of the Corinthian church craved love but needed to understand what it truly is. Paul could not be everywhere or everything to everybody. He was only a teacher, but Christ is the source of grace, salvation, and, of course, love. God's Holy Spirit dwelt in the midst of the people of the church, just as He lives in us now. The Spirit in our hearts is a true gift that prevails because God's love never, ever fails.

36. 2 CORINTHIANS

"But whenever anyone turns to the Lord, the veil is taken away."

\- 2 Corinthians 3:16

As Paul traveled, the Corinthians remained dear to his heart. All the things he wanted to tell them could not be contained in his first letter, so he sent a second message. This time, Paul spoke of the resurrection of Christ, coming judgment, and reconciliation to the Lord. He addressed matters such as giving, faithfulness, and grace amid suffering. He wanted to prepare them for his next visit when they would be joyfully reunited again.

First, he let them know about his current struggles. Paul faced great opposition anywhere he preached the gospel. In 2 Corinthians, he told the people about being beaten and stoned. He was shipwrecked, robbed, and threatened by many people, including Jews and Gentiles. He rarely slept, suffered hunger and thirst, endured cold and nakedness, and survived the wilderness and sea. Through all of this, he proclaimed the good news of Christ and gladly faced adversity in the name of the Lord. Paul assured the Corinthians that even though he constantly faced tribulations, God was faithful. The Lord comforted Paul, equipping him to comfort others who were in pain. Any trouble Paul faced was for the good of the people Paul served. He didn't complain or invite pity. Instead, he boasted! However, his pride was not in his own abilities or survival skills. He credited the grace of God for his perseverance.

Paul may have been physically far from the Corinthians, but he still maintained a connection. He continued to shepherd and guide them. For example, he addressed forgiveness for a church member that had sinned and was ready to be restored to the family of believers. He also reminded the church that they represented Christ to other believers as well as people in their community. While some people required letters of recommendation as proof of who they were, Paul said that the people of the Corinthian church acted as a living letter, a testament to Paul's character and work. When all this encouragement was done, it was time to focus on teaching his beloved church.

After centuries of following Jewish law, it was difficult for new believers in Christ to rest in faith about their righteousness. Often, they still acted as though they were responsible for earning their salvation through good works and rule-following. Paul taught the prevalence of grace. Jesus' death on the cross and resurrection are responsible for the salvation of believers, not the merit of the individual person. The law was a good thing for its time. In fact, he describes the glory on Moses' face when he received the law from the Lord on Mt. Sinai. However, that glory was minuscule compared to the glory of God's salvation through Christ. This miraculous grace outshines anything that existed previously.

To understand 2 Corinthians 3:16, we need to go back in time to that tremendous day in the Sinai wilderness. The account is recorded in Exodus 34 and begins with a conversation between Moses and the Lord. God had given Moses the law on stone tablets at a previous mountain meeting. However, when Moses returned to the Israelites, he found them worshiping an idol of a calf they made from melted gold. Moses was so upset that he threw the sacred tablets to the ground, smashing them to pieces! After a time of anger and consequences for the people, Moses had more time with God. During one of these meetings, God instructed Moses to replace the broken tablets. Again, the Lord wrote the words of the law on the stone. Besides the gift of the law itself, the Lord showed great mercy to His disobedient people by giving them a second chance and renewing His covenant. A true act of love!

When Moses came down from Mt. Sinai with the new tablets of the law, it was clear that he had been in the presence of God. His face was physically shining with God's glory! It was so magnificent that the people were frightened and refused to come near him. So Moses put a veil over his face to conceal the brilliant glory from the fearful Israelites.

Paul speaks of this veil in 2 Corinthians chapter three. The glory reflected on Moses' face was so strong that the people couldn't look at it. But, over time, it faded. Paul compares this to the law's passing glory in contrast to the everlasting brilliance of God's rescuing grace: "If the ministry that brought condemnation was glorious, how much more glorious is the ministry that brings righteousness!" (2 Corinthians 3:9). The law pointed out everything that people had done wrong, but God's grace brings forgiveness of those wrongs. This gives us hope, said Paul, and a reason to speak so boldly about Christ. We don't need to be like Moses and conceal the evidence of God's presence!

Another veil that represented the hearts of the people was found in the temple. A heavy fabric separated the place where the people worshiped from the Holy of Holies, where God's presence was. As we know, only consecrated High Priests could enter this area and only at specific times of the year. However, the minute Jesus died on the cross, the curtain of the temple was torn in two from top to bottom. This supernatural event signified the end of separation between God and people, marking the exact moment the universe was changed forever.

Unfortunately, a great number of the Jewish people were still clinging to the law. Many of us today tightly grasp the comfort of rules and good works. Perhaps the ancient believers felt as we do, more secure when we seem to be proactive in our own salvation. Checking off a list of good deeds instills a sense of self-manufactured righteousness. We like feeling in control of our own destiny and status before God. The problem is that it's not reality. We don't have the ability to make ourselves righteous. Our best effort isn't enough to erase the consequences of the sins we've committed, and human perfection is impossible. The single and only way to be made holy is by Christ's sacrifice on the cross. That's it. We have the choice to fight it or to rest in it. We can either trust God's reassurance of our salvation in the pages of His Word, or we can stubbornly insist on persistent doubt.

The early Jewish people could not bring themselves to rest in faith. Paul compared this to a veil blinding their minds and hearts. The miracle of love is explained in 2 Corinthians 3:16: "But whenever anyone turns to the Lord, the veil is taken away." Just like the miracle of salvation, God does the work of releasing us from the blinding veil. He opens our hearts and minds so that we can clearly see His truth, then the reality of mercy and grace becomes known to us. We can trust in the grace that we can't control. We understand that our part in salvation is simply to repent and accept His forgiveness, and then to follow where He leads.

In His loving kindness, God removes the barriers that prevent us from seeing Him clearly. These walls include bitterness, hatred, and jealousy. The blinders of materialism will be removed with His tender care. The fear that covers our eyes and hearts is dissolved so that we are no longer hindered by the things that scare us. We are then able to observe how the Lord protects us and works out each detail for our good. Our sins themselves are a barrier, as Isaiah explains in his prophecy: "But your iniquities have separated you from your God; your sins have hidden his face from you, so that he will not hear" (Isaiah 59:2). Yet, the minute Christ died for our sins, that barrier was obliterated. Romans 8:38-39 describes the hope that comes when God removes the obstacles between us and Himself: "For I am convinced that neither death nor life, neither angels nor demons, neither the present nor the future, nor any powers, neither height nor depth, nor anything else in all creation, will be able to separate us from the love of God that is in Christ Jesus our Lord."

Second Corinthians 3:17 continues the message of love. "Now the Lord is the Spirit, and where the Spirit of the Lord is, there is freedom." This is yet another gift we receive from God. The law was constrictive and kept people in a form of slavery as they tried in vain to keep every commandment. Grace unlocked the binding chains of the strict statutes and endless sacrifices of atonement. After Christ's final sacrifice, God's people experienced a freedom they had never known before, a freedom believers continue to rejoice in today. Love does not enslave; freedom is an expression of sacrificial love. When we sin today, forgiveness is available through repentance and a never-ending supply of grace. Jesus Himself said, "So if the Son sets you free, you will be free indeed!" (John 8:36).Our lives are not consumed by an extensive list of regulations anymore. This is what Paul desperately wanted the early believers to understand.

He closes this section of his letter with the following words: "And we all, who with unveiled faces contemplate the Lord's glory, are being transformed into his image with ever-increasing glory, which comes from the Lord, who is the Spirit" (2 Corinthians 3:18). There is no reason for a veil anymore. God has removed it for good. He gifts us with glimpses of His glory and the nearness of His presence. Little by little, He grows and changes us to make us more like Him. Before we know it, when people look at our faces, they will see the reflection of the Lord. They will be able to see His love shining on us.

37. GALATIANS

"The promises were spoken to Abraham and to his seed. Scripture does not say 'and to seeds,' meaning many people, but 'and to your seed,' meaning one person, who is Christ."

- Galatians 3:16

If you examine the book of Acts and trace Paul's journey, you might not see mention of Galatia. But look closer, and you'll find places like Lystra, Iconium, Derbe, and Pisidian Antioch. These are cities in the region of Galatia, and the stories in Acts 13-14 reveal the tumultuous beginnings of the churches there.

Paul's evangelical journey began in Pisidian Antioch. He was accompanied by a friend named Barnabas and perhaps a few other followers of Christ. While in this city, Paul delivered a passionate sermon that included a brief recollection of Israel's history leading up to Christ. He remembered John the Baptist's proclamations of the coming Messiah and the way the Jewish leaders had Jesus killed. Paul recounted the miracle of the resurrection and told the people that God had fulfilled His promises through Christ.

Many people believed Paul's words and begged to hear more. On the following Sabbath day, nearly the entire city showed up to listen to him preach. However, this made the Jewish leaders extremely jealous, so they began to oppose Paul. Paul's response was to point out that because the Jews rejected Christ, he would preach his message to the Gentiles. The Gentiles, of course, were quite happy to hear about the Lord's grace. But the angry Jews incited a crowd that kicked Paul and Barnabas out of town. So they moved on to

Iconium. While they were there, they again visited the synagogue to preach to the Jews as well as the Gentiles. Again, Jews who did not believe that Jesus was God's Son stirred up trouble. Despite witnessing many signs and wonders, the people were divided. Some believed Paul's message while others sided with the Jews. When Paul and Barnabas faced the threat of stoning, they escaped to nearby Lystra.

At this stop, they met a man who had been crippled since infancy. Paul noticed him and realized that he had faith, so he instructed the man to stand up and walk. The man immediately obeyed, and all the people marveled at the miracle! Enthusiastically, they exclaimed that Paul and Barnabas were the gods Zeus and Hermes. Promptly the people began worshiping the two men at Zeus' nearby temple.

Paul and Barnabas were so upset that they tore their clothes and pleaded with the people to stop. They insisted that they were only regular people serving the living God who created all things. It was no use; the mob could not be convinced. At the same time, the Jews from the previous two cities had also arrived in Lystra. Their influence over the multitude of people proved effective, and before anyone could stop it, Paul was violently pelted with rocks. His injuries were so severe that he appeared to be dead. But, with the support of his fellow believers, he was able to get up and move on to the next city—Derbe.

Paul preached and made disciples there, and then he boldly returned to the other Galatian cities to strengthen and encourage the emerging church. Once the believers were established, it was time for Paul and crew to move on and continue to spread the Word of the gospel. He would stay in touch by letter, and so we have the book of Galatians.

The Jewish influence was strong in Galatia. While the believers were growing in their faith in Christ, the Jews were persuading them that it was necessary to follow the law in order to please God. When Paul heard how influential they were, he quickly sent a message to clarify that faith and grace were what saved, not the law. He spoke of a curse from God to emphasize the severe consequences of contradicting the gospel and leading new believers astray. Then, he reminded the people of his own history and credentials as an apostle.

The issue of Gentiles following Jewish law had been discussed previously by the apostles (James, Peter, John, and Paul) and the leaders of the early church. They recognized that salvation was intended for both Jews and Gentiles. But they, too, struggled with the law. In fact, Paul and Peter had a significant argument when Peter was convinced by law-followers to quit sharing meals with Gentiles. Paul pointed out that Peter knew that righteousness comes from Christ alone and not the law. He reminded Peter of the power of the cross to destroy sin and give us life.

Paul urged the people of Galatia to come to their senses and stop listening to the Jews who were clamoring for the law. He reminded them of Abraham. Let's review Genesis 15, a story that those new followers of Christ knew well. God spoke to Abraham in a vision. He first said not to fear and that He Himself was Abraham's protection and great reward. Then He began to talk about family. God promised that Abraham, despite his old age, would have a son. But the blessings wouldn't stop there. God directed Abraham to look at the starry sky. He declared that Abraham's descendants would outnumber all those twinkling lights. God also promised to give him the land he currently occupied as a foreigner. After an offering that signified the official covenant between God and man, the Lord spoke to Abraham again. He described what we now know is the Hebrews' time of slavery in Egypt and the Exodus, wandering in the wilderness, then finally settling in the Promised Land.

In his letter to the Galatians, Paul pointed out that Abraham's belief in God made him righteous. So also, those who have faith in Christ (the Son of God who is both God and man) are also made righteous. Those who have faith are considered to be Abraham's descendants and are included in the promise of God.

Galatians 3:16 looks specifically at this: "The promises were spoken to Abraham and to his seed. Scripture does not say 'and to seeds,' meaning many people, but 'and to your seed,' meaning one person, who is Christ." We find this reference multiple times in Genesis when God said, "to your offspring (or seed) I will give this land." Paul explains that this means that Jesus Christ was the ultimate fulfillment of this covenant that God made with Abraham. It went beyond physical land and the count of descendants. Abraham's offspring included all believers in Christ, who are now also heirs of God's blessings. Paul writes in Galatians 3:26, "So in Christ Jesus you are all children of God through faith." Also, he says, "So you are no longer a slave, but God's child; and since you are his child, God has made you also an heir" (Galatians 4:7). These inherited blessings include, but are not limited to, life in heaven as well as provision here on Earth and gifts of the Holy Spirit.

As we've read through each of our 3:16s, we've seen the great lengths God went through to keep the covenant He established with Abraham, the Israelites, and, by extension, with us. The covenant has withstood disobedience and the trials of time. Nothing a human could do would break the promises from God's heart. His love is simply too great, too powerful, and too loyal to His children. He repeatedly demonstrates that He is the keeper of promises, and the covenant He made to Abraham was a promise for the ages.

"If you belong to Christ, then you are Abraham's seed, and heirs according to the promise," said Paul. In Christ, God made a new covenant that meant more than land. The Lord kept His promise to Abraham's people and opened His love to the whole world. We are now promised forgiveness, redemption of sins, and a life forever with Him in a beautiful eternity. We are recipients of the strongest, most enduring love in the universe. God had you, descendant of Abraham, in mind when He spoke that covenant on a star-filled night. By setting the promise into motion, He fully intended to include you personally in His abundant blessings. You are here to inherit the fullness of His love.

38. EPHESIANS

"I pray that out of his glorious riches he may strengthen you with power through his Spirit in your inner being..."

- Ephesians 3:16

Ephesus got a late start. When we meet a dozen Ephesian believers in Acts 19, we learn that although they were baptized and followed what John the Baptist proclaimed, they hadn't yet heard about Christ or the gift of the Holy Spirit. Paul changed that, and soon these men were baptized in the name of Jesus, prophesying and speaking in tongues. After this encounter, Paul continued preaching in the synagogue there as the Ephesian church slowly grew.

The supernatural seemed to congregate in Ephesus. This was a place where miracles of God outshone the acts of magicians. In the name of Christ, Paul healed those who were sick and cast out evil spirits. Some Jewish exorcists attempted to copy this by calling out demons while invoking Jesus' name. This backfired dramatically. When the Jews tried to confront one demon, the evil spirit defied them, saying, "I know Jesus and Paul, but who are you?" He then violently lashed out and overpowered them, sending the men scrambling away with wounds and without their clothes. When both Jews and Gentiles heard about this incident, they glorified God. More people believed in Christ, and some of the local magicians even burned their spell books. There were many victories in Ephesus.

Unfortunately, not everyone believed; the ancient gods still had a loyal following. In Ephesus, there were shrines to the goddess Diana (also known as Artemis, the deity of hunting). The old beliefs were deeply ingrained in many Ephesians, but the desire for money ran even deeper. One silversmith gathered the others and focused on their fear of losing profits since interest in idols was decreasing as the number of people turning to Christ increased. He united them against Paul, and their outrage developed into a cry of "Great is Diana of the Ephesians!" as they stirred up a large mob in the city. The crowd grabbed two of Paul's friends, and everyone rushed into a nearby amphitheater as the riot grew. Seeing that his men were in danger, Paul nearly raced in to help them. However, other Christ-followers held him back. It took a brave city clerk to calm the people enough to appeal to their love of Diana. He reasoned that there were courts to bring justice to anyone who had committed an actual wrong, and that their uproar was dishonorable. With that, the crowd dispersed, and the crisis was averted.

Paul could not always remain in Ephesus, of course. In Acts 20, he gave the elders of the Ephesian church some somber parting words. He knew that trouble was ahead as he prepared to travel to Jerusalem, so he encouraged them to be good shepherds of their fellow Christ-followers. Paul warned them of "savage wolves" that would be a threat to the church people. Even men within the church would fall away from God and become negative influences. Therefore, Paul instructed the elders to be vigilant. As Paul prayed that God would give them grace, they wept together, knowing they would never see one another again. Love was great between them.

Because godly friendship persists beyond great distances, Paul stayed in touch with his brothers and sisters. His heartfelt letter comprises what we now read in the book of Ephesians. As we observed in the Acts stories, the Ephesians were passionate people. It's no surprise that Paul's letter took on a passionate tone as he encouraged and instructed his church family. He immediately spoke of God's love for us before the world even existed. We were chosen from the time of creation to be adopted as children of God and blessed with His abundant grace. In beautiful language, Paul filled the first chapter of

Ephesians with truths about the Lord's incredible gifts to us. Then, tenderly, Paul expressed his gratitude for the support from his friends. He prayed that God would give them wisdom and that they would truly know the powerful reality of a life in Christ.

Next, he pointed out that while we were in the midst of our sin, before we knew Christ, it was as if our souls were dead. However, when Christ came, gave His life, and was resurrected from the dead, we, too, were brought to life! As we discovered in our previous 3:16s, we were given this gift of life even while we were in the thick of deathly sin. What an amazing miracle inspired by love! Paul reminded us that by grace we were rescued through faith; we were not saved by anything we did or earned. Instead, we were created by God to do good things that He planned for us. This is another truth filled with great hope.

The conflict between Jews and Gentiles remained heated. Paul continued to remind believers that the Ephesians who were Gentiles were formerly separated from God, but Christ brought them into the Lord's family. Jesus united the Jews and Gentiles into one group, and He desires peaceful unity among all believers. Paul encouraged the Ephesian Gentiles, telling them that they were included and belonged to the family just as much as their Jewish brothers and sisters. This remains true for all believers today as well. The exhortations in Paul's letter encourage us as sincerely now as they encouraged the Ephesians then.

In the third chapter, Paul wanted to make the bottom line of his message clear: the good news, the gospel of Christ, means that grace extends beyond the Jews and includes Gentiles as children and heirs of God. This grace is what makes Paul's story even possible, as he, too, was saved from an extremely sinful life in which he persecuted the people of Christ. He was not only saved but also given the privilege of preaching the gospel, spreading the message of Jesus, and leading young churches. His very life was a display of the Lord's goodness and glory. But God's plan wasn't limited to Paul's witness.

He intended the whole church to be a testament to the wisdom, glory, and purposes of Christ's kingdom. When outsiders looked upon the believers, they would see a reflection of Christ Himself.

Ephesians 3:16 is the beginning of another prayer that continues through verse 19: "I pray that out of his glorious riches he may strengthen you with power through his Spirit in your inner being, so that Christ may dwell in your hearts through faith. And I pray that you, being rooted and established in love, may have power, together with all the Lord's holy people, to grasp how wide and long and high and deep is the love of Christ, and to know this love that surpasses knowledge—that you may be filled to the measure of all the fullness of God" (Ephesians 3:16-19). There's a lot of love in this prayer!

First, Paul referenced God's glorious riches. This quickly calls to mind images from Revelation of streets of gold and jeweled thrones, but God's riches flow well beyond material wealth. Romans 11:33 names the Lord's wisdom and knowledge as riches. Ephesians 2:4 declares that He is rich in mercy, while Romans 2:4 includes qualities such as kindness and patience. Colossians speaks of the riches of His glory while Job treasured the words of God's mouth and David professed that God's law was more valuable than silver or gold. The Lord's riches are never-ending and from this bounty flow gifts for the children He loves.

God's gifts to us include strength and power. Psalm 28:7 boldly states, "The Lord is my strength and my shield; my heart trusts in him, and he helps me." In Psalm 68:34-35, the psalmist rejoices, "Proclaim the power of God, whose majesty is over Israel, whose power is in the heavens. You, God, are awesome in your sanctuary; the God of Israel gives power and strength to his people. Praise be to God!" The oft-quoted promise from the prophet Isaiah reminds us that, "He gives strength to the weary and increases the power of the weak. Even youths grow tired and weary, and young men stumble and fall; but those who hope in the Lord will renew their strength. They will soar on wings like eagles; they will run and not grow weary, they will walk and not be faint" (Isaiah 41:29-31).

God is not weak, and words are inadequate to fully describe the might of His strength. Combined with love, His power becomes a force so great that we can hardly comprehend it. To imagine that He would share that strength with us is nearly inconceivable. Yet, He gifts us, mere humans, with His divine power, which allows us to endure the trials and hardships that seem to come from all sides. That power helps us learn and grow as we develop His wisdom, knowledge, and maturity. It equips us to be His hands and feet as we love and support the people around us. His strength allows us to stare fear in the face and boldly refuse to back down. It enables us to hold onto truth when lies echo around us. God's presence never leaves us, and His strength fills us from head to toe. It is a gift out of His abundant riches, given lovingly to you, His dear child.

We also are "rooted and established in love." We're not floating around, hoping for the occasional collision with love. It does not come and go like the tide. It's there at the very core of our being. Love provides us with life. It is our foundation and the base for everything else we do. Love is our beginning. It's from this secure place of His love that God gives us His power. Furthermore, we have this power together with our fellow believers. If we thought we were strong individually, multiply that by the strength Christ has given our brothers and sisters and add it all together! The force of God's power and love is ginormous. Huge. Unable to be contained. And definitely exceedingly stronger than any problem, crisis, injustice, or even the devil.

Paul wanted us to be able to understand the expansive love of Christ. As if we could envision its dimensions, he described width and depth, length and height. But as we try to measure love, we find that it is immeasurable. Paul knew that, so when he expressed that we would be filled to the fullness of God's love, he meant it would be love overflowing from God's heart to ours. And so, he concluded this portion of his letter with the knowledge that

God can do so much more than we can even imagine. His power is working within us and His glory is displayed in our lives like the most brilliant fireworks show, dazzling everyone with His magnificent strength as they witness His work in us, through us, and around us. Love is not a sappy feeling that makes us weak. Instead, it's a powerful gift directly from God who gives us strength beyond our wildest dreams.

39. PHILIPPIANS

"Only let us live up to what we have already attained."

- Philippians 3:16

    Let's meet some Philippians. Many unique people inhabited the culturally diverse city of Philippi, a bustling trade center and colony of Rome in Macedonia. Paul and crew followed the Lord's direction and traveled to Philippi after Paul received a divine vision. They had been in town for only a few days when they met a woman named Lydia. She was successful in her business, specializing in the trade of fine purple cloth. When Lydia met Paul, her heart had already been touched by God. Motivated by his words, she and her family were baptized, and they welcomed Paul and friends into their home. Lydia represented the people of Philippi who followed Christ.

    Many others weren't as welcoming. Paul and his coworker, Silas, continued to preach, teach, and worship God. As they went to prayer one day, a slave girl tagged along. The girl was possessed by a demon that enabled her to tell fortunes. This was a big money-maker for her masters. Because demons know Christ and must submit to Him, the spirit in the girl knew who Paul and his companions were. She followed them, calling out, "These men are servants of the Most High God, who are telling you the way to be saved!" (Acts 16:17).

    After days of this, Paul couldn't help but be incredibly annoyed. Finally, he called out the spirit in the name of Christ, healing the girl. This, of course, took away her divination abilities. When her masters discovered that their source of income was depleted, they were furious. They grabbed Paul and

Silas, took them to the marketplace, and incited a crowd against them. The mob violently beat Paul and Silas and then imprisoned them.

It's interesting that God has a use for even the direst circumstances. We might see prison as the end of the road when we observed Paul and Silas in an inner dungeon, trapped and shackled with their feet in stocks. But this wasn't a stopping point for these men of God. They stayed up all night, praying and singing to the Lord. This strengthened them while also ministering to their fellow prisoners. Suddenly, an earthquake rattled and swayed the stone walls of the jail! The miraculous force opened every door and released the chains that secured each criminal. The jailer, who had been asleep, was sure that the prisoners had taken the opportunity to high-tail it to freedom. The terrifying thought of his punishment caused him to grab his sword. Killing himself would have been kinder than the wrath reserved for a prison-keep who lost his charges. But Paul quickly called out from the darkness, "Wait! We're all here!"

The jailer found a light and came to Paul and Silas to ask how to be saved. They replied that he should believe in Jesus, and he would be saved. The same invitation was extended to his entire household. Then they began to preach right there in the post-earthquake chaos. The prison-keeper took the men to his home, cleaned their wounds, and fed them. Next, his entire family was baptized! Lives continued to be changed in Philippi as the direct result of Paul's obedience to the Lord.

Just as Paul loved the people of Rome, Corinth, Galatia, and Ephesus, so he loved his brothers and sisters in Philippi. When another imprisonment kept him from returning to the Philippian church, Paul wrote and sent a letter from jail. He greeted them with a prayer of gratitude for their friendship and partnership in proclaiming the gospel. He asked God to increase their love and wisdom and then give them the ability to know what is true. Then they would be righteous through Christ and bring further glory to God.

Next, Paul addressed his jail time. He pointed out that his situation helped spread the message of Christ. His example also encouraged other believers to be brave and speak boldly about Jesus. Paul remained positive despite his circumstances, reassuring the Philippians that their prayer combined with God's provision would ultimately result in a good outcome. He was in a win-win situation. If he lived, more people would hear about Christ and he could continue to shepherd the churches. If Paul died, he would be with Christ. Knowing that either outcome glorified God and was also to Paul's benefit gave him peace. From this confidence, he encouraged the Philippians to live in a way that reflected Christ. This would unite them all by the Holy Spirit and strengthen them against fear of any opposition.

The love of God brought the Philippians together. This unifying love diminished self-centeredness and produced humility. When the people were more concerned about others than about themselves, God's love flourished. Christ Himself set the example of this humility. Even though He was God, He didn't parade around Earth exalting Himself and doing things only to make Himself happy. Jesus didn't build a fancy house and staff it with servants to do His bidding. He didn't commission banners to advertise His greatness. Nor did He sit around performing miracles for His own gratification. That would not be a life of love. Instead, Jesus Christ came to serve. He came not as a shining celestial deity but as an ordinary human person. All His actions were centered on directing God's love to people and people to God's love. He submitted to God the Father even though it meant physical pain and death. Because of this, God lifted Him up to a place of honor, a position above people and angels and everything else in heaven and on Earth. Everybody will know that Jesus is Lord, and God will receive every bit of glory. This reversal of honor extends to us as we follow Christ's lead. James 4:10 instructs us to "Humble yourselves before the Lord, and he will lift you up." This complex gift of humility and honor keeps us balanced. God will take care of the honor, and we will focus our time, energy, and efforts on loving Him and the people around us. This is another detail in the perfect picture of God's love.

Paul also needed to address the Jew/Gentile, law/faith, circumcision/uncircumcision argument with the Philippians. He again used his own background as a devout Jew to illustrate that even the most perfect adherence to the law is useless to save anyone; accepting the grace of Christ by faith brings salvation to the soul. Nothing was worth more to Paul than this truth. Everything else in the world was less valuable than trash compared to the beautiful treasure of Jesus Christ. Paul was willing to give up everything- even his own well-being—for the Lord. He wanted to truly know Christ and experience His power, including both suffering and resurrection into eternal life. For all that Paul had accomplished and as mature as he had grown, he remained imperfect. He still had things to learn, character to develop, and places to go with God. He continued to strive forward, allowing God to work in him. He described it as "straining toward a prize." That prize was completeness in Christ, wholeness only God can bring about in us, and a wonderful eternal life.

Paul urged the Philippians, and us, to live like this, too. Our lives are shaped by the gift of God's grace. Philippians 3:16 says, "Only let us live up to what we have already attained." God has given us so much love, forgiveness, and freedom. What is our response? Do we live recklessly with grace as our safety net? Should we go through life using this freedom to sin selfishly in the name of making ourselves happy? Of course not; that's nonsense. First, we've learned that living apart from God brings unhappiness. Then, to be blatantly disobedient to the Lord's commands would be to reject God's love. The Lord calls us to behave in a way that brings glory to Him and blessings to us. Our entire perspective shifts when we realize what it means for Christ to give us salvation. Paul explains in Philippians 3:20-21: "But our citizenship is in heaven. And we eagerly await a Savior from there, the Lord Jesus Christ, who, by the power that enables him to bring everything under his control, will transform our lowly bodies so that they will be like his glorious body." This, through our salvation, is what we have already attained. This has been given to us in pure love. When we see ourselves as citizens of heaven who are living on Earth temporarily, our view is transformed. This is another love gift. Problems that once consumed us with anxiety seem smaller and more manageable. The people around us are truly eternal brothers and sisters, which motivates us to greater kindness. The priorities of God's kingdom, such as caring for widows and orphans as well as passionately sharing the gospel message, become our priorities, too. Our hearts long to praise and worship our Heavenly Father. Reconciliation becomes more important than "winning" conflicts with our neighbor. We are part of the kingdom of God here on Earth as we wait, like Paul, for the day we experience resurrection power and enter eternal life in heaven. As Hebrews 13:14 explains, "For here we do not have an enduring city, but we are looking for the city that is to come." Looking forward to our forever home, greatly affects how we live here today.

Life in heaven is like a present from God that we eagerly anticipate. Life on Earth is another gift of love as we live in what Jesus called the kingdom of heaven. It also exists here, and God opens our eyes so we can see it and dwell in it. The fact that we don't have to wait until after our earthly death to experience life with God demonstrates how much He loves us right here and right now.

40. COLOSSIANS

"Let the message of Christ dwell among you richly as you teach and admonish one another with all wisdom through psalms, hymns, and songs from the Spirit, singing to God with gratitude in your hearts."

- Colossians 3:16

The beginnings of the church of Colossae are a puzzle. The book of Acts doesn't record much beyond mentioning Paul's travels in the region of Asia. All the clues we have about this group of believers are found in the short pages of the book of Colossians and a mention in Paul's letter to Philemon. In that single page, Paul appealed to Philemon, a Colossian, whom he addressed as a friend and co-worker. Philemon's slave, Onesimus, had been sent to assist Paul while he was imprisoned. In their time together, Onesimus became like a son to Paul. When it was time for Onesimus to go back to Colossae, Paul requested that the slave returned not as a servant, but as a free brother. This speaks to the compassion of the Colossian church and gives us insight into Paul's relationship with the people there.

Now, let's focus on the book of Colossians itself. Paul began his letter to the brothers and sisters of Colossae with prayer and gratitude. He and his co-workers were thankful for the Colossians' faith and their love for others. He prayed that God would continue to give them wisdom through the Holy Spirit, allowing them to please God while doing good works as they grew in the Lord. Paul also prayed that God would strengthen the Colossians, giving them endurance and patience through trials.

It's very possible that, like the churches of other cities, the Colossians were influenced by false teachings and groups that led them away from the truth of the gospel. Paul wrote to remind the believers that Jesus Christ is the Son of God and rules over all of creation. This also means that Christ is the head of the church. It's important to remember that Jesus was fully God; Christ not only reigns over all things in heaven and on Earth, but this is also what makes it possible to reconcile humanity to God through Christ's death. The Colossians needed a reminder of the basic truths to help them sort out what was real and what was false from people with self-interests or incorrect beliefs. However, Christ is the central focus of what Paul preached, as Christ is the very core of our salvation. Paul described the full Word of God as "the glorious riches of this mystery, which is Christ in you, the hope of glory" (Colossians 1:27). Paul emphasized that his reason for writing was so they would completely understand the gospel, attain wisdom, and be able to see through persuasive, untrue philosophies.

The pressure to follow Jewish law was another stumbling block to the Christ-followers in Colossae. Again, Paul reminded them that Jesus Christ was fully God, the head over everything, and the One who rescued us from the death of sin. Christ forgave all the many ways a person could violate the law and took every punishment on the cross for the sins of the whole world. This abolished the need to attain salvation by following the law to perfection, which is not humanly possible anyway. Christ also changed the landscape by making it no longer necessary to observe religious festivals or dietary restrictions. Those were all established to point the way to Christ and have now been fulfilled. To remain slaves to the law would be to remain in the past and miss the grace of the present.

Life in Christ is filled with more freedom than life consumed with legalism. Paul instructed the Colossians to look away from earthly things and to focus instead on the ways of the Lord. He broke it down in a list of things to avoid, such as lust, greed, anger, slander, and lying. He reminded the

Colossians that they were no longer divided by race or status but were instead united in Christ. He provided positive guidance to help them (and us) live as Christ intended. People of God are to be compassionate, kind, humble, gentle, and patient. Jesus forgave us, and so we are to forgive each other. Most of all, we are to love each other, which will also unify us, despite our differences. We need to allow the peace of God to permeate us, and we are to be thankful. During this encouragement, we find Colossians 3:16: "Let the message of Christ dwell among you richly as you teach and admonish one another with all wisdom through psalms, hymns, and songs from the Spirit, singing to God with gratitude in your hearts."

God didn't create us then release us onto Earth with no idea how to live. He does not sit above, watching humanity scramble in all directions trying to "get it right." Because He loves us, He gives us all the information we need to have blessed lives. Some of this guidance is found in the book of Colossians. By following these words, we live well both individually and collectively. Specifically, in Colossians 3:16, we find God's love in the gift of community. First, we are told to "let the message of Christ dwell among us." What does this look like in practical terms? It is proclaiming the good news of the gospel. It is teaching the Word of God to our children. It's sharing with one another where God is at work in our lives and where we saw Him recently. We are to learn together, speak with each other, and keep God's Word alive in our midst. This is not a secret we all know with closed mouths. We grow and are encouraged when the Lord is made known between us. This is not passive; this is a highly interactive process. No one sits out! We are all supposed to give and receive the good gifts of the Lord. Paul wrote, "Therefore if you have any encouragement from being united with Christ, if any comfort from his love, if any common sharing in the Spirit, if any tenderness and compassion, then make my joy complete by being like-minded, having the same love, being one in spirit and of one mind" (Philippians 2:1-2).

Paul said to admonish or to advise with wisdom. Proverbs 27:17 says, "As iron sharpens iron, so one person sharpens another." We are all flawed humans who will mess up occasionally (or even frequently). Often, this happens while we are sincerely attempting to do the right thing. In the mix of situations and emotions, we find ourselves distracted by details and unable to see the big picture. What a blessing to be part of a loving community full of friends who can see both the forest and the trees! We help each other discern the right way to handle circumstances as well as how to respond when we've veered off course into a path of sin. We help each other up when we fall, or, better yet, reach out to grab a friend before they slip into a mess. It's not always easy to speak the truth to someone on the brink of sin, but it is the loving thing to do. This is another gift from God, a safeguard to help us avoid greater catastrophes.

Life in community is not only about disaster prevention. There's also a great amount of joy that is multiplied when shared. Such joy cannot be contained merely through the spoken and written word. It can be expressed only through the gift of music. This might be why Paul encourages us to employ psalms, hymns, and songs of the Spirit to sing our praise and worship. It would be a mistake to ignore this instruction based on a perceived lack of talent or musical ability. We've allowed popular culture to shape our standards of acceptable offerings, forgetting that music was given to us by God as a way to go beyond what mere words can say. Psalm 95:1-2 invites us to "Come, let us sing for joy to the Lord; let us shout aloud to the Rock of our salvation. Let us come before him with thanksgiving and extol him with music and song!"

The psalms, which are poetry originally set to music, are full of calls to rejoice with singing voices or musical instruments. We can understand this, as our own experience has shown us how music can bring tears of sorrow or delightful dance. It gives us the ability to express emotion and relate to one another when words are inadequate. The vast number of songs and musical masterpieces about love are proof of music's ability to express ourselves when we can't speak exactly what is in our minds and hearts. Our supernatural God is beyond human linguistics, but music helps us relate to our Creator. We follow the examples of Miriam, David, and Mary, who sang at the most pivotal moments when God did something great in their lives. We are united when we take part in musical praise and worship together, which is why it is such a central part of church services and other gatherings. Even the mainstream world understands the unifying force of music at concerts and symphonies, unaware that they are experiencing a gift from a loving God to His children. The tones, cadences, notes, and rhythms were designed by the Creator to be a blessing. Just like the colorful details of a flower or the multi-hued jeweled shades of a sunset, music is something of beauty straight from the Lord, a present from our Heavenly Father.

Finally, Colossians 3:16 tells us to have gratitude in our hearts. The theme of thankfulness echoes throughout Paul's letters, and for good reason. It is part of what calms our anxiety and ushers in God's peace when Paul tells us not to be anxious in Philippians 4:6. When we combine it with rejoicing always and praying continually, we find God's will for us (1 Thessalonians 5:16-18). Thankfulness is a blessing to us, but it is also a way we can bless God. Psalm 106:1 exclaims, "Praise the Lord! Give thanks to the Lord, for he is good; his love endures forever!" With gratitude comes peace and contentment as we pause to open our eyes and appreciate the endless gifts God has lavished on us. When we are thankful, we are motivated to share what we have with others. Gratitude is an important part of living in community as well as a reflection of God's love for us.

The people of Colossae weren't very different from the people of God today. We all face the pressures of false doctrine in our diverse world of many faiths. The Lord utilizes our community to strengthen us as we live in a sinful world while being citizens of heaven. We need one another while we continue to grow in God's wisdom. As we express our praise through song, we discover the deep well of gratitude in our souls. All of this culminates as we abound in the Lord's love, living the joy of Colossians chapter three, verse sixteen.

41. 2 THESSALONIANS

"Now may the Lord of peace himself give you peace at all times and in every way. The Lord be with all of you."

- 2 Thessalonians 3:16

Being Paul's friend was not easy. As the apostle traveled and spread the gospel, he made many brotherly bonds and a great number of enemies. This remained true in the Macedonian city of Thessalonica, as well. After Paul and his co-workers left the earthquake-stricken jail cell in Philippi, they found a Jewish synagogue one hundred miles away in Thessalonica. For three weeks, they spoke of the wonders of Jesus Christ. Many believed the Lord and joined Paul and Silas. One man, named Jason, welcomed them into his home.

But many of the Jews were jealous of the attention given to Paul as people turned to Christ and away from the Jewish traditions. Just as in the previous cities, these Jews formed a mob with the intention of attacking Paul. The best they could do this time was to find Jason and a few other Christ-followers. The Jews brought Jason in front of the rulers of the city and accused him of sheltering Paul, whom they claimed was "turning the world upside down" with his teachings. Thankfully, after giving a bond, Jason was released, and Paul and Silas left town in the middle of the night. The Jewish leaders, however, followed them to the next town to stir up trouble again! Paul was able to move on safely, but Silas and Timothy remained in the region to support the people who believed. They helped the young church stay in touch with Paul, and his letters to these brothers and sisters are available for our reading in the books of 1 and 2 Thessalonians.

Despite the cold welcome from the Jewish leaders, many men and women were eager to follow Christ. Their zeal was met with the usual challenges, including the confusion that came from the influence of false teachers. Paul's letters helped clear up questions about doctrine and their faith foundation. First Thessalonians discusses living in a way that pleases the Lord, what happens to believers after death, and the second coming of Christ. The second letter to the Thessalonians begins with a great deal of encouragement. As was Paul's custom, he started out by expressing thankfulness and a prayer. Paul's gratitude came from the increasing faith of the believers in Thessalonica, as well as the ever-growing love they had for one another. They faced persecution as a result of their beliefs but were handling it with endurance and reliance on God. Paul encouraged them with reassurance that God would bring about justice at the proper time. He also told the Thessalonians that he and his co-workers were praying for them as they handled the opposition so that God would be glorified in them.

Paul also focused on what he called a "man of lawlessness." At that time, the people were still concerned about the details of the second coming of Jesus. Paul wanted to clear up misconceptions that were being spread in his name, including rumors that the day of the Lord had already come. This was not so. He told them that first a rebellion would happen, and the "man of lawlessness" would be revealed. He would declare himself as God and even perform signs and wonders. This is why it is extremely important to know truth in order to discern what is of the Lord and what is evil in the coming days. Then, Paul changed his tone and encouraged the Thessalonians again, thanking God once more for these people Paul also loved so dearly. He told them to stand firm and hold on tightly to the things they had been taught as God strengthened them.

In the third and final chapter of Thessalonians, Paul asked the believers to pray for him and those who traveled with him. He prayed that the gospel message would continue to spread rapidly to even more churches. Then, he advised the people not to be disruptive and lazy, but instead to work hard and continue to do good. He closed his letter with our 3:16: "Now may the Lord of peace himself give you peace at all times and in every way. The Lord be with all of you."

The "Lord of peace" is a beautiful description of Christ and an accurate portrayal of our Savior. One of Jesus' many names is the "Prince of Peace," and for good reason. He gives us this incredible gift of love that we can't find anywhere else, nor can we create on our own. A popular sticker on the bumpers of cars across the nation declares, "No Jesus, No Peace; Know Jesus, Know Peace." This is more than a catchy slogan; it's a proclamation of truth across bustling highways and in chaotic parking lots. Our world desperately needs the peace of Christ.

This peace is characterized by calm, a soothing confidence, and an inner quiet that comes from the Holy Spirit. We can experience it internally or collectively as a church or even as a nation. Sometimes, God handles the circumstances that cause stress or worry. In Mark 4:35-41, Jesus and the disciples sailed on the Sea of Galilee. A tremendous storm developed, threatening their safety and terrifying the disciples. Jesus stood up and told the storm to be quiet and the storm obeyed! Christ calmed the storm and He calmed the hearts of His disciples. Peace came externally and internally. Later, He told the disciples (and these words are also meant for us today), "Peace I leave with you; my peace I give you. I do not give to you as the world gives. Do not let your hearts be troubled and do not be afraid" (John 14:27).

Amazingly, the Holy Spirit can give us peace even when the storm rages around us. Paul writes in Philippians 4:6 that instead of giving into anxiety, we need to talk to God and focus on gratitude for our blessings. Then, "the peace of God, which transcends all understanding, will guard your hearts and your minds in Christ Jesus" (Philippians 4:7). This peace is not something we can make through logic or reasoning. This goes beyond our brain to comfort our hearts. This is a miracle that is often overlooked. The ability to have peace despite stressful situations is an act of God, a gift of love as He cares for us. Christ knew we would face all sorts of challenges and tragedies. He knew we would be stressed, exasperated, fearful, and anxious. So He said, "Come to me, all you who are weary and burdened, and I will give you rest. Take my yoke upon you and learn from me, for I am gentle and humble in heart, and you will find rest for your souls" (Matthew 11:28-29).

The world can fall apart around us, but God will still cover us with supernatural peace. "Though the mountains be shaken and the hills be removed, yet my unfailing love for you will not be shaken nor my covenant of peace be removed,' says the Lord, who has compassion on you" (Isaiah 54:10). Isaiah also speaks of God's love to us when he says, "You will keep in perfect peace those whose minds are steadfast, because they trust in you" (Isaiah 26:3). Because God keeps His promises and has given us peace in the past, we can trust Him to continue to quiet our anxious souls no matter what circumstances torment us. No crisis is too extreme, and no situation is out of control for the God who holds the whole world in His capable hands. He loves us so intensely that He refuses to stand by and do nothing while we cry in anguish. The God of love envelopes us with overwhelming peace, comforting our anxious souls with great compassion.

42. 1 TIMOTHY

"Beyond all question, the mystery from which true godliness springs is great:
He appeared in the flesh, was vindicated by the Spirit, was seen by angels, was
preached among the nations, was believed on in the world, was taken up in glory."

- 1 Timothy 3:16

A young boy from Galatia had a bright future. His dad was a Gentile and his mom and grandma were Jewish believers in Christ who raised the boy to study the Hebrew Scriptures diligently. When he was a teen, he met Paul and became like a son to the traveling apostle. Soon, young Timothy was part of a ministry that would change the world.

Timothy journeyed with Paul to places like Philippi and Thessalonica. He was entrusted with the responsibility of remaining behind to help build the Thessalonian church after Paul and Silas were run out of town. This began a pattern of traveling back and forth between various churches and wherever Paul was currently preaching. Soon, the young pastor grew into a mature leader.

Paul opens his first letter to Timothy by calling him a "true son in the faith." This endearing honor reflects that Timothy's rich spiritual legacy extended beyond his biological family. With great care, Paul encouraged and instructed Timothy, wasting no time addressing the serious issues. First, there was the threat of false teachers. Certain groups were promoting ideas contrary to the truth of Christ, and Paul advised Timothy to lovingly command such people to stop. He also clarified the purpose of the law. When used properly, it is good and useful for living a godly life. Though Paul gave a list of many types of sinners who could benefit from God's laws, he reminded Timothy that he, Paul, was also such a sinner, saved only by grace.

But this letter was about Timothy, so Paul turned his attention back to his son in the faith. He remembered prophecies regarding Timothy's calling and urged him to pray for all people. Next, Paul gave instructions for worship for both men and women in the congregation. Then, he focused on those who serve as deacons in the church. Paul outlined qualifications for individuals who are leaders so that they can honor God and fulfill their responsibilities well.

In the middle of his list of church instructions, Paul brought the focus back to the reason it all exists: Jesus Christ. First Timothy 3:16 sums it up: "Beyond all question, the mystery from which true godliness springs is great: He appeared in the flesh, was vindicated by the Spirit, was seen by angels, was preached among the nations, was believed on in the world, was taken up in glory." This summarizes the earthly life of Jesus, but the recap almost seems out of place after a description of church life matters. This is hardly the case; Christ is the very reason for all the details Paul provided. Without Jesus as the foundation, the details are useless.

Church life can be beautiful with all the blessings of community and the gift of Spirit-filled worship. But, as many can attest, church life can also be challenging. Many find it to be a barrier to Christ when they encounter disagreements, false teachings, greed, hypocrisy, or other dysfunction. The church is composed of people, and people come with flaws and mistakes along with good intentions and a genuine love for the Lord. Paul knew that it takes work to maintain a healthy church, and so he provided this important guidance to young Pastor Timothy. Paul also knew how crucial it was to keep sight of the very person who gave the church life, and so he stopped right in the middle of instructions in order to review the life of Christ.

In 1 Timothy 3:16, God's love is magnificently displayed in the life of Jesus. The fact that He came to Earth as a person is a remarkable miracle. John begins his gospel in wonder of this tremendous cosmic event. He describes Jesus as "The Word" who was with God and who was God from the very beginning. In Him was life; through Him all things were made. Then, "The Word became flesh and made his dwelling among us. We have seen his glory, the glory of the one and only Son, who came from the Father, full of grace and truth" (John 1:14). For an Almighty God who created an entire universe to walk in the sandals of a human being is nothing short of extraordinary. If the story ended there, it would be enough to leave us in jaw-dropping awe. From His very presence emanates a love for His children and there is more love to come.

To be "vindicated by the Spirit" means to be justified or proven right, in this case by the Holy Spirit. We can remember Jesus' baptism when the Holy Spirit came down and God spoke, proclaiming to all that Christ is His Son. The Holy Spirit is personally in us now, testifying to us individually. As Jesus explained to the disciples in John 16, the Holy Spirit lives in us. Through the Spirit, we experience part of the wonders of the Trinity. The Spirit of truth guides us into all truth, and He will tell us what is yet to come. Jesus said, "He will glorify me because it is from me that he will receive what he will make known to you. All that belongs to the Father is mine. That is why I said the Spirit will receive from me what he will make known to you" (John 16:14-15).

Jesus was seen by angels from the beginning, as all things in heaven were created for Him and through Him. Angels announced His conception to his mother, His earthly father, and even to local shepherds. When Jesus was tempted for 40 days in the desert, angels attended to Him. After His resurrection, angels were present at the empty tomb. These, of course, describe when the angels were visible to people. These creatures in the heavenly realm exist to serve the Lord night and day without ceasing.

We've witnessed firsthand how Christ was preached among the nations as Paul and the other apostles spread the gospel message far and wide. The word of the Lord was not limited to the Jews. All nations were welcomed into the family of God. Galatians 3:28 describes the unified family of Christ:

"There is neither Jew nor Gentile, neither slave nor free, nor is there male and female, for you are all one in Christ Jesus." Today, Christ is known across the globe on every continent. In Paul's time, the church saw the number of believers grow and multiply as the gospel spread like a wildfire. Even the violent threats of the Jewish leaders and various government officials could not contain the teachings of Christ or stop people from believing the truth of God. We continue to see the church grow throughout the world today, making the words of 1 Timothy 3:16 even more alive on the page as we read them with modern eyes. Though He was in the flesh, Jesus could not be confused with an ordinary person. The kingdom of God cannot be boxed in, and the love of Christ overflows to all nations.

The time came for Jesus to return to heaven, and the book of Acts tells the story of His ascension. He rose through the clouds until He could not be seen and promised to return the very same way, in clouds of glory. No person in this world has a story like Jesus. No human can love like God Himself. In great love He arrived, and in glorious love He returned to sit at His Father's right hand. In magnificent love, He will return to gather us all to Him. In the meantime, He is with us through the Holy Spirit, and we have His presence every minute of every day, no matter where we are. The psalmist rhetorically asks, "Where can I go from your Spirit? Where can I flee from your presence?" (Psalm 139:7). From the highest heavens to the depths of the sea, from sunrise to sunset, in darkness or in light, to the very nearness of our hearts, He is there.

From the creation of the world to His second coming, the life of Jesus is one full of love for us. While in earthly, human form, He spent his time teaching, healing, and making the kingdom of God known to all who encountered Him. Every single day was spent serving humanity, whether actively in front of a crowd or quietly in prayer during one-on-one time with the Father. He loved the multitudes and He loved individuals. He loved the people of the present, the past, and the future. His prayer in John 17 demonstrates how far

His love stretched as He shared His heart for His disciples and all believers. He led a simple life on a grand scale; to the outside observer, He was simply a traveling preacher or prophet, but to those who recognize God at work, Jesus is love embodied, greater than all miracles combined.

The daily workings of church life can distract us from the heart of the body of Christ. Jesus is the head of the church, yet we sometimes find ourselves looking in every direction but to His face. Paul wisely kept Christ in the middle of his guidance to Timothy, and it's no accident that these words are preserved for us to read today. As 1 Corinthians 13 reminds us, without love, we are nothing. If we do not love, our best efforts are of no use. But the greatest source of love—the only source of true love—is Christ. It's illustrated in His very life so that we could see it firsthand. Love walked the Earth centuries ago and remains with us today. Our lives are full of love because of the life of the One who loves us.

43. 2 TIMOTHY

"All Scripture is God-breathed and is useful for teaching, rebuking, correcting and training in righteousness..."

- 2 Timothy 3:16

Time was running out for Paul. As he was held in Roman custody, the threat of execution loomed ominously. He knew his death was near, so he composed a letter to Timothy. He urged Timothy to visit, preferably before winter, and to bring Paul's cloak and scrolls. However, even if Timothy didn't make it on time, the letter held plenty of encouragement and guidance for him to hold dear beyond Paul's life. The precious words would also outlive Timothy and be preserved for all believers through the centuries.

Paul spent a little time reflecting on his thankfulness and prayer for Timothy. Then, he addressed his persecution and the reason behind it: loyalty to the gospel. Paul urged Timothy to keep the faith and persevere despite any opposition. He compared serving Christ to a focused soldier unconcerned with civilian affairs, a disciplined, competitive athlete, and a hard-working farmer who reaps a harvest. Above all else, Paul reminded Timothy to remember Jesus Christ. He is worth enduring pain and suffering, as He, too, ultimately suffered. All persecution in the name of Jesus brings glory to God.

Again, Paul warned Timothy against false teachers and gave him advice about leading a congregation. His guidance included to avoid quarrels over petty things, be set apart for God's purposes, and "flee the evil desires of youth and pursue righteousness, faith, love and peace, along with those who call on the Lord out of a pure heart" (2 Timothy 2:22). Paul explained that terrible days would come and that we would need to be on our guard against sinful people who oppose truth. He said that everyone who lived for Christ would be persecuted, but that it is still crucial to confidently live the truth we know.

Timothy studied the Scriptures from childhood. Paul reminded him of this and told him that, "All Scripture is God-breathed and is useful for teaching, rebuking, correcting and training in righteousness, so that the servant of God may be thoroughly equipped for every good work" (2 Timothy 3:16-17). In a society full of false teachers and persecutors of faith, knowing that Scripture originates directly from God is of great importance. Picture the Lord exhaling the words and giving them to us. That's how powerful the Scriptures are! Hebrews 4:12 says that the Word of God is "living and active." God spoke through the prophet Isaiah and compared His words to the rain and snow that come from heaven and water the earth. "So is my word that goes out from my mouth: It will not return to me empty, but will accomplish what I desire and achieve the purpose for which I sent it" (Isaiah 55:11). This knowledge of the power of Scripture gave the Christ-followers of the early church strength in the face of opposition. Today, it gives us boldness to live truthfully and share the gospel with confidence. Knowing that these words (though written through man) are from God Himself helps us trust that what we read in the Bible is reality. They are not confined to the pages between a leather-bound cover but are bursting forth with the life from the breath of God. The same breath that gave life to humanity still speaks through the Word today! Because God loves us, He gives us His Word.

In love, God equips us through Scripture, which enables us to teach and to learn. Like Timothy's family, we pass on biblical truths to each new generation. Learning doesn't stop when we reach adulthood. The perpetual treasures of Scripture are continually revealed until the day we reach heaven. And then what a bounty of glorious treasures we will discover! It will be the ultimate grand finale of knowledge and wisdom as God reveals Himself through eternity. Again, He shares these truths because He loves us. Meanwhile, sinful humans occasionally need to be rebuked. The Scripture exists for that, too. To rebuke in the name of Jesus is an act of love. To allow a fellow believer to continue in sin is to be callous enough to not care whether they fall into a pit of self-destruction and negative consequences. A loving rebuke is a hand up, pulling them out of the darkness and pointing the way into safety and light. "My brothers and sisters, if one of you should wander from the truth and someone should bring that person back, remember this: Whoever turns a sinner from the error of their way will save them from death and cover over a multitude of sins" (James 5:19-20). But it isn't enough to rebuke and walk away. Second Timothy 3:16 continues with the purpose of Scripture to train and correct in righteousness. In love, God shows us the right way, the path that leads away from that destructive pit of sin. We are less likely to fall again if we are walking far from danger. This is how God's love protects us as He equips us for the good works He has prepared for us.

While the Scriptures themselves are a rich gift of God's love, flowing abundantly with truth and care for us, we have another gift in the pages of the letters to Timothy. The relationship between Paul and Timothy was special, like father and son. The presence of teachers and mentors in our lives is truly a gift from the Lord. In 1 Samuel, we see such a relationship between a very young boy, Samuel, and an elderly priest, Eli. Eli taught Samuel everything about serving God, and Samuel grew up to be a priest who led the Israelites in the ways of the Lord. This sounds pretty similar to Paul and Timothy! Ruth and Naomi also demonstrated how the blessing of a godly mentor can change the life of a younger person. Ruth was from Moab, but Naomi taught her how to serve the Lord. The love of Naomi combined with the love of God made it clear to Ruth that she would live with her mother-in-law and follow the Lord without any doubts or second-guesses. The teacher/student relationship was modeled by Jesus with His disciples. He taught more than spiritual knowledge; He loved His followers like brothers. Each biblical example of a teacher or mentor is filled with love. First, they lovingly pass on God's truth: "One generation commends your works to another; they tell of your mighty acts" (Psalm 145:4). This is done with great care. Paul described this relationship to the Thessalonians when he said, "Because we loved you so much, we were delighted to share with you not only the gospel of God but our lives as well" (1 Thessalonians 2:8). Mentors pour their hearts into ours, sharing their experiences, life lessons, and tender care. They extend the great love of God to us as the palpable extension of His nurture here on earth. As students, Hebrews 13:7 says that our response should be to "remember your leaders, who spoke the word of God to you. Consider the outcome of their way of life and imitate their faith."

We can hold a piece of God's love in our hands when we firmly grasp the Scriptures written in the Bible. We can experience His care when we look to our teachers and mentors. Much of our spiritual lives is unseen and wrapped up in faith and hope, but God gives us tangible pieces of His love so that we will live securely in Him.

44. HEBREWS

"Who were they who heard and rebelled? Were they not all those Moses led out of Egypt?"

- Hebrews 3:16

Think about everything you were taught as a child and which beliefs remain with you today. What if someone came and turned that all upside down? How would you know what is true? The early believers faced this dilemma. Their Jewish faith took a sharp turn when Christ changed the landscape. Altering their beliefs to include salvation from the death and resurrection of God's Son was no easy task. Just as Paul encouraged his churches in their new Christian faith, the writer of Hebrews explained how Jesus fit into their Jewish heritage and fulfills the traditions of their past.

Hebrews begins with angels. Though the celestial messengers were held in high regard, the writer wanted the people to understand that Jesus is higher than the angels. After all, God never referred to angels as His children as He acknowledged Jesus as His Son. Also, angels were commanded to worship Christ and to work as servants going about the Lord's business. Jesus, on the other hand, was honored with a position at God's right hand, reigning over all creation. Christ is exalted and praised while angels are described as "ministering servants sent to serve those who will inherit salvation" (Hebrews 1:14).

Even though Christ was fully God, He was also fully human. This can bewilder our minds as we attempt to grasp divine mysteries. Hebrews explains that Jesus was made lower in status than the angels while He walked on Earth as a man, but then He was lifted up and glorified in honor after His resurrection. Jesus was the first and we get to follow His path. We, too, will be lifted above the angels. What an honor, thanks to Christ who paved the way! Through His work on the cross, Jesus makes us holy and calls us brothers and sisters. Can we shout a hallelujah as we marvel at how literally amazing is the grace that God pours over us?

Chapter three boldly states that Jesus is greater than Moses. Our modern hearts quickly believe this, but to a devout Jew, this was a difficult truth to accept. Moses was a dear friend of God, the recipient and mediator of the law, the leader who brought the Israelites from slavery to freedom and nearly to the Promised Land. Moses was a great man, but Christ is even greater. The writer of Hebrews compared it to a house and its builder. While the house is great and deserves recognition, it is the builder who gets the credit and accolades. In this analogy, Moses served faithfully in God's house, but God is the builder and Christ the Son that rules over the house. We are right to place honor where it is due.

Moses bravely took the Israelites from Egyptian captivity to the wilderness, with the ultimate destination set for the Promised Land. God not only freed them from slavery, but He performed a colossal miracle when He parted the Red Sea to allow the people to escape Pharaoh's army. Then, He provided manna and quail for food as He led them by a cloud during the day and fire at night. When they complained of thirst, God gave the Israelites water out of a rock. Besides meeting their basic physical needs, the Lord gave them instructions for living and worshiping and provided laws that enabled the Israelites to have a blessed life. Yet, all of this was met with disobedience. The people not only whined and complained, but they built a golden calf to worship and some attempted a mutiny against Moses (for details, take a moment in Numbers 16). Repeatedly, the people turned their backs on the God who saved them. Their hearts were hard toward the Lord, and they were determined to do things their own way while feeling angry about their less-than-comfortable circumstances in the wilderness. The writer of Hebrews remembered this in our 3:16: "Who were they who heard and rebelled? Were they not all those Moses led out of Egypt?"

Before we discover the love here, let's find our place among the rebellion. It's easy to distance ourselves from the ancient desert-wanderers when we turn a blind eye to our own hardened hearts. Rebellion begins long before any defiant acts. It starts with discontent and dissatisfaction. When we aren't happy with our situation, we ask what is lacking. We compare ourselves to others who are seemingly better off. Then, we look for someone to blame for what we now perceive as unreasonable circumstances. Of course, we are never personally at fault, so we eye our family, our friends, and then, ultimately, God. After all, didn't He promise to supply all our needs? Aren't we supposed to ask for anything and He'll give it to us after making mountains move and all that? We take Scripture out of context once we decide that the Lord is to blame for our unfortunate situation and that makes us angry. Doesn't He love us? Everyone else gets what they want; it's not fair! What's the point in following His rules if we aren't going to benefit? Now, we will just do things the way we want to do them, because that's probably going to end up better anyway. We want instant gratification. We demand life to go our way and we'll do whatever it takes to make it so. Now there's room for doubt in our faith, and maybe we had it wrong all along. God isn't who He said He was. We are in control. And we like it better that way . . . we are in rebellion.

So what happened to the rebellious Israelites? Their consequence was that they would not enter the Promised Land after all. However, God's covenant with them included that inheritance, so the next generation would be the ones to step across the Jordan River into the land of milk and honey. God's love perfectly balanced the punishment for their sinfulness while keeping His word and providing for them. Israel's history with God is a continual ebb and flow of obedience and disobedience. Yet, God remains constant. He does not allow sin to go unpunished, but He never turns His back on His people. We can hold on to the promises of this very same God who loves us and deals with our rebellion.

Hebrews warns us to heed the good news we have heard: the good news of the gospel. We can learn from the mistakes of ancient Israel and listen "as the

Holy Spirit says: 'Today, if you hear his voice, do not harden your hearts as you did in the rebellion'" (Hebrews 3:7-8). We have the opportunity to reverse course, repent of our defiance, and turn our hearts back to God. He can soften us again. Nehemiah recounts the Israelites' wilderness obstinacy and says, "They refused to listen and failed to remember the miracles you performed among them. They became stiff-necked and in their rebellion appointed a leader in order to return to their slavery. But you are a forgiving God, gracious and compassionate, slow to anger and abounding in love. Therefore you did not desert them" (Nehemiah 9:17).

God will not desert us, either. He treats our repentance with kindness. As He promised in Ezekiel 36:26, He will replace our hearts of stone with hearts of flesh. When we recognize our rebellion, we take a deep breath and humbly turn back to our patiently-waiting God, who will accept us lovingly. In 2 Chronicles 7:14, the Lord assures us that "if my people, who are called by my name, will humble themselves and pray and seek my face and turn from their wicked ways, then I will hear from heaven, and I will forgive their sin and will heal their land." He heals more than our land; God heals our heart and souls. Then, He restores our relationship with Him so that we can continue to walk securely by His side. Because of His love, we can be confident that we will not be rejected when we reach out to Him. Our rebellion doesn't ruin our relationship with God because His love is so much stronger than any tantrum we can throw. We might betray him, but He will never walk away from us. Rebellion isn't permanent, but it's up to us how much damage we will do before we finally relent and allow Him to heal our broken pieces.

Israel's rebellion could not shatter the love of God. Disobedience has consequences, but it does not cancel the covenant made by our Heavenly Father. The only way this is possible is through the powerful force of God's forgiving and patient love, a love that can withstand the sin of our betrayal. How long until we allow His kindness to lead us out of our stubborn darkness and into His loving, forgiving light?

45. JAMES

"For where you have envy and selfish ambition, there you find disorder and every evil practice."

- James 3:16

Living in the shadow of an older brother is a challenge. If that brother is great at everything, the challenge increases. He could be the team captain, homecoming king, lead in the school play, or the valedictorian, and yet, still he is your brother. Pride mixes with jealousy, a competitive spirit, and gratitude for all the things he teaches you. Perhaps there's a little frustration or feeling like you don't measure up. But you can also feel safe knowing he'll protect you if anything goes wrong. Big brothers are a gift from God, and James' older brother was sent directly from heaven.

We don't hear much about Jesus' siblings, except for a brief mention in Mark and Matthew. It takes some creativity to imagine growing up with a Messiah in the family. James was a boy like every other human kid, and it must have been difficult not to compare his flaws and mistakes to his perfect older brother. Yet, as the years passed, James supported Jesus' ministry. After the resurrection, James became a leader in the early church, described by Paul in Galatians as a "pillar" and one "held in high esteem." It's strongly believed that Jesus' little brother wrote the letter to Jewish Christians that we now have as the book of James.

Brothers usually give good advice, and brotherly guidance is plentiful in this letter. James began by addressing a tough issue: trials. The early Christians endured persecution, but James suggested that the approach to tribulation was not merely survival. He boldly said that we should find joy in life's overwhelming problems! After all, he reasoned, this tests our faith. That testing leads to perseverance, maturity, and an opportunity to seek the Lord's wisdom.

James also warned against the dangers of doubt. The guidance flows from paragraph to paragraph. He touched upon matters such as temptation while reminding readers that all good gifts come from God. He emphasized the need to do more than simply listen to the word; action must be the result of hearing the gospel. It's possible that the early church had problems with favoritism because James addressed this as well. He used a story to illustrate that the Lord loves equally those who are rich and poor and that we should follow His example. He then reminded the people again that both faith and action are necessary in the life of a Christ-follower. Believing without actively living the word of God is useless and doing good works without faith motivated by Christ is empty. A believer needs the combination of faith and good works in order to live an effective life that serves the Lord.

Next, James gave attention to the power of our words. Just as a horse can be led by a small bit and a ship directed by a rudder, so our mouths can lead us into trouble if we are not mindful of our words. We have the choice to use what we say to either praise God or tear down our brothers and sisters. James urged us to choose our words wisely. Then, he discussed wisdom, again pointing back to the necessity of using our actions to demonstrate that we have godly understanding. When we aren't guided by the Holy Spirit, we risk being affected by bitterness and selfishness in our hearts. "For where you have envy and selfish ambition, there you find disorder and every evil practice" (James 3:16).

A heart focused on self is toxic. We have only so much energy and effort available to us, and if we focus it all on ourselves, little to nothing is left for others and God. Any barrier between us and the Lord is destructive. Perhaps that's even more true when that barrier is self-absorption, because the foundation of that wall is so deeply-rooted in our hearts that it's extra difficult to tear down. A heart concerned only with oneself breeds envy as it compares itself to others and finds dissatisfaction. Any perceived wrongs cause deep wounding where bitterness digs deep and grows. Outwardly, all decisions and actions are in the best interest of self, often causing harm to the people around us. Meanwhile, these conditions have created an internal greenhouse where anger and greed thrive. Few things are more destructive to our souls than selfishness. God knows this and will not tolerate anything that is harmful to His children.

Envy is another beast that needs to be tamed. If we allow jealousy to consume us, it will destroy us from the inside out. It transforms our hearts from caring for our neighbor to viewing our neighbor as a competitor. We no longer bear one another's burdens, come before the Lord in intercessory prayer, or find ways to reach out in love. Instead, we keep to ourselves, use our resources to keep up or outdo our friends, and find ourselves tearing them down instead of building them up and encouraging them. After all, it takes a lot of effort to have and do all the good things that they do. It's easier to bring them down to our level, therefore elevating ourselves above them and placating our envious hearts that never seem to get enough. Envy not only eats away at us, but it obliterates relationships and hurts the people in our lives.

Because God loves us, He wants to protect us from the toxins of envy and selfish ambition. First, He calls attention to the problem with Scriptures like James 3:16 and Romans 2:8, which warns, "But for those who are self-seeking and who reject the truth and follow evil, there will be wrath and anger." Once we recognize that our heart is poisoned by selfishness and envy, we are moved to do something about it. We are repulsed when we get a clear look at the unholy things that reside in us. Yet, we are not capable of cleaning up our own mess. Our best efforts at removing the self-absorption from our own hearts make a little difference, but as we focus on self-improvement, we are still focusing on . . . ourselves. We're stuck in a cycle that can't go very far. We must reach out beyond ourselves to the One who is able to break that cycle and bring us into freedom. Only the Lord can restore us to a healthy balance of **JOY**: **J**esus first, then **O**thers, and finally **Y**ourself.

How does this healing from self-obsession happen? James 3:17 provides a description: "But the wisdom that comes from heaven is first of all pure; then peace-loving, considerate, submissive, full of mercy and good fruit, impartial and sincere." When we allow God to work with our hearts and minds, He gives us heavenly wisdom. It pushes out all the envy, greed, and anger that come from self-focused living. Then, God replaces all of that with the things James tells us about. We become peace-loving, considerate, submissive to the Lord, merciful, sincere, and more. The Holy Spirit begins to grow fruits like love, joy, patience, kindness, and self-control in hearts that were once like bitter, barren soil. Our transformation is like a desert wasteland becoming a verdant garden. Not only does He soften our hearts, but He produces good things from our new-found interest in Him. Suddenly, we are glorifying Christ instead of ourselves. Though we once hurt our neighbor, we now are instruments of God's blessings. This great turn-around is a product of the Lord's magnificent love for us. We are not abandoned to wither away in our selfishness; He changes the story into one overflowing with healing and goodness.

"But seek first his kingdom and his righteousness, and all these things will be given to you as well" (Matthew 6:33). We can rest easy without fighting and scrambling for the things we need. God provides them while we are focused on His way of life. While we are looking heavenward and loving our neighbor, our needs and even some of our wants are given to us by our Heavenly Father. We aren't missing a single thing when we release our tight grasp on selfishness. In fact, we will find that we receive more good things from the Lord than we could ever obtain by our own efforts. God lovingly designed this world and our existence. His gifts are good and for our benefit. He is not about to allow even one of His precious children to waste away in the desert of selfish ambition and envy. He loves us far too much for that.

46. 1 PETER

"... keeping a clear conscience, so that those who speak maliciously against your good behavior in Christ may be ashamed of their slander."

- 1 Peter 3:16

He was just fishing. That was the day that Christ stepped into his life and changed everything. No longer was time marked by the rhythm of the sea, but each day as a disciple meant something new. Jesus set the pace with teaching, miracles, and questions that challenged their beliefs. Peter stumbled along as his relationship with the Lord grew deeper. The more he learned, the more he was tested. Then, just when he thought he understood it all, his friend and teacher was killed on a cross. His world was shattered, and he barely had a chance to catch his breath when, in a flash, life was transformed again. This time, he could barely believe the miracle! The tomb was empty, and his heart was full! Jesus was standing right in front of Peter again. This restoration of hope was more than Peter ever could have imagined.

The next change began a new phase in Peter's life. Jesus returned to heaven, leaving the Holy Spirit to work in the lives of His disciples. Peter was no longer the young man prone to mistakes; he had matured into a leader of the emerging church. His time with Jesus, the questions and answers, the tests and miracles, the betrayals and forgiveness . . . all of these produced an apostle who was equipped to shepherd new believers in the face of violent persecution. His letter found in 1 Peter is an example of encouragement to Christ-followers who were struggling to exist in a society that rejected the

Lord. As his words were passed around provinces and cities, Peter was able to guide the Christians through trials of faith.

"Praise be to the God and Father of our Lord Jesus Christ! In his great mercy he has given us new birth into a living hope through the resurrection of Jesus Christ from the dead . . . " (1 Peter 1:3). He began with praises, reminding the people of the great joy they had in Christ, a joy that could not be taken from them by anyone. Keeping that hope front and center provided strength that could withstand any oppression. Peter wanted the believers to keep their circumstances in perspective, so he pointed out that their trials were only temporary. However, the glory of the Lord is eternal.

How do believers conduct themselves when faith collides with life in the Roman Empire? Peter instructed the Christians to remain holy, as God called them to be. Focusing on hardship would be easy, but their lives were to be built on love. Peter wrote, "Now that you have purified yourselves by obeying the truth so that you have sincere love for each other, love one another deeply, from the heart" (1 Peter 1:22). Already, God's love is seeping through the lines of this letter, spilling out to each reader with its crucial message. No matter what the situation, God calls us to love. Every action and intention will honor Him when we are filled with and directed by His love. Additionally, Peter calms their fears of persecution by telling them that they have been born again into eternal life and that the word of God endures forever. No opposing force can undermine the Lord.

In case there was any question, Peter added more instructions: Avoid deceitfulness, hypocrisy, and envy. Continue to grow in faith. Realize that you have been chosen by God. It was important to be set apart from non-believers and to be good examples to others. Ideally, the life of a Christ-follower should glorify God, even to those who do not worship Him. Peter also advised that believers should be submissive to human leadership and obey the law. First Peter 2:17 explains that a Christian should respect everyone, love other believers, fear God, and honor government rulers. Though they may face harsh treatment for their faith, it was better to be punished while innocent than to do something wrong and deserve the consequences. Blameless suffering shares in Christ's pain and testifies to any witnesses that the Christian believes so strongly in the truth that they are willing to endure the resulting persecution. This is extremely difficult, but the Lord provides strength. Peter urges the people to not be frightened by any threats. Even if they do suffer for doing what is right, they will be blessed.

The letter continues its instructions, including to love each other with compassion and humility. We should not take revenge on someone who wrongs us. Also, we must always be ready to share the good news of Christ. "Always be prepared to give an answer to everyone who asks you to give the reason for the hope that you have. But do this with gentleness and respect, keeping a clear conscience, so that those who speak maliciously against your good behavior in Christ may be ashamed of their slander" (1 Peter 3:15-16).

God's love is protective. The early Christians were living in a dangerous situation, and many of them were exiled from their homes because of their beliefs. Their faith was still new and not widespread. It was counter-cultural in a society where differences were often seen as a threat to the peace of the Roman Empire, and people were physically harmed because they followed Jesus. Living in faith can be challenging, but a hostile environment made it even more difficult. However, the Christians were not left to fend for themselves; God was with them, never leaving them for a single moment. He provided strength to endure oppression and peace to calm fears. They never had to question what was right because the Lord provided clear direction. Through letters like 1 Peter, He told them how to live and how to make wise choices. He equipped them to survive persecution and thrive as children of God. Their faith would be preserved, and the good news of the gospel would continue to spread.

Thankfully, in the Western world today, many of us do not experience the level of hardship that the ancient believers faced. However, we do find that our faith can be counter-cultural and not always welcomed enthusiastically. Often our beliefs are criticized and mocked. We feel rejected, belittled, frustrated, and out of place. We aren't comfortable praying or worshiping in many public spaces. Frequently, non-believers don't understand our opinions or decisions. We are constantly reminded that this world is not our home and that we are in the world, but not of it. Our persecution is not life-threatening, but God is just as protective of us as He was of the early church. This is because of His great love.

We can take the guidance of 1 Peter just as seriously today as when the letter was penned. The directions for living are more than good advice. They're not merely suggestions for a good way to behave. These are direct instructions from God on how people of faith are to conduct themselves. Think of these directions not as guidelines, but as commands. As always, God doesn't demand things of us arbitrarily—every word is for our good and benefit. His commands provide a loving path to blessing and protection in the face of opposition. This includes 1 Peter 3:16. By following this guidance, we are protected from further persecution by our enemies. If we live sinfully, we give them more fuel for their fire, more reason to mock and criticize, and our suffering could increase. Furthermore, we would no longer endure the blessed suffering in the name of Jesus, but instead, experience the consequences of straying from God's word. We would be in pain that does not glorify God. No blessings ever result from our disobedience.

Following instructions for holiness is about more than pain avoidance. If anyone were to speak maliciously against our good behavior in Christ, justice would eventually prevail. In our previous 3:16s, we've seen how strongly God enforces what is right in His perfect timing. Those who are doing the persecuting will eventually be put to shame. Romans 8:33 asks, "Who will bring any charge against those whom God has chosen? It is God who justifies." Also, 2 Thessalonians 3:3 offers hope to the persecuted: "But the Lord is faithful, and he will strengthen you and protect you from the evil one."

When we are persecuted for our faith, the Lord can bring about a bounty of fruit for His kingdom. When non-believers see the steadfast faith of a believer under persecution, their heart can be turned to Christ. Holding tightly to beliefs despite opposition suggests a faith worth fighting for. Why would people tolerate so much hardship if what they believed was untrue? When we are prepared to explain the reason for our hope with gentleness and respect, we are giving a precious gift to another person. We can share the gospel in the most genuine, heartfelt, and impactful way by living obediently through persecution. Just as Saul once oppressed Christ-followers and was changed by God, our oppressors can experience transformation. What an honor for us to be instrumental in God's heart-changing work!

Peter continued to address persecution in 1 Peter 4:13-14: "But rejoice inasmuch as you participate in the sufferings of Christ, so that you may be overjoyed when his glory is revealed. If you are insulted because of the name of Christ, you are blessed, for the Spirit of glory and of God rests on you." Because God loves us, He enables us to survive oppression. He is with us through any persecution and transforms it into something that produces glory. We are no longer victims but partners with God in His incredible work. He blankets us with the protective covering of His love, and we can extend that love in the face of adversity. Then, the people who intended to do us harm become brothers and sisters as they experience the grace of the gospel. This is a love that continues to multiply, growing despite any efforts to quench its goodness. The love of God is mighty, overpowering opposition as it protects and equips His dear children.

47. 2 PETER

"He writes the same way in all his letters, speaking in them of these matters. His letters contain some things that are hard to understand, which ignorant and unstable people distort, as they do the other Scriptures, to their own destruction."

- 2 Peter 3:16

Peter's story was about to end, but he had a few more things to say. He sent a second letter to the Christ-followers to make sure they understood more about Christ. He wanted them to know that they were called to live in a way that glorified the Lord, and Peter highlighted a few qualities that were important for a fruitful, faith-filled life: goodness, knowledge, self-control, perseverance, godliness, mutual affection, and love. He also emphasized that it was crucial to know one's purpose in the Lord in order not to stumble. All of this would result in eternal rewards.

Peter wanted to be sure the believers recognized that everything the apostles taught about Jesus was true, as they were credible eyewitnesses to the ministry of Christ. Unfortunately, false teachers were also preaching to the people. Their words were destructive and misleading, often to the point of denying the Lord. Tragically, these false teachers would lead many people astray. Peter warned the believers to be aware and avoid anyone who contradicts the gospel. False teachers face severe consequences delivered by a God who consistently judges between the righteous and the unrighteous.

In the final chapter of 2 Peter, the discussion turned to the final days of earth, or the Day of the Lord. Peter wanted to be clear that his purpose was to lead Christians to wholesome thinking and to remind them of the Lord's commands. He told of people who were full of contempt, motivated by evil or greed, who would mock the idea of Christ's second coming. No one knows when Christ is returning, and we could easily be discouraged while we wait for God's perfect timing. Peter offered reassurance that our view of time is not the same as the Lord's. God isn't slow or running late; instead He is patiently waiting for the right time to come so that everyone has a chance to repent. However, He will not wait forever. Christ will come again, and the old heaven and Earth will be destroyed to make way for the new, where righteousness will dwell.

How does this glimpse of God's big picture affect the way we live today? Peter instructed us to be righteous and at peace with the Lord. God's patience gives hope because it means salvation for us. Paul wrote about this in his letters, too. Peter referenced these in our 3:16: "He writes the same way in all his letters, speaking in them of these matters. His letters contain some things that are hard to understand, which ignorant and unstable people distort, as they do the other Scriptures, to their own destruction." The false teachers would not relent, even manipulating Paul's teachings for their own gain.

God's protective love intervened to guard against the lies, and He continues to do so today. First, He gives us a heads up so that we are aware that there is a problem. Through the writings of Peter and Paul, the believers were warned about the trouble. We must still heed these warnings now. Once we know about the problems, we are told to be on our guard. We must grow in grace and knowledge of Jesus Christ in order to strengthen our faith. This will enable us to discern between truth and the fiction of misleading teachings.

Part of the challenge described in 2 Peter 3:16 is that Paul's letters contain information that's difficult to understand. This is another opportunity to observe God's great love for us. The ways of the Lord are much greater than human comprehension, so it's no wonder that parts of Paul's writing are confusing. But our loving God doesn't leave us scratching our heads in ignorance as we wonder at His ways. Through the Holy Spirit, God personally helps us comprehend what He teaches us. Second Corinthians 2:12 explains, "What we have received is not the spirit of the world, but the Spirit who is from God, so that we may understand what God has freely given us." We need help, and no person on Earth is able to grasp completely the ways of God without the Holy Spirit.

In a grand gesture of His love, Jesus promised the disciples that an Advocate or Helper was coming after He left. He explained how the Holy Spirit would be in us and help us know the ways of God. Paul described the ways the Holy Spirit helps us in 1 Corinthians 12. There are different kinds of gifts, but they all come from the same Spirit. These gifts include wisdom, knowledge, faith, healing, miracles, prophecy, and more. Every person is uniquely given some of these gifts so that we can all serve God together as a family, as the body of Christ. None of these are man-made; they come only through the Holy Spirit to enable us to fully live the life God designed for us as we serve Him.

In addition to providing divine wisdom, the Holy Spirit is a gentle but firm reminder. Jesus said that the Holy Spirit will teach us all things and remind us of everything He said. When faced with false teachings, the Spirit points out the truths we have learned. We are then able to tell the difference between God's truth and twisted lies. The Holy Spirit declares God's glory and convicts us of sin. The more time we spend with the Lord, the more we recognize the promptings of the Spirit. We stop relying on our gut feelings and understand when the Spirit indicates that something is wrong. Our time spent in the word of God combined with reliance on the Holy Spirit is a strong safeguard against any distortions of Scripture. We will no longer be in danger of being led astray when we are led by God Himself.

In John 10, Jesus compares Himself to a shepherd and we are His sheep. The sheep are familiar with the voice of the Shepherd and they respond to Him. When a thief comes in and speaks with an unfamiliar voice, the sheep know that this is not their Shepherd and they will not follow. When we spend time with God, we learn to tell His voice apart from anyone else. We can trust Him and serve Him faithfully without being deceived by manipulators. Of course, when we neglect our time with Him, it's difficult to recognize His voice. Jesus also talked about wolves coming to scatter the sheep. As the good Shepherd, He will go so far as to give His own life to protect His flock. This is exactly what Jesus did through His death and resurrection. Then He lives in us through the Holy Spirit who continues to help us discern what is of God and what is not. When the Spirit of truth comes, He will guide us into all the truth.

Because God loves us so dearly, He protects us from false teachers who have ulterior or sinister motives. He personally shows us what is true. There is no risk when we are listening to the Lord; He will always lead us to safety—whether here on Earth or ultimately eternally—as a good shepherd lovingly leads his beloved sheep.

48. 1 JOHN

"This is how we know what love is: Jesus Christ laid down his life for us. And we ought to lay down our lives for our brothers and sisters."

- 1 John 3:16

To be called "beloved" is a joy. We find secure comfort in knowing that someone loves us. To be named beloved by someone we hold in high esteem is an honor, one that might feel unbelievable one minute and inspire pride the next. To be considered beloved by people we admire is a greater gift because we value their opinions and affections above others. John experienced all of these as Jesus' beloved disciple. His dear friendship with his teacher and Messiah was a uniquely close relationship. In addition to the plentiful blessings of being called a brother by the Son of God, this friendship also gave John a unique perspective; he saw and experienced miraculous events and intimate moments. While he personally treasured these things in his heart, he also generously shared many of these gifts with us.

Like Peter, John began his adulthood as a fisherman. When Jesus called him to discipleship, the trajectory of his life was forever altered. John's purpose changed from a fish-centric existence to one passionately devoted to spreading the gospel. His brief years walking alongside Christ were a far cry from a string of long, damp nights on a wave-tossed boat. Though the disciples still occasionally sailed across the Sea of Galilee as they traveled from town to town, their sandals quickly became worn as they walked the miles, listening as Jesus explained the kingdom of God. Before, most of John's time had been spent with his brother, father, and partners, Peter and Andrew. Now, he was surrounded by eleven other disciples and Jesus, as well as additional followers and crowds of people seeking miracles. The steady routine he once knew was disrupted. Each day held a fresh revelation that stretched the limits of John's faith. Witnessing acts of healing and casting out evil spirits was amazing, but perhaps the changes in John's heart as he spent more time with Christ were the most incredible.

Then it all came crashing down. Jesus seemed invincible, but suddenly angry hatred brought Him low, tied Him to a cross, and raised Him up to a public, humiliating death. Defeat weighed heavily on the disciples for a few days that seemed to never end. Then one morning, their world was flipped upside down and their dark despair became jubilant hope. Jesus, who had raised others from the dead, had overcome mortality Himself and stood right there before them! John and the disciples would soon learn that this meant more than simply being reunited with their teacher. Christ's resurrection affected the entire planet, reaching all of humanity throughout all the ages. The reality of this, the greatest miracle, would consume the rest of their lives.

After Christ ascended, John's days were filled with the Holy Spirit. He continued Jesus' legacy of teaching and healing. As a pillar of the early church, John put quill to parchment and shared the story of Christ. He personally knew the love of God and was determined to help new believers understand a remarkable truth: Jesus loved them just as dearly as He loved John. The tangible love of a Savior we can't currently see face-to-face can be difficult to comprehend, but John knew that God's love is very alive and real here and now. Christ loved John like a younger brother, and He also calls us dear brothers and sisters. Through his gospel and letters, John revealed many of the marvelous truths of life in Christ.

John was there. The stories were true. The blind did see, evil spirits fled, dead people woke up and took breaths again. Jesus was just as incredible as they said He was, if not more. As John began the letter, we now have in 1 John, he assured his readers that it was all real; this was an eye-witness account. They could and should believe every word that John was about to write, and it would resonate with believers for generations.

He started off with some basics: God is light and there is no place for darkness in Him. We are sinners, but there is no place for sin in the light. We must acknowledge that we have sinned, and Christ will forgive and purify us. He makes light out of our darkness. But life in Christ doesn't stop inside our hearts. Our relationship with others is another crucial part of the kingdom of God. God's love for us turns into our love for others. John said that if we claim to love God but don't love other people, we are liars. These words might seem harsh, but the bold message underscores the importance of John's message.

He also addressed the false teachings that threatened to steal truth from the believers. John spoke of antichrists, those who seemed to start out as Christ-followers but then turned away. He also emphasized the importance of knowing what was true in order to distinguish between the gospel and lies. John wanted to protect the people of the early church and guide them in God's reality.

Next, John moved on to what might be his favorite subject: God's love. He expressed his wonder in John 3:1: "See what great love the Father has lavished on us, that we should be called children of God! And that is what we are!" Out of this love, Christ purifies us and makes us like Him. John continued to move back and forth between God's love for us and our love for others, demonstrating the important connection between the two. This is where we find our 3:16. "This is how we know what love is: Jesus Christ laid down his life for us. And we ought to lay down our lives for our brothers and sisters" (1 John 3:16). Love is something we all experience, yet it takes a lifetime to understand its complexities. To help us understand, John pointed us to the greatest example of love there is: Christ's sacrifice of His own life. Then he instructed us to do the same thing for other people. But isn't this too much to ask?

Before we imagine taking a bullet for our neighbor, let's read on to 1 John 3:17: "If anyone has material possessions and sees a brother or sister in need but has no pity on them, how can the love of God be in that person?" Laying down our life means more than physical death. When we sacrifice our own well-being to provide for another person, that is a form of laying down our life. We can do this with physical possessions or by setting aside our best interests in favor of our neighbor. We can sacrifice our time to volunteer and serve our community. We can choose to vote on issues that help those in need, even if it means that our own situation would not benefit. We have the ability to push aside selfish ambition and devote our lives to the good of the people we love. And since God calls us to love both our neighbors and our enemies, we have infinite opportunities to lay down our lives for a brother or sister. If we begin to feel like this is unjust or a bit too much to ask, our complaining is silenced by the realization that Christ did more than merely inconvenience Himself for us. He suffered, He endured death, and He did what only He could do by overcoming the sins of the world at a great cost to Himself. How much more are we able to actively love others since the love of Jesus equips us? First John 3:18 continues to encourage us: "Dear children, let us not love with words or speech but with actions and in truth."

God's love is sacrificial. Jesus foreshadowed His death when He told the disciples that there is no greater love than to lay down one's life for one's friends. While on Earth, Christ sacrificed a comfortable life in exchange for a life of service to the people He loved so passionately. In the story of God and His people, beginning with Adam and continuing today, we see an all-powerful Deity acting for the good of humanity. We do not serve a God who sits on a heavenly throne uninterested in the affairs of people. Our loving God is so invested in His dear children that He gave the most precious thing to save us: God sacrificed His Son. He sacrificed Himself. It was no easy thing to live on Earth and serve the masses. He survived spiteful ridicule, venomous mockery, and physical torment. His body endured the maximum amount of attack possible until it gave out completely. He experienced the terrors of death and emerged victorious. None of this was easy, not even for the Messiah. He went through the most extreme punishment because of love. This was the only way that we could be saved, and our sins be purified, and so He did it. It mattered so much to God to keep us with Him eternally that He literally went through hell and back to secure our place in heaven. This is ultimate love and it is the love that lives in us. This is the extreme love that is meant to overflow from us onto our brothers and sisters. Such great sacrifice brings such great love.

49. REVELATION

"So, because you are lukewarm—neither hot nor cold—I am about to spit you out of my mouth."

- Revelation 3:16

Exiled. Thanks to his bold profession of faith, John was no longer welcome on the mainland. Government officials banished him to the small island of Patmos, about sixty miles out to sea. Surely from there he would no longer be able to persuade the masses to follow Jesus Christ. But God never wastes an opportunity to advance His kingdom and He never allows our trials to be in vain. Punishment by exile on a desert island was transformed into a powerful concluding book of Scripture.

Right from the start, John explained that his writing was a revelation from Jesus Christ. An angel was sent to John, who recorded what he experienced to share with the believers. Much of the revelation is prophecy that describes the last days of Earth and Christ's second coming, but first God had a message for the seven churches in the province of Asia. The Lord spoke of each church's strengths and weaknesses, and we can learn from their example. It's possible to see what we have in common with the churches and where we need to grow as they did.

John was "in the Spirit" on the Lord's Day when he received this word of God. He heard a loud voice telling him to write a letter to the seven churches. When John turned around, he saw seven golden lampstands and "someone like the Son of Man." The Son of Man was shining and holding seven stars.

From his mouth came a double-edged sword. John was so stunned at the sight of Him that he fell to the Son of Man's feet. At that moment, the Son of Man placed His hand on John and told him not to be afraid and then declared that He was the First and Last, the Living One. He instructed John to write what he was about to see and explained that the seven lampstands represented the seven churches and the seven stars in His hand represented the angels of each church. From this dramatic beginning came the individual messages.

The church in Ephesus was commended for perseverance and diligent work. When they encountered unrighteous people who falsely claimed to be apostles, they handled the situation well. Despite extreme hardship, the Ephesians were still pressing on as if they weren't tired. However, they had some issues. They once had great love, but over time they had fallen. Christ urged them to repent and return to the intense love they had before. Next, He declared that everyone should listen, and whoever was victorious would have the right to eat from the tree of life.

The church in Smyrna survived hardship and poverty, but Christ called them wealthy. He encouraged them not to be afraid of what they would soon suffer and warned of impending prison time and persecution. He urged them to remain faithful, even if it meant facing death, and promised a reward. The one who was victorious would not be harmed by what was referred to as the second death.

God had much more to say to the church in Pergamum, which was situated amid evil and wickedness. Despite being surrounded by unrighteousness, the believers in Pergamum were loyal to Christ. They professed their beliefs even as Christians were being killed and oppressed. Unfortunately, they also ascribed to false teachings. Christ instructed them to repent as He warned them that He would come fight against the lies. The one who was victorious would receive something called hidden manna and a white stone with their new name written on it.

Thyatira held a church that was known for love, faith, service, and perseverance. While the Christians there had been growing in their faith, they were being misled into immorality and trouble. The Lord would not allow the one misleading them to continue, and anyone who followed wickedness would face consequences. Those who remained faithful to Christ would avoid this trouble, and they should continue in righteousness. The one who was victorious would have authority over the nations.

Harsh words were given to the church in Sardis. Though they were known for life, the followers there were dead in faith. Christ told them to wake up! They had little faith left that could be revived. However, they must repent and return to an active life of faith or they would miss Christ's return. There was hope in the few people in Sardis who walked with Christ, and the one who was victorious would be like them. Their name would be included in the book of life.

The church in Philadelphia had only a little strength, but they were true to the Lord and proclaimed His name. The false teachers would soon fall at the feet of the believers and declare the love of God for His people. Because the Philadelphians endured persecution, Jesus would protect them from the coming trials. He encouraged them with the news that He is coming soon and told them to hold on because their reward could not be taken away by anyone. The one who was victorious would be a pillar in the temple of God.

The final church was in Laodicea, and their deeds were pretty much just okay. They couldn't be described as cold or hot. This is where our 3:16 comes in: "So, because you are lukewarm—neither hot nor cold—I am about to spit you out of my mouth." The Laodiceans thought they were rich but didn't realize they were in poor shape. They needed to return to the Lord once more. Jesus reminded them that He disciplines those He loves and that He is figuratively standing at their door and knocking. He was available to them, but they needed to welcome Him into their church and into their hearts again.

The one who was victorious would be given the right to sit with Christ on His throne.

Love was lacking in Laodicea. The people knew the gospel; the knowledge of Christ was in their heads. But the good news was not rooted deeply enough in their hearts to produce the actions of people who truly believe in Jesus. We're not given specific details about what they were doing or avoiding, but we can make some educated guesses. Perhaps they were not caring for widows or orphans. Maybe they refused to forgive a brother or sister who wronged them. Did they decide that they were glad to be saved but they didn't feel the urgency to share God's love with their neighbor? They might have allowed false teaching or idolatry to mingle with the true teachings from the apostles. While they were called to be set apart, it was likely that any person who knew a member of the Laodicean church would be surprised to discover that they were believers. They were neither on fire for God or coldly pushing Him away. They were just . . . lukewarm.

God's love is not lukewarm. The love of God is passionate! If the Laodiceans were anything like Him, their love would have been known for miles! The love of God is enthusiastic. It is exuberant. The intensity of His love burns so wildly that we can see it in action. It's possible that we've allowed life-filled Scriptures to become routine memory verses and downplayed the fierceness of God's love for us. Familiar passages like Psalm 117:2 should pack a punch: "For great is his love toward us, and the faithfulness of the Lord endures forever." We've printed this on mugs and notebooks, then tucked it away as a nice sentiment. But we miss the power behind it. God's love is *great*! It is huge! It is dynamic! It is so great and huge and strong that it can withstand anything and everything in order to endure forever. Time can't kill it. Hardship can't kill it. Wars and famines and cultural divides are weak compared to the strength of God's love. Nothing can take it away or dilute it. Forever is a very long time, but God's love will still be at maximum strength then just as it is now.

Isaiah compares this love to that of newlyweds: "As a young man marries a young woman, so will your Builder marry you; as a bridegroom rejoices over his bride, so will your God rejoice over you" (Isaiah 62:5). A groom isn't lukewarm about his new wife. He is excited! He is ready to slay dragons and take on the world for her. Any wish she has, he will do everything in his power to grant it. No obstacle is too great for his love. A groom is willing to go to the ends of the Earth if it would benefit his bride in any way. If human love is so passionate, imagine how great such a love would be flowing from the Creator of the universe!

God's zeal is demonstrated in His jealousy for His children to worship Him and Him alone. After instructing the Israelites to avoid idolatry, Moses says, "For the Lord your God is a consuming fire, a jealous God" (Deuteronomy 4:24). Like fire, God's love is a wild force. It is not lukewarm; it burns hotly. We see the Lord's great love in Isaiah 37:32: "For out of Jerusalem will come a remnant, and out of Mount Zion a band of survivors. The zeal of the Lord Almighty will accomplish this." God demonstrated His zealous love by preserving His beloved people after the years of exile in Babylon. Generations later, He would send His Son to preserve all His beloved children. Jesus is the greatest demonstration of God's passionate love. "Of the greatness of his government and peace there will be no end. He will reign on David's throne and over his kingdom, establishing and upholding it with justice and righteousness from that time on and forever. The zeal of the Lord Almighty will accomplish this" (Isaiah 9:7).

Throughout time, God has gone to extreme lengths to actively love His people. He is a passionate God. When His love fills the hearts of His dear children, we display His zeal in our own lives. Enthusiastic, exuberant love spills over onto everyone we encounter. It is not like any earthly love and is immediately recognized by anyone who experiences it. The Laodiceans were missing this love, and many of us miss it as well. It wasn't too late for them to turn back to it, and it's not too late for us. When we ask the Lord to pour out His fiery love on us, He is happy to fulfill our need. When we ask for anything in the name of Jesus, the Lord will provide. The passionate love of God is intended to overwhelm us, and it is limitless. Like a blazing fire, we are consumed by love. It is a love that cannot be tamed and a love that will satisfy our deepest longing as we constantly cry out for more. A love so extreme is beyond accurate description, but we can know it intimately. It is alive and crashing over us like unrelenting ocean waves. Are our hearts open to receiving the overflow?

50. JOHN, THE CONCLUSION

"For God so loved the world that he gave his one and only Son, that whoever believes in him shall not perish but have eternal life."

- John 3:16

The night was cool and breezy, but there was something else in the air that couldn't quite be described. It was something like expectation, but maybe a little more like uncertainty. Nicodemus was an important man, a Pharisee who ruled on the Jewish council. Most of his friends were skeptical of the teacher named Jesus, but Nicodemus was also a little curious. Something drew him to the man who claimed to be the Son of God. It was too risky to speak publicly to Jesus unless it was to rebuke Him for blasphemy, so Nicodemus chose this quiet night to meet Him.

Nicodemus began by acknowledging what they both agreed on: Jesus was a teacher who came from God. Jesus replied with a perplexing truth, telling him that the only way to see the kingdom of God is to be born again. Immediately, Nicodemus was confused. How could a person be physically born a second time? Jesus elaborated by saying that there is physical birth and spiritual birth. To enter the kingdom of God, we must be born by water and the Spirit. Nicodemus still had difficulty understanding what Christ meant.

Jesus focused on the heart of the matter. Belief in Him, the Son of Man, was the way to live forever. He said, "For God so loved the world that he gave his one and only Son, that whoever believes in him shall not perish but have eternal life" (John 3:16). He continued by explaining that He didn't come to condemn the world, but to save it. He was light in the world, but people still preferred to be in darkness. However, when believers live by truth, they come into the light. This ended the conversation between the two men. Nicodemus took Jesus' words to heart, because we later discover him somewhat defending Jesus in front of the council in John 7 and then bringing spices to the tomb in John 19 as Christ was prepared for burial.

John 3:16 is the anchor Scripture in our 3:16 journey. It summarizes the wondrous love of God in a way that even young children can understand. This one sentence holds a truth so great that it takes a lifetime to let its full impact absorb into our souls. Because God loved the people of the world in such a way—so greatly, so passionately, so completely, so boldly, so faithfully—He did something so simultaneously fantastic and horrible. He sacrificed what had the greatest value, His Son. The Father, Son, and Holy Spirit are one because of the mystery of the Trinity. This means that God sacrificed Himself in place of humanity's sin. Christ gave Himself for all the selfishness, the mistakes, and the deliberate evil in the hearts of people. His love was so great that He took on the ultimate rescue mission for an undeserving humanity. He did it in order that anyone—no matter who they are or what they have done—anyone who simply believes in Him won't truly die. Instead, they will live forever with Christ in heaven. This eternal gift is the most expensive present ever given, and it holds all the love in the entire universe and beyond.

When we commit John 3:16 solely to mental memory, we risk dulling its dazzling brightness. When we hide its beautiful truth in our hearts, however, that brightness of God's love shines in us. This sentence is made to be delightfully common in the way that it is frequently celebrated and shared. It would be tragic to reduce it to a nifty catchphrase without considering the awe-inspiring reality of each word. At first glance, it appears that the gospel fits nicely and neatly in one verse. Yet, as we examine its meaning, we realize that it is the key that unlocks God's endless treasures of love.

Every other 3:16 is summarized and reinforced here in John. Each verse describes part of the love that saved the world. On our journey, we've discovered new perspectives and seen God's love through the lens of each unique attribute. Love is found in discipline and in grace. We found His love in sacrifices and woven into intimate relationship with our Heavenly Father. We have been honored by being entrusted with responsibilities that give Him glory and advance His kingdom. We've witnessed miracles and seen the beauty of His attention to intricate details. We've been pursued by Him and we are slowly beginning to understand His justice. His consequences, consistency, and compassion are reaching out to us across the ages. We've heard His warnings and felt the warmth of His loving restoration, all the while soaking in divine wisdom. We've danced with joy and wept tears of grief, all while He never left our side. We've only begun to experience the holiness of God, but the amazing thing is that we have, in fact, begun to experience a little bit of the holiness of God. With each 3:16, the love of the Lord takes on another dimension. We are beginning to see how complexly gorgeous it is, more complicated than a tapestry woven with incredible detail, yet simultaneously as simple as Him drawing near to us.

When we realize the full extent of God's love, our whole lives reflect Him. We are transformed as children of the Lord. Every moment of each day is affected by our awareness of His love. Once we trust that God keeps His promises, we begin to live more securely. His love soothes our fears and assures us that our unknowns are quite known to Him—and He's taking care of the details with our well-being in mind. Filled with His love, we are given the boldness of an apostle, ready to speak truth to a world in need. We know that God will handle any backlash that we might receive for standing up in His name, so we have no need for cowardice. Love from God settles in our hearts and emerges as love for others. His love enables us to show compassion—both to our neighbors and our enemies—that we are not capable of demonstrating on our own. We are meeting the needs of others, encouraging and supporting them as our own hearts are continually refueled by the love of the Father. Inhibitions and prejudices are drowned out by His great inclusive love. He continues to change the world and allows us the privilege to be His instruments. Additionally, His love changes our approach to sin. It motivates us to keep His commands and avoid living in ways that feel like adding another nail to His cross. Our love for Him compels us to desire following Christ while sin becomes detestable in our eyes, too. But our understanding of His love leads to acceptance of His grace. This enables us to cast aside guilt and shame that would otherwise weigh us down and hold us back. We discover the freedom of forgiveness and are no longer slaves to perfectionism and legalism. Love releases even the chains that we shackle on ourselves.

Without God's love, we would lack the wisdom we need to navigate life's complications. His loving hand orchestrates details beyond our control. When we are fully aware of the role His love plays in our lives each day, our decision-making and control issues are adjusted. When we align ourselves with His love, we begin seeking His glory instead of our own. Once that happens, bountiful blessings begin to unfold before our eyes. Love transforms our big-picture view moment by moment. Where we once struggled to keep up with the rushing speed of our lives, we are now able to stop and enjoy His friendship. Our stressful pace is disrupted by His peace. Additionally, our very personalities and character are lovingly developed by the Holy Spirit. We are shaped into people who reflect God's love with kindness, patience, faithfulness, self-control, goodness, and joy. We seek community, knowing that we were designed to live together in unity bound together in love. Now that we know that God is speaking to us, we take the time to listen to Him. Our prayers become more than eager wish lists; love changes them into thoughtful conversations. When we know that God is lovingly pursuing us, we stop running away from Him.

The ways that God's love transforms our lives are never-ending and as unique as each individual. Often, when we say, "God loves me," what we really mean is "I think God likes me a lot." We might even go so far as to say, "God cares about me." But now that we've taken a stroll through the 3:16s, we realize that God gives us much more than a fond emotion or adoring sentiment. God's love is active and tangible. It is so multifaceted that even the 3:16s aren't able to describe it fully. They, too, are keys that unlock greater treasures, an invitation to dig deeper and discover what other Scriptures reveal. The Bible gives us the opportunity to witness how God worked in ancient lives, how He works universally, and what He is doing in our lives personally. If His words were only for the people of the past, God would not have gone through all the trouble to make sure Scripture was preserved for us today. His love for you is incredibly immense and He wants you to know it! He wants his love to affect every aspect of your life right now.

May your 3:16 journey be the beginning of a new adventure with Christ. Let the love of God enfold you where you are, where you've been, and where you are going. "May the God of hope fill you with all joy and peace as you trust in him, so that you may overflow with hope by the power of the Holy Spirit" (Romans 15:13). Truly know that He loves you with an everlasting love that will never be shaken or removed. Let us love one another, because love is of God. Rest in the promise of His love that is faithful from generation to generation. Amen.

ACKNOWLEDGMENTS

First and ultimately, all glory goes to God for this project. He alone inspired the journey and made it happen. Thank you to the team at Ambassador International for publishing *The Other Three Sixteens*. Additionally, this book would not exist without the help of some wonderful people in my life. Many thanks to Clayton Prescott, Karen Todd, Beth Collins, Emily Taylor, Matt Bowler, Bethany Douglas, and Brooke Daughtery. A special thank you to Lindsay O'Conner, Jennifer Jacobs, Kikanza Nuri-Robins, Dr. Gary Phillips, Leonard Sweet, June Tompkins, Lisa Snyder, and Lauren Steward for your help and encouragement! I forever treasure the support from my family and friends, as well as the love from my church community. Without all of you, *The Other Three Sixteens* would not have been discovered.

RESOURCES CONSULTED

The Nelson Study Bible NKJV, by Earl D. Radmacher, Ronald B. Allen, and H. Wayne House. Published by Thomas Nelson, 1997.

The Expositor's Bible Commentary (with the New International Version) (Volumes 1-12), edited by Frank E. Gaebelein. Published by Zondervan, 1990.

DISCUSSION QUESTIONS

If your group is studying *The Other Three Sixteens*, choose your track: 6-week plan: read 8 chapters a week, or 10-week plan: read 5 chapters a week. The following discussion questions will help guide your group time.

6-WEEK PLAN

WEEK 1: CHAPTERS 1-9

- How has God forgiven one of your sins and helped you grow from it?

- At what troubled time in your life did you hope God was watching? Were you aware of His presence then or in retrospect?

- Sacrifice, by definition, includes a cost. What have you given to the Lord that was difficult? Were you motivated by love to sacrifice or something else?

- What responsibilities has God given you? Do you see it as a burden or a privilege?

- Think of a poor decision you've made in the past. Can you recognize God's prevailing love? How does this affect future decisions?

- What obstacles currently seem impossible to overcome? Talk to God about them.

- What makes you unique? How has God used your uniqueness for His purposes?
- Make a list of the ways God has provided for you this week, month, or year.

WEEK 2: CHAPTERS 10-17

- Recall a time when you were brokenhearted like Hannah. How did God comfort you?
- Has your experience in a flawed human relationship colored your perception of God's love? Explain.
- What have you experienced in life that seems unfair? How can you see the God of justice at work?
- Have you ever united with someone unexpected? How did God bless that?
- When have the consequences of your sin kept you from falling further into disobedience?
- What can you sacrifice to express your love to the Lord?
- Think about your own season of rebuilding and restoration. Where do you see God at work?
- What questions do you have that God hasn't yet answered?

WEEK 3: CHAPTERS 18-25

- Which proverbs resonate most with you?
- Which injustice in our world today breaks your heart the most? How can you trust that God is in control despite current injustices?

- Humility can be a difficult lesson. When has God adjusted your pride?

- When have you turned your back on God? How did He call you back to Him?

- How do you experience grief? In the past, how has God comforted you while still allowing you to experience emotions?

- Who are the watch-people in your life? Take time to pray for them today.

- What circumstances have been fiery furnaces in your life? How did God stand with you?

- Where do you find refuge with God?

WEEK 4: CHAPTERS 26-33

- Have you ever felt like an outsider? Did anyone welcome you or show you love? Who are the outsiders in your life? How can you share God's love with them?

- What was the last thing that inspired wonder for you?

- What scares you the most? How can you surrender it to God's capable hands? Ask Him for peace today.

- When have you felt lost in a crowd? Have you ever "gone against the flow" and lived differently than the majority? How do you experience God's love for you personally?

- Does the parallel between God's love and a parent's love encourage you or bring up complicated emotions? How can you find reassurance in God as a Heavenly Father?

- What does your name mean? What other names do you think God has given you?

- Describe a time you were in a refining fire. How did God change you?
- What needs healing for you right now? Talk to God about it.

WEEK 5: CHAPTERS 34-41

- How would you describe yourself before Christ transformed your life?
- What teachers has God used to help you grow? Have you ever been tempted to put your trust in them instead of the Lord?
- Do you still find yourself trying to earn God's favor by being a good person? How do you follow God's commands without falling into legalism?
- What have you inherited from your earthly family? Possessions? Traits? How is our inheritance from God similar or different?
- When have you experienced a strength you knew was from the Lord?
- How do you experience the Kingdom of God on Earth?
- Who is in your community? How do you serve and glorify God together? What does fellowship mean to you?
- Where do you find peace? When have you experienced God's peace in stormy circumstances?

WEEK 6: CHAPTERS 42-50

- What is your favorite Bible story about Jesus? How does it demonstrate love?
- Choose a Scripture and commit to memorizing it. As you study the Word, what does God reveal to you?

- When have you found yourself in rebellion?

- What are three things you can (and will) do this week to take your focus off self and onto the Lord and other people?

- Have you ever felt persecuted for your faith? How did you respond?

- Have you ever believed something that turned out to be false? How clearly do you feel that you hear God's voice?

- What have you sacrificed for another person? How did that feel? How do you react to the knowledge that God sacrificed for you personally?

- What makes you the most passionate? Do you experience that same amount of enthusiasm in Christ?

- Which attribute of God's love means the most to you? What surprised you in this 3:16 journey? How are you changed after closing this book?

10-WEEK PLAN

WEEK 1: CHAPTERS 1-5

- How has God forgiven one of your sins and helped you grow from it?

- At what troubled time in your life did you hope God was watching? Were you aware of His presence then or in retrospect?

- Sacrifice, by definition, includes a cost. What have you given to the Lord that was difficult? Were you motivated by love to sacrifice or something else?

- What responsibilities has God given you? Do you see it as a burden or a privilege?

WEEK 2: CHAPTERS 6-10

- Think of a poor decision you've made in the past. Can you recognize God's prevailing love? How does this affect future decisions?

- What obstacles currently seem impossible to overcome? Talk to God about them.

- What makes you unique? How has God used your uniqueness for His purposes?

- Make a list of the ways God has provided for you this week, month, or year.

- Recall a time when you were brokenhearted like Hannah. How did God comfort you?

WEEK 3: CHAPTERS 11-15

- Has your experience in a flawed human relationship colored your perception of God's love? Explain.

- What have you experienced in life that seems unfair? How can you see the God of justice at work?

- Have you ever united with someone unexpected? How did God bless that?

- When have the consequences of your sin kept you from falling further into disobedience?

- What can you sacrifice to express your love to the Lord?

WEEK 4: CHAPTERS 16-20

- Think about your own season of rebuilding and restoration. Where do you see God at work?

- What questions do you have that God hasn't yet answered?

- Which proverbs resonate most with you?

- Which injustice in our world today breaks your heart the most? How can you trust that God is in control despite current injustices?

- Humility can be a difficult lesson. When has God adjusted your pride?

WEEK 5: CHAPTERS 21-25

- When have you turned your back on God? How did He call you back to Him?

- How do you experience grief? In the past, how has God comforted you while still allowing you to experience emotions?

- Who are the watch-people in your life? Take time to pray for them today.

- What circumstances have been fiery furnaces in your life? How did God stand with you?

- Where do you find refuge with God?

WEEK 6: CHAPTERS 26-30

- Have you ever felt like an outsider? Did anyone welcome you or show you love? Who are the outsiders in your life? How can you share God's love with them?

- What was the last thing that inspired wonder for you?

- What scares you the most? How can you surrender it to God's capable hands? Ask Him for peace today.

- When have you felt lost in a crowd? Have you ever "gone against the flow" and lived differently than the majority? How do you experience God's love for you personally?

- Does the parallel between God's love and a parent's love encourage you or bring up complicated emotions? How can you find reassurance in God as a Heavenly Father?

WEEK 7: CHAPTERS 31-35

- What does your name mean? What other names do you think God has given you?

- Describe a time you were in a refining fire. How did God change you?

- What needs healing for you right now? Talk to God about it.

- How would you describe yourself before Christ transformed your life?

- What teachers has God used to help you grow? Have you ever been tempted to put your trust in them instead of the Lord?

WEEK 8: CHAPTERS 36-40

- Do you still find yourself trying to earn God's favor by being a good person? How do you obediently follow God's commands without falling into legalism?

- What have you inherited from your earthly family? Possessions? Traits? How is our inheritance from God similar or different?

- When have you experienced a strength you knew was from the Lord?

- How do you experience the Kingdom of God on Earth?

- Who is in your community? How do you serve and glorify God together? What does fellowship mean to you?

WEEK 9: CHAPTERS 41-45

- Where do you find peace? When have you experienced God's peace in stormy circumstances?

- What is your favorite Bible story about Jesus? How does it demonstrate love?

- Choose a Scripture and commit to memorizing it. As you study the Word, what does God reveal to you?

- When have you found yourself in rebellion?

- What are three things you can (and will) do this week to take your focus off self and onto the Lord and other people?

WEEK 10: CHAPTERS 46-50

- Have you ever felt persecuted for your faith? How did you respond?
- Have you ever believed something that turned out to be false? How clearly do you feel that you hear God's voice?
- What have you sacrificed for another person? How did that feel? How do you react to the knowledge that God sacrificed for you personally?
- What makes you the most passionate? Do you experience that same amount of enthusiasm in Christ?
- Which attribute of God's love means the most to you? What surprised you in this 3:16 journey? How are you changed after closing this book?

For more information about
Malinda Fugate
and
The Other Three Sixteens
please connect at:

www.malindafugate.com
www.facebook.com/malthewriter
@malthestar

For more information about
AMBASSADOR INTERNATIONAL
please connect at:

www.ambassador-international.com
@AmbassadorIntl
www.facebook.com/AmbassadorIntl

If you enjoyed this book, please consider leaving us a review on Amazon, Goodreads, or our website.

More from Ambassador International

We live in an unpredictable, uncontrollable world where things change often, and fear can plant itself deeply within our hearts. *Chickening IN* is a practical approach to defeating the fear and doubt that is preventing us from becoming brave, bold women of God.

Chickening In
by JJ Gutierrez

Nathan and Tammy Whisnant were once overweight, exhausted, and unable to enjoy their grandchildren. But one day, the Holy Spirit convicted them of their need to be the best version of themselves, and together they have now lost nearly a hundred pounds. After working off the weight themselves, the Whisnants decided to share their secret to success with others, and *Imagine Not as Much* was born.

Imagine Not As Much
by Nathan and Tammy Whisnant

Using her own personal journey during an adventurous move to Paris, Anne shares healing truths of Scripture and methods she found to help others find freedom from their baggage. You will be inspired and refreshed as you realize you no longer have to carry your baggage either.

Pack Your Baggage, Honey, We're Moving to Paris!
by Anne Farnum

www.ingramcontent.com/pod-product-compliance
Lightning Source LLC
Chambersburg PA
CBHW070139100426
42743CB00013B/2760